Mountain Biking Oregon

Northwest and Central Oregon

Help Us Keep This Guide Up to Date

Every effort has been made by the author and editors to make this guide as accurate and useful as possible. However, many things can change after a guide is published—trails are rerouted, regulations change, techniques evolve, facilities come under new management, etc.

We would love to hear from you concerning your experiences with this guide and how you feel it could be improved and kept up to date. While we may not be able to respond to all comments and suggestions, we'll take them to heart and we'll also make certain to share them with the author. Please send your comments and suggestions to the following address:

The Globe Pequot Press
Reader Response/Editorial Department
P.O. Box 480
Guilford, CT 06437

Or you may e-mail us at:

editorial@GlobePequot.com

Thanks for your input, and happy trails!

Mountain Biking
Oregon

Northwest and Central Oregon

Lizann Dunegan

FALCON®

GUILFORD, CONNECTICUT
HELENA, MONTANA
AN IMPRINT OF THE GLOBE PEQUOT PRESS

A FALCON GUIDE ®

Maps created by XNR © The Globe Pequot Press

Photo credits: Lizann Dunegan and Ken Skeen

Library of Congress Cataloging-in-Publication Data
is available.

ISBN 0-7627-2575-3

Manufactured in the United States of America
First Edition/First Printing

Contents

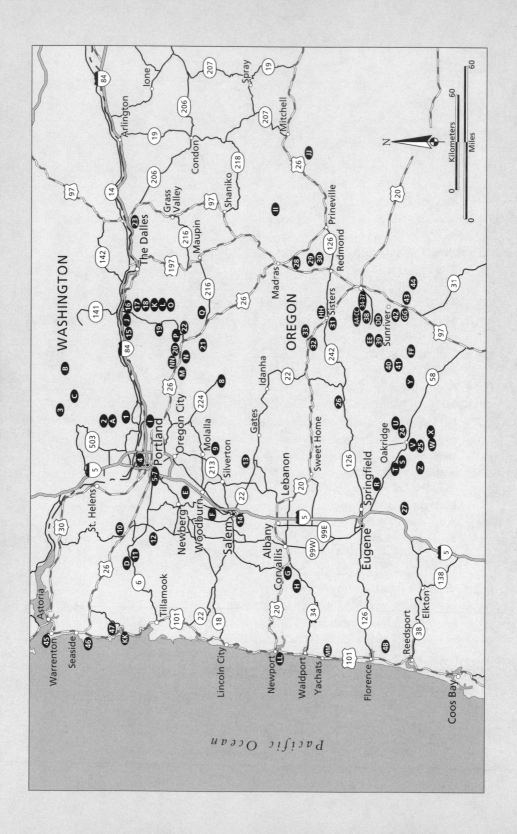

Eugene and Oakridge

Bend and Central Oregon

Oregon Coast

Acknowledgments

Thanks to my trail riding partners who helped me to research the new trails that have been added to this updated guidebook. This also includes my canine trail partners, Levi and Sage, who always add some extra spice to my mountain bike adventures. Also, thanks to Scott Adams and all of the other folks at Falcon for their help and advice.

Introduction

This guide features 87 mountain bike rides in northwest and central Oregon through some of the most scenic and varied landscapes in the state: from the northwest corner where rocky coastline meets the pounding waves of the Pacific Ocean, to majestic Mount Hood in the Cascade Mountain Range, to the high desert in central Oregon where Smith Rock rises from the Crooked River.

As the largest city in Oregon, Portland has been called an "urban nirvana." Forest Park, one of the world's largest city parks, rests right in the heart of city limits. This 5,000-acre park features more than 60 miles of trails and fire roads that you can explore. There are many other off-road opportunities within or not far from Portland's city limits as well.

Located north of Portland, southwest Washington is host to fabulous singletrack rides that should not be missed. Two of the best are the Tarbell Trail in the Yacolt Burn State Forest and the Plains of Abraham in the Gifford Pinchot National Forest.

A quick 30-minute drive east from Portland takes you into the scenic Columbia Gorge. Carved by the massive Columbia River, the gorge is lined with cascading

Cruising on the Gray Butte Trail.

waterfalls, colorful wildflowers, and beautiful windswept forests. Thanks to 1986 legislation, it was declared a National Scenic Area, allowing it to remain undeveloped for all of the public to enjoy. The gorge is crisscrossed with biking trails that wind through a variety of ecological zones, offering mountain bikers a firsthand glimpse at the spectacular scenery this unique place has to offer.

Travel just another hour farther and you reach Hood River, gateway to the Hood River Valley, Mount Hood, and the Mount Hood National Forest. Here you'll find miles of inspiring singletrack trails that circle high alpine lakes and rivers and offer stunning views of 11,235-foot Mount Hood.

An hour east of Eugene is the small community of Oakridge, another premier mountain biking destination. Many epic singletrack rides are found in this region. You can ride past lava flows on the McKenzie River Trail, crank on the technically challenging Moon Point–Youngs Rock Loop, or ride through old growth forest on the Larison Creek Trail.

Excellent singletrack can be found in the dry and sunny central part of the state, known for its high desert ecosystem of sagebrush, juniper, and ponderosa pine; amazing gorges; and unique rock formations. Carving this landscape is the mighty Deschutes River, beginning high in the Cascade Mountains and traveling north to south through the heart of Bend, central Oregon's largest city. Luckily, you can bike along this gem on the Deschutes River Trail.

Bend is considered by many to be the gateway to the Cascade Lakes and Deschutes National Forest. Located just a few minutes to a few hours from Bend, cyclists will find scores of accessible mountain bike trails that travel through pine forests, circle high glacial lakes, and offer stunning views of the Central Cascade Mountains. One classic singletrack trail that should not be missed is the Newberry Crater Rim Loop Trail—located approximately 38 miles southeast of Bend in the center of the Newberry Crater National Monument. This route circles Paulina and East Lakes, both of which are cradled in a huge caldera.

Northeast of Bend is the Crooked River National Grassland and Ochoco National Forest, both of which have hundreds of remote forest service roads and singletrack trails through a sagebrush-and-juniper steppe surrounded by buttes and canyons. Two great rides in this area are located at Smith Rock State Park and Gray Butte. The Smith Rock State Park Route leads you through a canyon carved by the Crooked River and lined with 400-foot cliffs. The Gray Butte Loop winds its way around Gray Butte, one of the tallest buttes in the region, and then sends you careening into Sherwood Canyon. Both of these rides offer challenging terrain, magnificent scenery, and spectacular views of the Central Cascade Mountains.

Northwest of Bend is the small, western town of Sisters—the hub for an excellent linked mountain bike trail system managed by the Deschutes National Forest. There are dozens of trails in the Sisters area that take you through open, ponderosa pine forests and next to picturesque alpine lakes and meadows.

For those who settled the northern Oregon coast in the late 1800s and early 1900s, fishing, logging, and agriculture dominated the region. In 1910 the state government set aside the entire coastline as public land. Today, forest, rivers, and beaches are publicly accessible for a good mountain bike ride any day of the week. A fun beach ride you can check out is Cannon Beach. If you are craving a singletrack adventure, pedal the Siltcoos Lake Trail. Recommended family rides that travel through dune and forest environments include Fort Stevens State Park, Nehalem Bay State Park, and South Beach State Park.

Weather

The weather in northwest Oregon varies depending on what area you're visiting. The climate in the western valleys encourages biking all year. Moderated by the prevailing ocean breezes, the temperatures rarely go below freezing or exceed 90 degrees Fahrenheit. The late fall, winter, and spring bring the majority of this region's 40 inches of annual precipitation. The summer and early fall months are usually quite dry and are the best time to ride. The temperatures along the coast are moderated to a greater extent, with average summer temperatures in the 60s and winter temperatures in the upper 40s. It's not uncommon to be sweltering in the valley summer heat while your friends at the coast ride in their winter gear. The average annual rainfall along the coast jumps to about 80 inches.

Heading into the Cascade Mountain Range from the valley, you'll see lower temperatures and higher precipitation. Expect routes above 3,000 feet to be snow-packed from November through June. Though rare, snow squalls can occur during summer months. Hood River and central Oregon have excellent biking weather during most of the year (except for mountain trails above 3,000 feet). The temperature ranges are more extreme with summer highs into the 90s and winter lows in the teens. Annual precipitation ranges between 8 and 30 inches for most areas. Summer thunderstorms and winter snowstorms are much more common than on the western side of the state.

Flora and Fauna

The Cascade Mountains are the dividing line between the east and west sides of northwest Oregon. The west side of the mountains represents a wetter ecosystem than its dryer cousin to the east. The forests on the west side are denser and are primarily made up of Douglas fir. Joining this predominant tree species in the coastal regions are the Sitka spruce, red cedar, western hemlock, maple, and oak trees. Other distinctive forest-floor plants include the purple-fruited Oregon grape, brightly flowered rhododendrons, vine maple, salmonberries, and numerous mosses and ferns. There are also a variety of berry plants that make a tasty treat while mountain biking. Some examples of these are juicy marionberries, thorny blackberries, and

bright red huckleberries. However, be sure you are familiar with a type of berry before you decide to pop one in your mouth—you wouldn't want to mistake a poisonous one for a harmless snack. In the spring and summer months, a myriad of wildflowers, such as trillium, foxglove, bleeding hearts, white bunchberry, phlox, columbine, Indian paintbrush, and purple lupine, can also be seen.

Birds that you may glimpse on the Oregon coast include gulls, cormorants, pelicans, and puffins. In coastal tidepools, it is common to see mussels, barnacles, sea anemones, starfish, and hermit crabs. Majestic gray whales can be seen in several locations during their semiannual migration from December through June. Sea lions and seals also frequent the rocky headlands and mouths of the coastal rivers to feast on salmon and steelhead. Mammals that roam the coastal forests include mule deer and black bear. Along streams and marshes blue herons, mallard ducks, belted kingfishers, and black-necked loons can be seen feeding.

Oregon's only poisonous snake is the western rattlesnake, which is found in all parts of the state except the coast, Coast Mountain Range, and the northern portion of the Willamette Valley. This snake is 2 to 4 feet in length, has a diamond-shape head, and is brown with large rounded blotches along the back and black and white crossbars on the tail. A rattle is on the end of the tail. Western rattlesnakes prefer dry, sunny locations such as sagebrush-covered grasslands, rocky habitat found in creek and river canyons, and open pine forest.

On the drier eastern side of the Cascade Mountains, the forests are mainly filled with ponderosa pine, lodgepole pine, and Douglas fir. The stately ponderosa pine forms parklike stands on the sunny mountain slopes and plateaus. Trails in the Cascade Mountains have a tendency to be dry and dusty during the summer months due to the high pumice content in the soil.

The dominant tree species on the savannas and plateaus of central Oregon is the western juniper tree. This part of the state is home to the second-largest juniper forest in the world. These hardy trees grow well in hot sun and can thrive on less than 8 inches of rain per year. Stands of juniper trees are interspersed in a landscape dominated by sagebrush mixed with rabbitbrush and native grasses. Other trees that flourish along rivers and streams are poplars and cottonwoods. These fast-growing trees are a common sight on farms and ranches, where they provide shade and serve as windbreakers. Wildflowers that give splashes of color to the landscape include the purple lupine, Indian paintbrush, yarrow, and yellow balsamroot.

Many species of raptors, including red-tailed hawks and kestrels, can be seen soaring in the skies, and osprey are common along streams and lakes. Coyotes thrive in Oregon and their haunting, serenading calls are very distinct and can often be heard in the late evenings. These hardy individuals feed on rabbits and small rodents.

◀ *Foxglove.*

Wilderness Restrictions and Regulations

Oregon is a magical place for those mountain bikers wanting to explore its beautiful trails. The Bureau of Land Management and the U.S. Forest Service manage most of the public lands here. Trailhead fees are $5.00 per day; or you can buy an annual Northwest Forest Pass, which is good at all participating national forests and scenic areas in Oregon and Washington. You can find out participating national forests, as well as locations for purchasing a Northwest Forest Pass by calling (800) 270–7504 or going online at www.naturenw.org.

The majority of Oregon's state parks require a $3.00 day use pass or you can purchase a $30.00 State Park Annual Pass. If you are mountain biking on the Oregon coast, you can also purchase an Oregon Pacific Coast Passport. It is valid for entrance, day use, and vehicle parking fees at all state and federal fee sites along the entire Oregon portion of the Pacific Coast Scenic Byway (U.S. Highway 101) from Astoria to Brookings. An annual passport, valid for the calendar year, is available for $35. A five-consecutive-days passport is available for $10. Call (800) 551–6949 to purchase an Oregon State Park Pass or Oregon Pacific Coast Passport.

Before you head out to explore northwest Oregon's trails, find out what type of permits and restrictions are in place for the area you are going to visit. Trail Park Passes can be purchased at local ranger stations, at participating outdoor outlets, and at some trailheads.

How to Use This Book

Mountain Biking Oregon: Northwest and Central Oregon features forty-eight mapped and cued rides and thirty-nine honorable mentions, as well as everything from advice on getting into shape to tips on mountain bike camping and getting the most out of cycling with your dog.

Each region begins with an introduction where you're given a sweeping look at the lay of the land.

Now to the individual ride. Each ride starts with a short summary that gives you a taste of terrain and surprises the route has to offer. Just below this you'll find the quick, nitty-gritty details of the ride: where the trailhead is located, the nearest town, ride length, approximate riding time, difficulty rating, type of trail terrain, total climbing (in feet), if dogs are permitted, what other trail users you may encounter, any fees or permits required, reference maps, and the organizations who can give you information about the trail. Our **Finding the Trailhead** section gives you dependable directions from a nearby city right down to where you'll want to park. **The Ride** is the meat of the chapter. Detailed and honest, it's our carefully researched impression of the trail. While it's impossible to cover everything, you can rest assured that we haven't missed what's important. In our **Miles and Directions** section, we provide mileage cues to identify all turns and trail name changes, as well as points of interest. Between this and our **route map,** you simply can't get lost.

The **Ride Information** box contains more useful information including: local information sources such as visitors centers and chambers of commerce, where to stay, where to eat, and what else to see while you're riding in the area.

The **Honorable Mentions** section details additional rides that will inspire you to get out and explore. Short descriptions of each ride are included that cover the rides' length, direction on how to get to the trailhead, and contact information. The Honorable Mention rides, designated by letters, are located after the numbered rides in each region.

The Maps

We don't want anyone, by any means, to feel restricted to just the routes and trails that are mapped here. We hope you will have an adventurous spirit and use this guide as a platform to dive into northwest Oregon's backcountry and discover new routes for yourself. One of the simplest ways to begin this quest is to just turn the map upside down and ride the course in reverse. The change in perspective is fantastic and the ride should feel quite different. With this in mind, it will be like getting two distinctly different rides from each map.

You may wish to copy the directions for the course on a small sheet to help you while riding, or photocopy the map and cue sheet to take with you. Otherwise, just slip the whole book in your pack and take it all with you. Enjoy your time in the outdoors and remember to pack out what you pack in.

Elevation profile: This book uses elevation profiles to provide an idea of the length and elevation of hills you will encounter along each ride. In each of the profiles, the vertical axes of the graphs show the total distance climbed in feet. In contrast, the horizontal axes show the distance traveled in miles. It is important to understand that the vertical (feet) and horizontal (miles) scales can differ between rides. Read each profile carefully, making sure you read both the height and distance shown. This will help you interpret what you see in each profile. Some elevation profiles may show gradual hills to be steep and steep hills to be gradual. Elevation profiles are not provided for rides with little or no elevation gain.

Route map: This is your primary guide to each ride. It shows all of the accessible roads and trails, points of interest, water, towns, landmarks, and geographical features. It also distinguishes trails from roads, and paved roads from unpaved roads. The selected route is highlighted, and directional arrows point the way.

Map Legend

═══(84)═══	Limited access highway
══(97)══	U.S. highway
──(35)──	State highway
──────	Paved road
══════	Gravel road
═ ═ ═ ═ ═	Unimproved road
- - - - - - - -	Singletrack trail
▬▬▬▬▬▬	Featured trail
┼┼┼┼┼┼┼┼	Railroad
•───•	Powerline
⋈	Bridge
⚠	Campground
†	Cemetery
🐎	Horse trail
•—◦	Gate
⌘	Golf course
◼	Overlook/viewpoint
🅿	Parking
)(	Pass
▲	Peak
⊞	Picnic area
▮	Ranger station
🚻	Rest room
🚴	Featured trail start
🚴	Trailhead
⫽	Waterfall

START

● Easy   ■ Moderate   ◆ Difficult   ◆◆ Very Difficult

Southwest Washington, Portland, and Salem

Cyclists from Portland, Oregon's largest city, frequently cross over the Columbia Gorge and ride the Cascades to the north. Southwest Washington is host to classic singletrack riding, with many of its premier rides located in the Yacolt Burn State Forest, Gifford Pinchot National Forest, and the Mount St. Helens National Volcanic Monument. Before spinning off on a knobby adventure in the Beaver State, be sure to check out the Tarbell Trail, Ape Canyon–Plains of Abraham–Windy Point, Lewis River, and Siouxan Creek–Horseshoe Creek Falls–Chinook Falls.

Back on the southern side of the river, Portland is host to Forest Park, one of the world's largest city parks, right in the heart of the city limits. This 5,000-acre forest is home to more than 62 species of mammals and 112 species of birds and offers mountain biking on 60-plus miles of trails and fire lanes, challenging all levels of off-road cyclists. Portland's southeast district is host to two beautiful forested parks located atop extinct volcanic buttes. Powell Butte Nature Park and Mount Tabor Park offer many miles of singletrack that weave through shady forest, offer opportunities for lung-bursting workouts, and phenomenal views of Portland and Mount Hood. A classic river trail that should not be missed is the Riverside Trail, an hour east of the city in the Mount Hood National Forest. This gorgeous river trail takes you through mossy old-growth forest and past secluded swimming holes and spectacular viewpoints of the dynamic Clackamas River. Recommended trails within an hour of Portland (heading west off Highway 26) are the challenging Tillamook State Forest and the sinewy singletrack trail that circles Hagg Lake.

Salem, Oregon's state capital, is located 60 miles south of Portland off I–5. Beginning cyclists will enjoy a leisurely ride along the Willamette River and through rolling farmland on paved and wood chip paths in Minto–Brown Island Park. Other mellow rides around Salem can be found in the Champoeg State Heritage Area and Willamette Mission State Park. If you are looking for a challenging singletrack ride, head to Silver Falls State Park—Oregon's largest state park.

1 Three Corner Rock

This is a favorite local ride in the Yacolt Burn State Forest in southwest Washington. The first half of the ride is steep and uneventful on a rough gravel road. But once you hit the singletrack trail, all of the gravel road riding is well worth it. The trail descends at a rapid pace, interspersed with bursts of intense hill climbing, through cool forest to a creek crossing at Stebbins Creek. Navigating switchbacks is the predominant theme in this mountainous terrain as you crank pedals and test your quads on a steep climb out of the creek canyon, and then you'll enjoy more ups and downs on buff singletrack back to your starting point.

Start: The Three Corner Rock Trailhead is located about 30 miles northeast of Portland off Washington Highway 14 in southwest Washington.
Length: 16.9-mile loop (with longer options).
Approximate riding time: 3.5 to 5 hours.
Difficulty: Difficult, due to technical difficulty, elevation gain, and numerous switchbacks.
Total climbing: 2,150 feet.
Trail surface: 7.4 miles of singletrack; 9.5 miles of rough gravel road.
Land status: State forest.
Seasons: May through October.
Nearest town: Washougal, Washington.
Other trail users: Hikers and equestrians.
Canine compatibility: Dog friendly.

Wheels: A bike with front shocks is nice to have due to the rough gravel road and numerous technical obstacles on the trail.
Trail contacts: Washington Department of Natural Resources, Southwest Region, 601 Bond Road, Castle Rock, WA 98611; (360) 577-2025; www.parks.wa.gov/ada-rec.
Fees and permits: No fees or permits required.
Maps: Maptech maps: Bobs Mountain, Washington; Beacon Rock, Washington. Yacolt Burn State Forest Map available from the Bureau of Land Management, P.O. Box 2965, Portland, OR 97208; (503) 808-6001; www.or.blm.gov/lo/index.htm.

Finding the Trailhead

From the intersection of I-205 and Washington Highway 14 in Vancouver, travel 10 miles east (from I-5 in Vancouver, go 16 miles east) on Washington Highway 14 to Washougal. In downtown Washougal turn left on Fifteenth Street (this turns into Washougal River Road). Follow Washougal River Road for 17.2 miles to a road fork. Turn right on Forest Road W-2000 toward Three Corner Rock. Continue for 3.3 miles to the signed trailhead parking area on the left side of the road. *DeLorme: Washington Atlas & Gazetteer:* Page 23 B8.

The Ride

Southwest Washington is filled with awesome singletrack riding that will challenge your stamina and your technical prowess. This ride is located about 30 miles northeast of Vancouver in the Yacolt Burn State Forest. A severe fire devastated this area in September 1902. It is thought to have started from sparks that blew into the dry forest from smoldering burn piles. Fueled by the hot gorge winds, the deadly

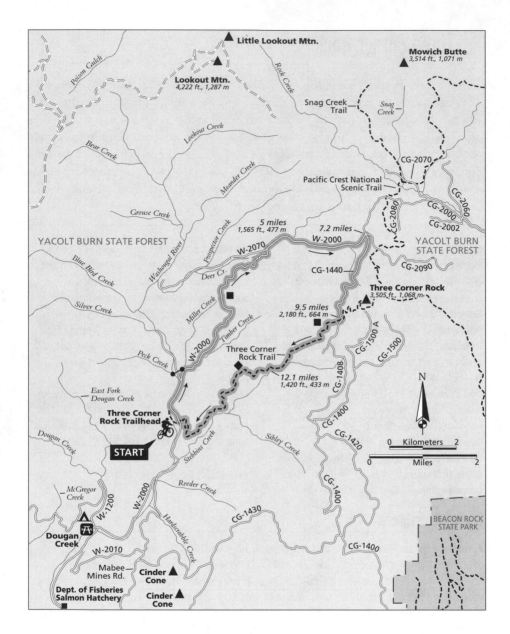

fire swiftly traveled 30 miles in just 36 hours, killing 38 people and charring 238,000 acres in Skamania, Clark, and Cowlitz Counties. The fire came within a half mile of the small community of Yacolt before it turned north, sparing the town. As a result of the sheer devastation, stronger fire protection laws were passed. Between 1933 and 1942 the Civilian Conservation Corps replanted the area with millions of seedlings, built fire roads, and helped to fight fires. Today a second–growth forest of Douglas fir, hemlock, western red cedar, and blue spruce covers the once charred hills. This forest of fifty-to-seventy-year-old trees provides shelter and food for deer, elk, and coyotes. Hawks, owls, and grouse also thrive here.

Admittedly, the start of this ride is not fun—you'll climb 1,295 feet for 9.5 miles on a rough gravel road past the ugly scars of clear-cuts. To avoid this brutal road, consider completing this ride as an out-and-back (see Miles and Directions for details). Bright spots on this uphill trek are glimpses of the bouldery Washougal River and rambling Deer Creek. Additional roadside distractions include splashes of color from wild daisies, foxglove, and lupine as well as a good viewpoint of the rocky pinnacle of Three Corner Rock at the 8.6-mile mark. Just before you start the singletrack section of the ride at the 9.5-mile mark, you'll have the option of hiking 1,325 feet in 2 miles to the 3,505-foot summit of Three Corner Rock. (This section of the trail is also open to mountain bikes but is very steep and technical.) From the rocky summit you'll have far-reaching views of Mount Adams, Mount Hood, and the Columbia River Gorge.

Just past the turnoff for the Three Corner Rock summit trail, you'll turn right on a singletrack trail and immediately begin a fun downhill surf. The trail descends at a rapid pace through sections of broken rock and tight switchbacks in a maze of green made up of vine maple, salal, and sword fern. This mad pace is periodically broken by some short intense uphills that test your lungs and quads. At 12.1 miles you'll arrive at rambling Stebbins Creek. This watery oasis is a great spot to take a break. You'll also want to fuel up for the steep climb out of the creek canyon, where you'll ascend 425 feet in 1.3 miles. At 13.4 miles you'll enjoy another fun downhill dash before you begin another hard uphill crank at mile 15. This last hill climb continues to the 15.9-mile mark and then the trail pounces downhill on some curvy switchbacks until it intersects with FR W–2000 at the 16.7-mile mark. From here you'll ride 0.2 mile on FR W–2000 back to the trailhead.

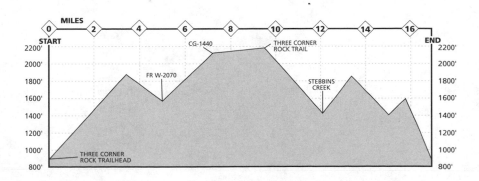

Miles and Directions

0.0 Start by turning left out of the parking on FR W–2000. **Option:** If you don't want to ride up the gravel road, you have the option of completing this route as out-and-back on the singletrack trail. To find the trail, turn right out of the parking area on FR W–2000 and pedal 0.2 mile to the Three Corner Rock Trail on the left.

1.0 Turn right following FR W–2000.

3.4 Arrive at Deer Creek Divide and a road junction. Turn right toward the signed FR W–2000. Begin a fast descent.

5.0 Turn right toward W–2000 ROAD/ROCK CREEK PASS 2/THREE CORNER ROCK. Continue your uphill climb. (Note: FR W–2070 goes left.)

7.2 Turn right on FR CG–1440 toward Three Corner Rock.

8.6 (FYI: Admire Three Corner Rock on your left.)

9.5 Immediately after crossing a creek, turn right on the Three Corner Rock singletrack trail. Begin a fast, technical descent. **Option:** Just before this junction you can turn left and hike (or bike) 2 miles (and 1,325 feet) to the summit of Three Corner Rock.

12.1 Arrive at Stebbins Creek. Cross the creek and continue uphill on the singletrack trail.

13.4 Arrive at the top of the pass and begin descending.

15.0 Cross a creek and begin a steep uphill climb.

15.9 The steep hill climb ends and you'll begin descending.

16.7 Turn right on FR W–2000.

16.9 Arrive back at the trailhead parking area on the left.

Ride Information

Local Information

Camas–Washougal Chamber of Commerce,
422 NE Fourth Avenue, Camas, WA 98607;
(360) 834–3472; www.cwchamber.com.

Scenic waterfall on the Three Corner Rock Trail.

2 Tarbell Trail

Located in the Yacolt Burn State Forest, this route is one of the best in southwest Washington. It combines the perfect mix of climbing, technical obstacles, views of Pyramid Rock, and inspiring downhills. As an added bonus you'll also get to admire two cascading waterfalls.

Start: The Tarbell Trail starts at Rock Creek Campground, about 40 miles northeast of Portland off Washington State Route 503 in southwest Washington.
Length: 19.5-mile loop.
Approximate riding time: 3.5 to 6 hours.
Difficulty: Difficult, due to distance, elevation gain, and brief technical sections.
Total climbing: 2,400 feet.
Trail surface: 14 miles of singletrack; 5.5 miles of gravel road.
Land status: State forest.
Seasons: May through October.
Nearest town: Battleground, Washington.
Other trail users: Hikers and equestrians.
Canine compatibility: Dog friendly.

Wheels: A bike with front suspension is nice to have due to the moderate rock gardens, roots, and water bars on this route.
Trail contacts: Washington Department of Natural Resources, Southwest Region, 601 Bond Road, Castle Rock, WA 98611; (360) 577-2025; www.parks.wa.gov/ada-rec.
Fees and permits: No fees or permits required.
Maps: Maptech maps: Larch Mountain, Washington; Dole, Washington.
The Yacolt Burn State Forest Map is available from the Bureau of Land Management, P.O. Box 2965, Portland, OR 97208; (503) 808-6001; www.or.blm.gov/lo/index.htm.

Finding the Trailhead

From the intersection of I-205 and I-84 West in Portland, head 9.5 miles north on I-205 to the Washington State Route 500 East exit 30. Go 1.5 miles to the stoplight at NE Fourth Plain Road. Continue straight (north) on Washington State Route 503 toward Battleground. Continue 14 miles north on SR 503 (you'll pass through Battleground after 8 miles) and turn right on Rock Creek Road. Go 2.8 miles to a stop sign, where the road name changes to Lucia Falls Road. Continue straight another 5.9 miles to the junction with Sunset Falls Road. Turn right and continue 2.1 miles to the junction with Dole Valley Road. Turn right (eventually this turns into Forest Road L-1000) and travel 5.1 miles to Rock Creek Campground. Turn left into the campground entrance road and go 0.1 mile to a brown pump house and parking area on the right side of the road. *DeLorme: Washington Atlas & Gazetteer:* Page 23 B6.

Fording Rock Creek. ▶

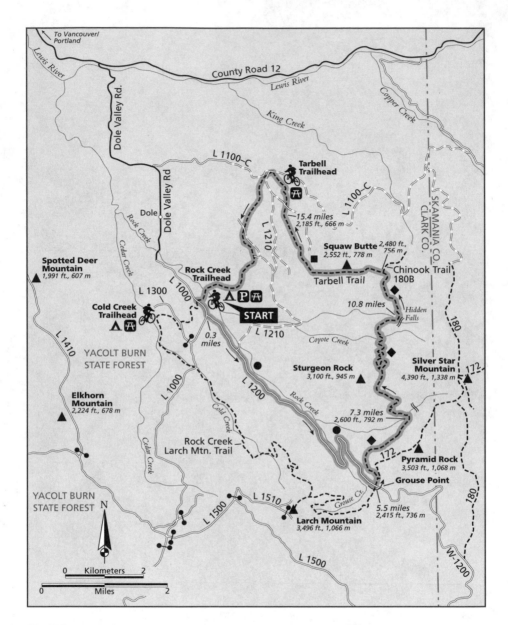

The Ride

The Yacolt Burn State Forest in southwest Washington is host to some excellent singletrack rides within an hour's drive of Portland. This route follows a 14-mile section
of the Tarbell Trail, which winds through a Douglas fir, cedar, and blue spruce forest
beneath the prominent spire of Pyramid Rock and Squaw Butte.

You'll warm up by pedaling over 1,300 feet on a well-graded gravel road for 5.5 miles to Grouse Point. From here you'll turn on the Tarbell Trail and begin cranking up a steep grade. After about a mile of mixed climbing and cruising through a forested setting carpeted with purple lupine and red Indian paintbrush, the route heads into the open, where you'll have a great view of the summit pinnacle of 3,503-foot Pyramid Rock. In the fall months the bright oranges and reds of vine maple put on a showy color display. At the 7.3-mile mark you'll cross Rock Creek on a partially broken wooden bridge, where you can view a small, rocky waterfall.

Over the next 1.4 miles, you'll continue your ascent as the trail continues north. At 8.7 miles you'll reach the trail's high point at 3,075 feet. From here get ready to surf on a smooth and fast downhill on a set of long switchbacks for the next 2 miles until you reach magnificent Hidden Falls at the 10.8-mile mark. Watch out for little sinkholes in the fast sections on this part of the trail. Hidden Falls is a good spot to take a break and get fueled up for the climb out of the creek canyon.

From Hidden Falls the trail has many fun ups and downs as it travels through a shady forest carpeted with big clumps of bear grass, sword fern, and vine maple. At the 14.1-mile mark, you'll start a long descent on a sometimes rocky, root-strewn trail. Beware of water bars that are prevalent on this section of the trail. The last 3 miles tend to be muddy early in the spring and are overgrown in spots. Also remember to yield to equestrians and hikers you may encounter as you near Rock Creek Campground. This last section will challenge you with its multiple rock gardens and roots. At 19.2 miles, near the end of your singletrack adventure, you'll get to hop across picturesque Rock Creek. Note that the creek can be deep and swift during the spring. After crossing the creek you'll ride 0.2 mile through the campground back to your starting point.

Miles and Directions

- **0.0** Ride out the campground entrance road.
- **0.1** Turn left on FR L-1000.
- **0.3** Turn left on FR L-1200.
- **0.9** Continue straight (right) on FR L-1200.

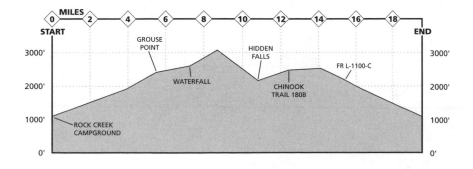

3.9 Cross Grouse Creek on a concrete bridge.

5.5 Arrive at Grouse Point. Turn left on the signed Tarbell Trail and begin a short but steep ascent.

5.6 Turn left at the trail fork. (FYI: The trail that heads right goes to Pyramid Rock.)

6.3 FYI: You'll have great views of the 3,503-foot summit of Pyramid Rock.

7.3 FYI: You'll ride past a small waterfall on the right.

8.7 Cross a doubletrack road where a sign indicates HIDDEN FALLS 2 MILES. Begin a long, fast descent.

10.5 Cross a singletrack trail and continue descending.

10.7 Cross a bridge over the South Fork of Coyote Creek and continue on a rocky descent.

10.8 Cross a bridge over Coyote Creek and stop to admire the mesmerizing cascade of Hidden Falls. After crossing the creek you'll start ascending on steep switchbacks.

12.4 Continue straight (left) at the trail fork. Chinook Trail 180B heads right.

14.1 Cross a singletrack trail and start descending. (Note: Watch your speed on the descent, as there are many water bars on this section of the trail.)

14.3 Cross a doubletrack road and continue descending.

15.4 Cross FR L-1100-C.

16.0 Turn left toward Rock Creek Campground. (FYI: The trail that heads right goes to Tarbell Campground.)

16.2 Cross a gravel road and continue descending on a rocky, root-strewn singletrack.

17.2 Turn left on a gravel road. Ride about 100 yards and turn right on an unmarked single-track trail.

18.0 Continue straight and ignore the faint trail that heads left.

19.2 Cross Rock Creek, then head upstream about 50 feet. Then turn left and head up a slight incline on a singletrack trail toward Rock Creek Campground.

19.3 Turn right on the gravel road that takes you through Rock Creek Campground.

19.5 Arrive at the trailhead.

Ride Information

Local Information

Camas–Washougal Chamber of Commerce,
422 NE Fourth Avenue, Camas, WA 98607;
(360) 834-3472; www.cwchamber.com.

3 Ape Canyon–Plains of Abraham–Windy Point

This strenuous tour winds through a mystical red cedar and Douglas-fir forest and then takes you through part of the eruption zone in the Mount St. Helens National Volcanic Monument. Additional highlights are stunning views of Ape Canyon and Mount St. Helens.

Start: The ride starts at the Ape Canyon Trailhead, located 66.5 miles northeast of Portland off Washington State Route 503.
Length: 21 miles out and back.
Approximate riding time: 4 to 6 hours.
Difficulty: Difficult, due to steep terrain, technical obstacles, and a steep section of stairs.
Total climbing: 2,030 feet.
Trail surface: 17.4 miles of singletrack; 3.6 miles of gravel road.
Land status: National monument.
Seasons: May through October.
Nearest town: Cougar, Washington.
Other trail users: Hikers.
Canine compatibility: Dog friendly.

Wheels: A bike with suspension is recommended to handle tight switchbacks, rocky creek crossings, occasional roots, and rock gardens.
Trail contacts: Mount St. Helens National Volcanic Monument Headquarters, 42218 N.E. Yale Bridge Road, Amboy, WA 98601; (360) 449-7800; www.fs.fed.us/gpnf/mshnvm.
Fees and permits: $5.00 Northwest Forest Pass, which can be purchased by calling (800) 270-7504 or online at www.naturenw.org.
Maps: Maptech maps: Smith Creek Butte, Washington; Mount St. Helens, Washington.

Finding the Trailhead

From the intersection of I-205 and I-84 West in Portland, head 9.5 miles north on I-205 to the Washington State Route 500 East exit 30. Go 1.5 miles to the stoplight at NE Fourth Plain Road. Continue 44 miles north on SR 503 (you'll pass through Cougar after 37.5 miles). Turn left on Forest Road 83 toward Ape Canyon Trailhead. Go 11.5 miles and turn left into the Ape Canyon Trailhead parking area. *DeLorme: Washington Atlas & Gazetteer: Page 33 C7.*

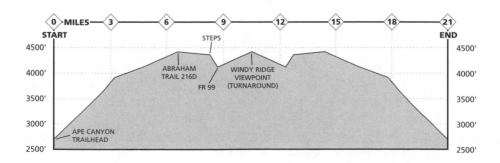

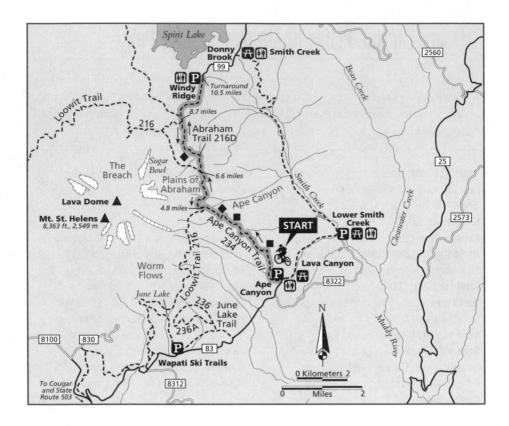

The Ride

This inspiring route takes you through the contrasting landscapes of the 110,000-acre Mount St. Helens National Volcanic Monument. The centerpiece of this national monument is spectacular Mount St. Helens. On May 18, 1980, this fiery giant came alive. The north side of the mountain gave way in a huge explosion that sent a plume of ash 14 miles into the sky, and pyroclastic flows of hot gases, pumice, and ash blasted down the mountain at speeds of up to 100 miles per hour destroying everything in their path. This violent volcanic activity caused snow and glaciers to melt, sending hundreds of tons of water down the mountain, which turned into giant mudflows. These mudflows caused further destruction in many of the river valleys surrounding the mountain. More than 55 million cubic yards of debris flowed down the Cowlitz River, eventually emptying into the Columbia River, where they blocked the path of oceangoing ships for over 9.5 miles.

The singletrack trail starts climbing immediately as it parallels the Muddy River. Over the next 4.6 miles, you'll ascend over 1,400 feet through a red cedar and Douglas fir forest carpeted with sword fern, salal, and vine maple. After 4.6 miles you'll

Pedaling through a moonlike landscape on the Plains of Abraham Trail.

exit out of the trees and continue climbing on the exposed edge of Ape Canyon. Over the next 2.2 miles, the trail surface changes from hard-packed to soft and dusty. Your technical expertise will be challenged as the trail crosses over several dry creekbeds. At 6.6 miles continue on Abraham Trail 216D and follow it as it weaves in and out of creek canyons over a moonlike landscape with great views of Mount St. Helens. After 8.3 miles and a total elevation gain of 1,660 feet, you'll be rewarded by a fast descent down the skinny spine of a prominent ridge. On the final section of this descent, you'll have to hop off your bike and walk down a series of steps. After 8.7 miles the singletrack trail ends at the junction with FR 99. From here you'll climb another 300 feet over 1.8 miles until you reach a spectacular viewpoint at Windy Ridge, where you can view Spirit Lake and Mount St. Helens. Take a break and refuel for the fun ride on the same route back to the trailhead.

Miles and Directions

- **0.0** Start riding on a steep uphill on the signed Ape Canyon Trail 234.
- **4.6** You'll exit out of the trees and start riding along an exposed ridge. Use caution over the next 0.2 mile as the trail snakes its way along the edge of the canyon.
- **4.8** Continue straight (right) at an unsigned trail junction. Continue your ascent of the ridge.

6.6 Continue straight (right) on the signed Abraham Trail 216D toward Windy Ridge and FR 99. (FYI: The Loowit Trail 216 heads left at this junction.)

8.3 Begin a very steep descent on the spine of a steep ridge. You'll have to walk down a series of steps.

8.7 Turn right on FR 99.

10.5 Arrive at the Windy Ridge Viewpoint and your turnaround point. Retrace the route back to the trailhead.

21.0 Arrive at the trailhead.

Ride Information

Local Information

Mount St. Helens National Volcanic Monument Headquarters, 42218 N.E. Yale Bridge Road, Amboy, WA 98601; (360) 449-7800; www.fs.fed.us/gpnf/mshnvm.

4 Marine Drive Multiuse Path

Located off Marine Drive in north Portland, this paved tour is great for families and beginning mountain bikers. The route parallels the Columbia River and offers outstanding views of majestic Mount Hood.

Start: The trailhead is located off Marine Drive at Broughton Beach in north Portland.
Length: 7.6 miles out and back.
Approximate riding time: 1 to 1.5 hours.
Difficulty: Easy, due to smooth paved surface.
Total climbing: 5 feet. Elevation profiles are not provided for rides with little or no elevation gain.
Trail surface: Paved path.
Land status: City park.
Seasons: Open year-round.
Nearest town: Portland.
Other trail users: Hikers, runners, in-line skaters.

Canine compatibility: Leashed-dog friendly (dogs are not allowed on Broughton Beach).
Wheels: A hybrid bike will work fine on this route due to the smooth paved surface.
Trail contacts: Portland Parks & Recreation, 1120 SW Fifth Avenue, Suite 1302, Portland, OR 97204; (503) 823-2223; www.parks.ci.portland.or.us.
Fees and permits: No fees or permits required.
Maps: Maptech map: Mount Tabor.

Finding the Trailhead

To get there from the intersection of I-5 and I-84 in Portland, travel 4.2 miles north on I-5 and take exit 307 for 99E/Delta Park/Marine Drive. After 0.4 mile turn right toward Marine Drive East and the Portland Airport. Go 0.3 mile to a T-intersection and stop sign. Turn left and follow signs for Marine Drive East. At the next four way junction, continue straight and go 3 miles east on Marine Drive. Park in a dirt pullout on the left side of the road just before a flashing yellow light at a bike crossing. If this parking lot is full, continue east on Marine Drive and pull into a large dirt parking area on the right side of the road just past the flashing yellow light. *DeLorme: Oregon Atlas & Gazetteer:* Page 66 D3.

The Ride

You'll share the route with walkers, joggers, and in-line skaters. It is part of a 40-mile loop that connects parks and green spaces in Portland. The Olmsted brothers, the well-known landscape architects, originally proposed the 40-mile loop in 1903. In a report to the Parks and Recreation board, they said, "Parks should be connected and approached by boulevards and parkways . . . they should be located and improved to take advantage of beautiful natural scenery. The above system of scenic reservations, parks and parkways and connecting boulevards would . . . form an admirable park system for such an important city as Portland is bound to become." This original idea has been expanded, and when the trail is completed, it will be

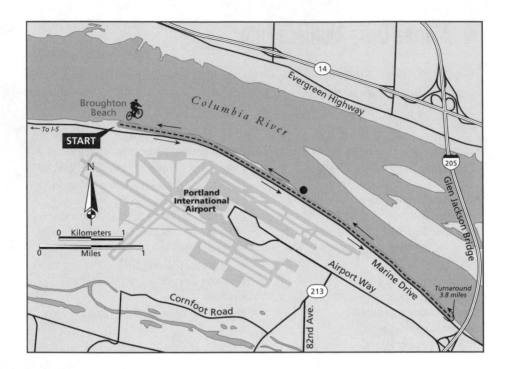

more than 140 miles in length and will connect more than thirty parks and green spaces in Portland and Multnomah County.

The route starts at Broughton Beach and heads east along the banks of the majestic Columbia River. To the east the river has carved the magnificent Columbia River Gorge, which has one of the highest concentrations of waterfalls in North America. From your starting point at Broughton Beach, the river heads west until it reaches Hayden Island in north Portland and then turns north. It continues its northern journey and joins the Willamette River at the southern tip of Sauvie Island, located 10 miles north of Portland off Highway 30. From that point it travels in a northwest direction for about 80 miles to Astoria, where it empties into the Pacific Ocean.

As you ride you'll most likely see fishing boats of all shapes and sizes bobbing on the river. This is the most heavily fished section of the Columbia River, and spring chinook salmon and sturgeon are the main catch. This stretch of the river is also popular with sailing enthusiasts, and on a nice day you can watch all types of sailboats with their colorful spinnakers catching the wind offshore.

The route also travels past the Portland International Airport, so you'll have the opportunity to watch jets take off and land. The gorgeous views of Mount Hood to the east are another highlight.

The Columbia River.

Miles and Directions

0.0 Start the ride by heading east on the paved path that parallels the Columbia River and Marine Drive.

3.8 Arrive at a paved parking area on the left just before the I-205 freeway (your turnaround point).

7.6 Arrive at the trailhead.

Ride Information

Local Information
Portland Visitors Information and Service Center, 701 SW Sixth Avenue, Portland, OR 97204; (877) 678-5263; www.pova.com/visitor/index.html.

5 Leif Erikson Drive–Firelane 1

Portland's Forest Park is a wilderness setting in a world–class city providing a spectacular loop that combines both gravel and dirt roads and pavement. You'll ride for 6 miles on Leif Erikson Drive, winding through a landscape of hardy bigleaf maples, dark green sword fern, Oregon grape, and red elderberry. After a short paved section, you'll ride a steep descent on Firelane 1, where you may have to dodge a few boulders, roots, and rocks. Nowhere else can you be so close to a city, yet feel so far from it all.

Start: The end of NW Thurman Road in northwest Portland.
Length: 15-mile loop.
Approximate riding time: 1 to 2 hours.
Difficulty: Moderate, due to a steep, rocky descent on Firelane 1.
Total climbing: 620 feet.
Trail surface: 0.9 mile of singletrack; 11.2 miles of gravel and dirt roads; 2.9 miles of paved road.
Land status: City park.
Seasons: Year-round.
Nearest town: Portland.
Other trail users: Hikers and joggers.
Canine compatibility: Leashed dogs permitted.

Wheels: The Leif Erikson portion of this ride is fine for bikes without front suspensions. Front suspension would be nice for the 0.9-mile singletrack descent on Firelane 1.
Trail contacts: Portland Parks & Recreation, 1120 SW Fifth Avenue, Portland, OR 97204; (503) 823-2223; www.parks.ci.portland.or.us/Parks/ForestPark.htm.
Fees and permits: No fees or permits required.
Maps: Maptech maps: Portland; Linnton. Forest Park One City's Wilderness map: Oregon Historical Society, 1200 SW Park Avenue, Portland, OR 97203; (503) 306-5230; www.ohs.org.

Finding the Trailhead

From I–405 North in downtown Portland, take the U.S. Highway 30 West–St. Helens exit (3). At the end of the off-ramp, stay in the right lane, which turns into NW Vaughn Street. At the first stoplight, turn left on NW Twenty-third Avenue. Go one block and turn right on NW Thurman Street. Go 1.4 miles to the end of the street and park near the green metal gate. Leif Erikson Drive starts at the gate. *DeLorme: Oregon Atlas & Gazetteer:* Page 66 D3.

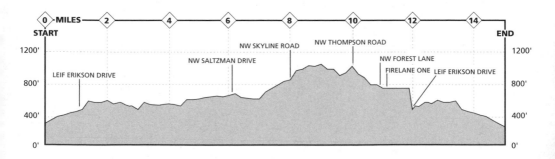

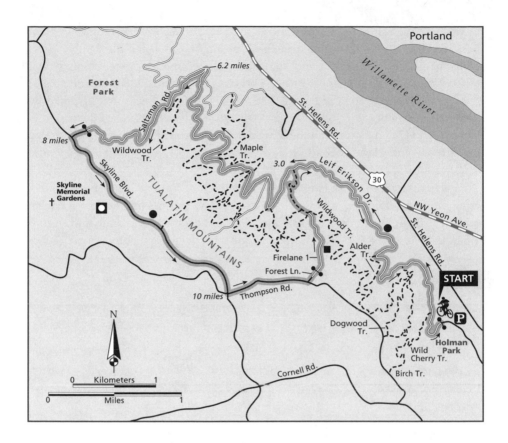

The Ride

There aren't many city parks where cyclists can pedal through a 5,000-acre forest that is home to more than 62 species of mammals and 112 species of birds. But, as one of the largest city parks in the world, Portland's Forest Park is just such a place. Thanks should go to those who lived in Portland at the turn of the century who had the foresight to secure what today is a wonderful park system enjoyed by mountain bikers, runners, and hikers alike.

Forest Park is part of a forested ridge local Indians referred to as "Tualatin Mountain." As settlements sprang up along the Willamette River and the west side of the mountain in the early 1800s, the original Indian routes over the mountain were improved and expanded. These improvements allowed farmers on the west side of Tualatin Mountain to take advantage of export opportunities and expanding settlements along the Willamette River. This also allowed for extensive logging on the mountain. What would have been an evergreen forest of Douglas fir, western hemlock, and western red cedar is now covered with a canopy of mostly red alder and bigleaf maple.

In the Olmsted report of 1903, John C. Olmsted, a landscape architect from

Brookline, Massachusetts, recommended to the Municipal Park Commission of Portland that the woodlands of Tualatin Mountain be purchased for a public park. Unfortunately, between 1915 and 1931, the land became embroiled in shifty real estate schemes. As a result, more than 1,400 acres of residential lots were forfeited to the city of Portland, and additional land on Tualatin Mountain was acquired by Multnomah County due to delinquent taxes. No land was purchased for park use. Finally, in 1947 and 1948, Multnomah County and the City of Portland transferred 2,500 acres of this land back to the Portland Parks & Recreation. Forest Park was, at last, dedicated in September of 1948.

A descriptive sign about Forest Park's history, plants, and wildlife makes for interesting reading before you start this 15-mile loop. The first 6.2 miles of the route are on Leif Erikson Drive; then the ride turns left on NW Saltzman Road and ascends 1.8 miles to paved NW Skyline Boulevard. You'll hit the pavement for almost 3 miles

BRIDGE TRIVIA

Bridges and people are the lifeblood of Portland. Every day, thousands travel over multiple bridges that span the Willamette River, tying the east and west sections of the city together.

- Phillip Marquam, for whom the Marquam Bridge was named, was a prominent nineteenth-century attorney and judge who owned vast real estate holdings in Portland. One was Marquam Hill, now the location of the Oregon Health Sciences University.

- The Hawthorne Bridge was built in 1910 and was designed to carry streetcars, wagons, and early motor vehicles. Presently, more than 30,000 vehicles cross the bridge daily. It is also a main commuting route for pedestrians and cyclists.

- Portland's Morrison Bridge is its oldest, built in 1887 as a toll bridge. It was rebuilt in 1958 at a whopping cost of $12.9 million.

- The Burnside Bridge is owned by Multnomah County and shelters the Portland Saturday Market under its west side.

- The Steel Bridge is owned by the Southern Pacific and Union Pacific Railroads, which lease the bridge to the Burlington Northern Railroad and the state of Oregon.

- Portland's newest bridge, the Fremont Bridge, was built in 1973. It is famous for its 902-foot center arch.

- The top of the St. John's Bridge is 205 feet above the Willamette River. It is the highest bridge crossing in Portland.

- The Broadway Bridge was named for SW Broadway Street, originally called Seventh Street.

- The Ross Island Bridge supports two large water mains that bring drinking water to Portland from the Bull Run Reservoir.

and then you'll hit the dirt again for a dizzy descent on Firelane 1 back to Leif Erikson Drive. From here you'll have a leisurely ride back to the trailhead.

Miles and Directions

0.0 Start the ride at the end of Thurman Street. Go past the green gate and begin pedaling along Leif Erikson Drive. There's a drinking fountain here.

3.0 Leif Erikson Drive intersects Firelane 1. Continue straight (right) on Leif Erikson Drive. This is where the loop will rejoin Leif Erikson Drive.

4.2 Leif Erikson Drive intersects Firelane 3. **Side trip:** If you want a short, thigh-burning side trip, turn left here and crank up Firelane 3.

6.2 Arrive at a four-way intersection. Turn left on NW Saltzman Road. **Side trip:** If you're hankering for more mileage and a more leisurely ride, pedal to the end of Leif Erikson Drive at Germantown Road, for a total workout of 22 miles. To continue on Leif Erikson Drive, head straight through this four-way intersection. The road gets a bit wilder and the forest deeper on this optional section.

7.9 Reach an iron gate. Continue straight.

8.0 Turn left on NW Skyline Boulevard to begin the pavement portion of the ride.

10.0 Turn left on NW Thompson Road.

10.7 Turn left on NW Fifty-third Drive and ride up a short, steep hill.

10.8 Turn left on NW Forest Lane.

10.9 The pavement turns into a gravel road.

11.1 The road turns into Firelane 1. Go around a green metal gate. Then ride a steep, 0.9-mile singletrack descent back to Leif Erikson Drive.

12.0 Turn right on Leif Erikson Drive and ride 3 miles back to your starting point.

15.0 You'll arrive back at your starting point at the green gate at NW Thurman Street.

Ride Information

Local Information

Portland Visitors Information and Service Center, 701 Sixth Avenue, Portland, OR 97204; (877) 678-5263; www.pova.com/visitor/index.html.

Local Events and Attractions

Oregon Brewers Festival, held in Waterfront Park in July, Portland; (503) 778-5917.
Oregon Museum of Science and Industry (OMSI), Portland; (503) 797-6674; www.omsi.org.
Oregon Zoo, Portland; (503) 226-1561; www.oregonzoo.org.
Pittock Mansion, Portland; (503) 823-3624.
Providence Bridge Pedal, Portland; (503) 281-9198; www.providence.org/oregon/services/cancer/bridge_pedal/default.htm.

Portland Rose Festival, held from June 1 through July 1, Portland; (503) 227-2681.
Waterfront Blues Festival, held in Waterfront Park in July, Portland; (503) 973-FEST.
World Forestry Center, Portland; (503) 228-1367.

Accommodations

Heron Haus, 2545 NW Westover Road, Portland; (503) 274-1846; home.europa.com/~hhaus.

Organizations

Portland United Mountain Pedalers (PUMP), 818 SW Third, # 228, Portland, OR 97204; (503) 690-5259; www.pumpclub.org.

6 Mount Tabor Park

Mount Tabor Park is one of those urban sanctuaries where you can still find wild in the city. This prominent volcanic butte rises above Portland's skyline bursting with urban greenery. Where else can you ride to the top of a three-million-year-old volcano covered with a Douglas fir and conifer forest? This 200-acre park is crisscrossed with dirt trails that are a mountain biker's dream, and views from the western summit are stellar. This short route is a good introduction to this beautiful urban park that promises a fun adventure right in the heart of the city.

Start: Mount Tabor Park in southeast Portland.
Length: 2.8-mile loop.
Approximate riding time: 30 minutes to 1 hour (with longer options).
Difficulty: Easy, due to smooth trail surface and no technical obstacles.
Total climbing: 450 feet.
Trail surface: Singletrack and paved road.
Land status: City park.
Seasons: Year-round (the driest time to ride is July through October).
Nearest town: Portland.
Other trail users: Hikers, runners, skateboarders.

Canine compatibility: Leashed dogs permitted.
Wheels: A bike without front suspension will do just fine due to the smooth riding surface on this route.
Trail contacts: Portland Parks & Recreation, 1120 SW Fifth Avenue, Portland, OR 97204; (503) 823-PLAY; www.parks.ci.portland.or.us/ Parks/MtTabor.htm.
Fees and permits: No fees or permits required.
Maps: Maptech map: Mount Tabor.

Finding the Trailhead

From downtown Portland, head 5.5 miles east on I–84 toward The Dalles. Leave the freeway at Eighty-second Avenue (exit 5). At the end of the off-ramp, turn right and go one block to a stoplight and the intersection with NE Eighty-second Avenue. Turn left (south) on NE Eighty-second Avenue and travel 1.1 miles to its intersection with SE Yamhill Street. Turn right and proceed 0.3 mile west to the intersection with SE Seventh-sixth Street. Turn right and then take an immediate left back onto SE Yamhill Street and continue heading west for 0.3 mile. Turn left on SE Sixty-ninth Street, go one block, and turn right on an unmarked paved road at the base of Mount Tabor Park. Continue 0.2 mile to a parking area on the right side of the road. *DeLorme: Oregon Atlas & Gazetteer:* Page 66 D4.

The Ride

Located 5.5 miles east of downtown Portland, 195-acre Mount Tabor Park has plenty of smooth singletrack for you to get in a quick workout. The park is located on an extinct three-million-year-old volcano and from its 643-foot summit you can

Mount Tabor Park is a fun urban ride.

enjoy stunning views of Portland's east side and sneak peeks of Mount Hood through the trees to the west. Plympton Kelly, an early Portland resident, named Mount Tabor after the mountain in Palestine. In the early 1900s this park was in a semirural area that was dominated by fruit orchards. Luckily the city recognized this area as a place to preserve and the Parks and Recreation Department began purchasing land for the park in 1909.

Mount Tabor is in the center of Portland's southeast district. You'll see a wide variety of human-powered crafts cruising on the roads and trails in the park. The canine crowd also likes to hang out in the park with their humans in tow. Multiple paths crisscross the butte, making an endless possibility of routes to explore.

The ride described here is a mix of singletrack and paved roads and gives you a quick tour of the park's highlights. It begins adjacent to the rest rooms on a wide smooth track that swerves around the west side of the park through a large grove of shady Douglas fir trees. It swoops downhill past a set of tennis courts and then travels past one of three reservoirs that store drinking water from Bull Run. After

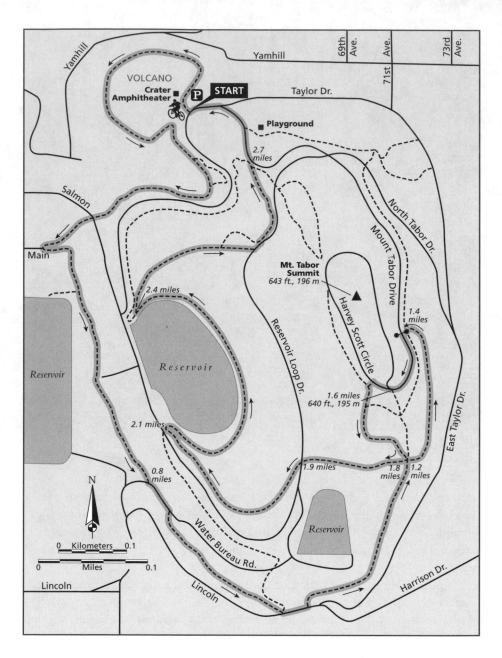

the twin towers of the World Trade Center were destroyed on September 11, 2001, security around these reservoirs was stepped up. In 2002, security consultants warned the Portland Water Bureau that the three open reservoirs in Mount Tabor Park and two reservoirs in Washington Park are vulnerable to terrorist attack. In response, the Portland Water Bureau may spend $65.5 million to reconstruct the reservoirs so the water is stored in underground tanks so they are less vulnerable. This money will also help fund a water bureau security force. The proposed project will span a period of five years and is still waiting for approval.

After a short uphill crank, you'll sail around the east side of the park, where you'll have opportunities to view Mount Hood through the trees. The route then hits the pavement and heads to the summit, where a bronze statue of Harvey W. Scott, former editor of the *Oregonian,* is prominently displayed. Here you'll find many park enthusiasts enjoying the great summit views and soaking up the sun's rays on warm summer days. The ride's grand finale is a quick downhill dash with a quick spin around a smaller butte and then one last downhill jaunt to your starting point.

This is one of the few parks in the city that has trails open to mountain bikes. To keep it that way, watch your speed on descents and don't ride on the park's trails when it's wet out. You can check out the ride described here or make up your own route on the park's many trails.

Miles and Directions

0.0 Start riding on the dirt path that starts in the northeast corner of the parking area next to the rest rooms. After a short jaunt you'll arrive at a trail fork. Turn right and pedal past shady Douglas fir trees along the west side of Mount Tabor.

0.3 Cross a gravel road and continue straight on the dirt path.

0.4 Arrive at a four-way junction. Continue straight on the singletrack trail. Go 25 yards and arrive at a T-junction. Go right and continue on the singletrack trail.

0.5 Cross a paved park entrance road and continue straight on the singletrack trail on a fun descent. Go 50 yards and take a sharp left at the drinking fountain and ride parallel to the tennis courts, which are on your right.

0.6 Arrive at a trail junction. Stay to the left and crank uphill. You are now above the reservoir. Turn left after crossing a paved path.

0.7 Go right at the trail fork.

0.8 Turn left on the paved Water Bureau Road and continue about 50 yards uphill on the road shoulder and then peel right on a dirt path. Ignore spur trails that head left.

0.9 Turn right on a dirt path and go about 35 yards. Turn left on a paved road. Continue about 50 yards along the road shoulder and then swing a left on a dirt path. Go 15

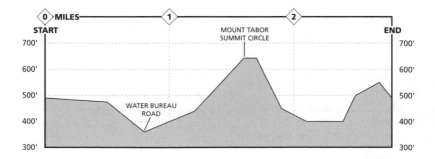

yards to a T-intersection. Turn right and crank uphill. At the next trail junction, turn right and continue powering up the steep grade. Ignore a spur trail that heads to the left.

1.2 Turn right at a five-way junction and continue pedaling on the wide dirt path as it goes around the east side of Mount Tabor. You'll have sneak peeks of Mount Hood through the trees. At the next trail junction, turn right and continue sailing on the smooth singletrack trail.

1.4 The trail intersects with paved Mount Tabor Drive. Continue straight on Mount Tabor Drive for about 50 yards. Take a very sharp left and ride around a white gate and continue riding uphill on the paved road toward the summit.

1.6 Arrive at the paved Mount Tabor Summit Circle. Turn left and continue on the paved road.

1.7 Turn left on a singletrack trail that heads downhill. Go about 15 yards to a trail junction. Turn right on a singletrack trail and continue on your descent. At the next trail junction, veer right.

1.8 Turn right at the five-way junction and continue descending on the dirt path.

1.9 Cross a paved road, pass a drinking fountain on your left, and turn left on a dirt singletrack trail that goes around the base of a small butte.

2.1 Turn right at the trail junction and continue riding on the singletrack trail. At this point the reservoir is located on the left side of the trail. At the next trail junction, veer left on a dirt path. This path parallels the reservoir, which is on your left.

2.2 Enjoy views of Portland's skyline to the west.

2.4 Turn right on a dirt path, which heads up a steep hill. Go about 10 yards to another trail junction. Continue straight (right) and continue cranking up a steep grade.

2.5 Ignore a paved road on your right and continue straight on the singletrack trail. In a short distance the path intersects another paved road. Turn left on the paved road.

2.7 Turn left on a dirt path. It forks almost immediately; go right and descend on a singletrack trail. Go about 200 yards and then turn left on a paved road opposite a little kiddy playground.

2.8 Arrive at a T-junction and stop sign. Turn left on a paved road and then take an immediate right into the parking area and your starting point.

Ride Information

Local Information

Portland Visitors Information and Service Center, 701 SW Sixth Avenue, Portland, OR 97204; (877) 678-5263; www.pova.com/visitor/index.html.

Local Events and Attractions

Providence Bridge Pedal, Portland; (503) 281-9198; www.providence.org/oregon/services/cancer/bridge_pedal/default.html. This annual event (held in mid-August) is a 27-mile bike ride crossing eight of Portland's historic bridges—the Hawthorne, Ross Island, Marquam, Burnside, Steel, Fremont, St. Johns, and Broadway.

Restaurants

Ya Hala Lebanese Cuisine, 8005 SE Stark Street, Portland; (503) 256-4484.

Organizations

Portland United Mountain Pedalers (PUMP), 818 SW Third #228, Portland, OR 97204; (503) 690-5259; www.pumpclub.org.

7 Powell Butte Nature Park

This 570-acre park has more than 9 miles of trails for mountain bikers, hikers, and horseback riders to explore. Rich in plant and animal diversity, this urban park is characterized by forests of bigleaf maple, Douglas fir, and Pacific dogwood; rolling meadows; and an old apple, pear, and walnut orchard. It's common to see birds of prey, black-tailed deer, coyotes, raccoons, and squirrels here. What more could you ask for?

Start: Powell Butte Nature Park at the end of SE 162nd Avenue in southeast Portland.
Length: Varies depending on trails selected.
Approximate riding time: Varies depending on trails selected.
Difficulty: Easy to moderate, depending on the trails selected.
Total climbing: Varies depending on trails selected.
Trail surface: Singletrack, doubletrack, and paved path.
Land status: City park.
Seasons: Open year-round.
Nearest town: Portland.
Other trail users: Hikers and equestrians.

Canine compatibility: Leashed-dog friendly.
Wheels: A dual suspension is recommended to avoid arm jarring on some of the technical singletrack in this park.
Trail contacts: Portland Parks & Recreation, 1120 SW Fifth Avenue, Portland, OR 97204; (503) 823-PLAY; www.parks.ci.portland.or.us/ Parks/PowellButteNature.htm.
Fees and permits: No fees or permits required.
Maps: Maptech maps: Gladstone; Damascus. The Powell Butte Nature Park brochure is available at the trailhead or by calling Portland Parks & Recreation, (503) 823-PLAY.

Finding the Trailhead

From I-205 in southeast Portland, take the U.S. Highway 26, Powell Boulevard, Division Street exit. At the end of the off-ramp, turn east on SE Division Street. Proceed 3.5 miles and turn right on Southeast 162nd Avenue. Travel 0.7 mile to the entrance of Powell Butte Nature Park. Continue 0.3 mile to the parking area at the top of Powell Butte. *DeLorme: Oregon Atlas & Gazetteer:* Page 60 A4.

The Ride

The city of Portland is full of surprises and Powell Butte Nature Park is one of the best. George Wilson, the original owner of Powell Butte, leased the property to Henry Anderegg in the early 1900s. Anderegg grew crops and raised cattle here. In the early 1920s the City of Portland purchased Powell Butte, intending one day to construct a reservoir. A 500-million-gallon reservoir was finally built in the early 1980s and is now part of the Bull Run water system, which is the primary water source for the Portland metropolitan area.

Powell Butte Nature Park is part of the interconnected park system in the Portland area that was brought under the Metropolitan Greenspaces Master Plan in 1992. This plan consists of a system of more than 350 miles of trails linking parks,

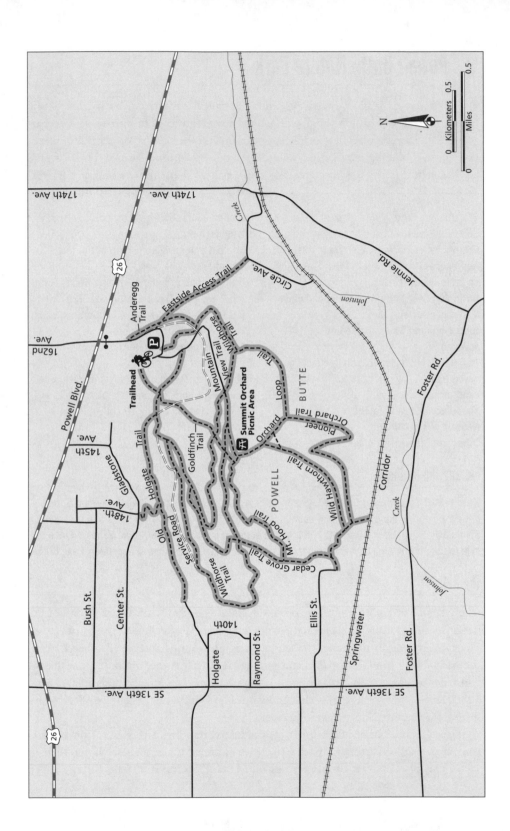

natural areas, open spaces, and greenways. But it was not the first. The Olmsted Report, written in 1903 by John and Frederick Olmsted, landscape architects from Brookline, Massachusetts, was an inspiration for the current system of parks. These brothers were contracted by the Municipal Park Commission of Portland to perform a park-planning study. Their report recommended a 40-mile looping trail system around the city of Portland that connected a series of parks. The report concluded, "A connected system of parks and greenways is manifested far more complete and useful than a series of isolated parks." Linking natural areas together provides a larger habitat for plants and animals, ultimately increasing biodiversity, improving air and water quality, and promoting wellness to people by supplying them with open spaces to run, bike, and hike.

Many of the trails that are part of the Metropolitan Greenspaces Master Plan are old rail corridors built along valleys, ridgelines, and streamsides during the nineteenth and early twentieth centuries. As motor vehicles became a more dominant presence and road building was more economically feasible, many of these early rail lines were abandoned. Today the National Trail System Act allows unused railway corridors to be redeveloped into trails for public use. The Springwater Corridor is one example of this rails-to-trails development. This former rail corridor now serves as a 16.8-mile-long multiuse trail stretching from the town of Boring to SE McLoughlin Avenue in Portland. The Springwater Corridor Trail, used by walkers, runners, hikers, and cyclists, links Powell Butte Nature Park to the rest of Portland's greenspaces and parks. It can be accessed from Powell Butte Nature Park via the Pioneer Orchard Trail.

At the parking lot is a sign with a detailed trail map, as well as rest rooms, drinking water, and picnic tables. The trails in the park can be as intense or easygoing as you like. Tight, tree-laden curves, steep ups and downs, and technical singletrack trails invite the hard-core adventurous types; while level, easy curves and wonderful scenery invite those who simply want to take it easy and enjoy the view.

A PENNY FOR A NAME ...

Portland has a history worth every penny of its name. In 1843 William Overton wanted to lay claim to a 640-acre site along the banks of the Willamette River. He, however, lacked the 25 cents needed to file a land claim. He convinced his traveling partner, Asa Lovejoy, to loan him the 25 cents and, in return, split the ownership of the site. Eventually, William Overton sold his share of the claim to a man named Francis W. Pettygrove. With the popularity of the land increasing, the new partners decided they needed a name for the site.

Lovejoy wanted to name it Boston. Pettygrove wanted to name it Portland. They decided to flip a penny—best out of three tosses. The obvious winner was Pettygrove.

This fruit orchard is a reminder of this area's farming history.

Miles and Directions

There are many trail options available for cycling in the park. All of these trails are fairly well marked and offer combinations of singletrack and doubletrack with short, steep ups and downs, tight curves, and varying scenery from open meadows to thick forest. On a clear day, you'll have some great views to the north of Washington State's Mount St. Helens and Mount Adams, while to the east and southeast Oregon's Mount Hood and Mount Jefferson command the view.

Ride Information

Local Information
Portland Visitors Information and Service Center, 701 SW Sixth Avenue, Portland, OR 97204; (877) 678-5263; www.pova.com/visitor/index.html.

Organizations
Portland United Mountain Pedalers (PUMP), 818 SW Third, #228, Portland, OR 97204; (503) 690-5259; www.pumpclub.org.

8 Riverside Trail

This is simply the best river riding close to Portland. It is a blend of short, intense uphills and downhills with a fun mix of technical obstacles. Immense red cedars, cool mossy forest, and the soothing sounds of the Clackamas River are the backdrop to this fun ride. Additional distractions that will keep you grinning include superb swimming holes and stunning viewpoints of the river.

Start: The trailhead is located 25 miles east of Estacada (or 42.5 miles east of Portland) off Forest Road 46 in Rainbow Campground.
Length: 8.4 miles out and back.
Approximate riding time: 2 to 3 hours.
Difficulty: Moderate, due to steep ascents and descents, bridges, roots, and rocks in the trail.
Total climbing: 170 feet.
Trail surface: Singletrack, paved walk, wood ramps, and wood bridges.
Land status: National forest.
Seasons: April through October.
Nearest town: Estacada.
Other trail users: Hikers.

Canine compatibility: Dogs permitted.
Wheels: A bike with front suspension is nice to have to handle the creek crossing, wood ramps, and occasional root and rock sections on the trail.
Trail contacts: Mount Hood National Forest, Estacada Ranger Station, 595 NW Industrial Way, Estacada, OR 97023; (503) 630-8700; www.fs.fed.us/r6/mthood/crtrails.htm.
Fees and permits: $5.00 Northwest Forest Pass, which can be purchased by calling (800) 270-7504 or online at www.naturenw.org.
Maps: Maptech map: Fish Creek Mountain.

Finding the Trailhead

From I-205 in southeast Portland take exit 12A for Oregon Highway 212/Highway 224/Clackamas/Estacada. Head east for 3.5 miles and then veer right on Highway 224 toward Estacada. You'll reach Estacada in about 14 more miles. From Estacada continue 25 miles east on Highway 224 to a road junction, which is right after you cross the Oak Grove Fork of the Clackamas River. Continue right toward Detroit/Bagby Hot Springs on Forest Road 46. Almost immediately, veer right into Rainbow Campground. Continue 0.3 mile through the campground to the trailhead at the end of the campground loop road. *DeLorme: Oregon Atlas & Gazetteer:* Page 61 D8.

The Ride

This scenic river trail begins at Rainbow Campground on the Oak Grove Fork of the Clackamas River. This tributary of the river, about 25 miles in length, flows into Timothy Lake and then flows for about 16 miles finally emptying into the Clackamas River at Rainbow Campground. The trail doesn't give you much time to warm up, because almost immediately you are hopping over creek boulders, riding on ramps, and cranking up a short intense hill, all within the first half mile. The route

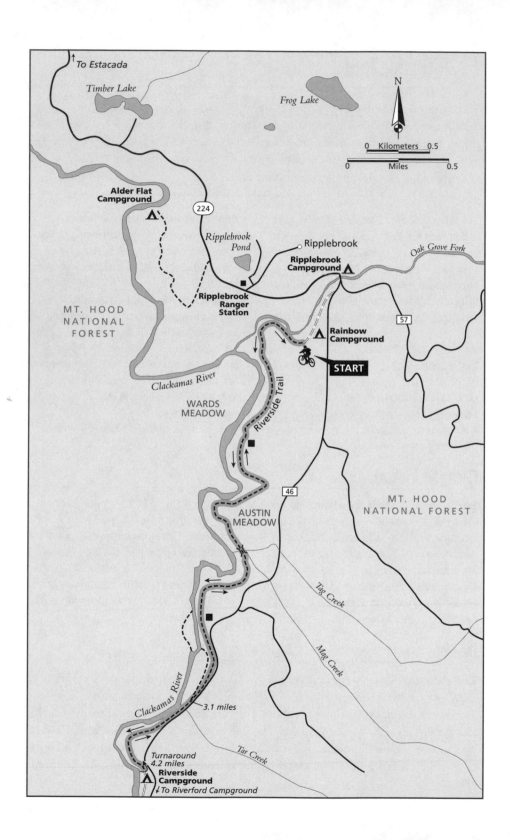

To Estacada

Timber Lake

Frog Lake

N

0   Kilometers   0.5

0   Miles   0.5

Alder Flat
Campground

224

Ripplebrook
Pond

Ripplebrook

Ripplebrook
Campground

Oak Grove Fork

MT. HOOD
NATIONAL
FOREST

Ripplebrook
Ranger
Station

Rainbow
Campground

57

START

Clackamas River

WARDS
MEADOW

Riverside Trail

46

AUSTIN
MEADOW

MT. HOOD
NATIONAL FOREST

Tag Creek

Mag Creek

Clackamas River

3.1 miles

Tar Creek

Turnaround
4.2 miles

Riverside
Campground

To Riverford Campground

keeps you grinning from ear to ear as it turns south and parallels the Clackamas River, where you'll be constantly challenged by fast, twisting descents and numerous hill climbs.

As you ride this radically fun trail, immense red cedars surrounded by a shimmering green carpet of sword ferns will keep you cool. These amazing trees, which thrive in areas with a moist environment, are in demand by lumber mills. Trees that have escaped the logger's axe can grow to be 8 to 10 feet in diameter and up to 200 feet tall. You'll pass by a boggy area at mile 1.4 that is filled with yellow skunk cabbage. This curious plant gives off a skunklike odor that is produced by sap in the flowers. The odor attracts pollinating insects. Native Americans soaked the roots of this plant for many days before eating them. This soaking process helped to leech out calcium oxalate, a chemical compound that causes the throat and tongue to swell and can also cause temporary paralysis of the salivary glands. Flour was also made out of the dried roots and the leaves were used to make water containers and to relieve headaches and fevers.

Additional highlights on this trail include awesome swimming holes and many spectacular viewpoints of the Clackamas River. After 4.2 miles of lung-popping singletrack riding, you'll arrive at Riverside Campground (your turnaround point). After taking a break retrace the same route back to the trailhead.

Miles and Directions

0.0 Start by heading south on the singletrack trail. Cross a creek with some large boulders.

2.5 Pass a great viewpoint of the Clackamas River on the right.

2.6 Cross a wood bridge over a side creek. After crossing the bridge, turn right and continue cruising on Riverside Trail 723.

2.9 Pass a great viewpoint of the Clackamas River on the right.

3.1 Continue straight (left).

3.6 Pass a great swimming beach on the right.

4.0 Pass another great swimming hole on the right.

4.1 Arrive at the crest of a hill that gives you a commanding view of the river. From here enjoy a steep, fun descent.

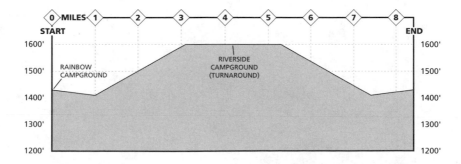

4.2 Arrive at Riverside Campground (your turnaround point). (Note: Rest rooms and water are available here.) From here, retrace the route back to your starting point.

8.4 Arrive back at the trailhead at Rainbow Campground.

Ride Information

Local Information

Estacada Chamber of Commerce, 24101 South Entrance Road, Estacada, OR 97023; (503) 630-3483; www.estacadachamber.org.

Accommodations

Rainbow Campground is located at the trailhead and features large, shady campsites along the river. For more information contact the Mount Hood National Forest, Estacada Ranger Station, at the address given above.

Organizations

Portland United Mountain Pedalers (PUMP), 818 SW Third, #228, Portland, OR 97204; (503) 690-5259; www.pumpclub.org.

◀ *The Riverside Trail is very canine friendly.*

9 Molalla River Trail System

This trail system has several miles of technical pathways suitable for the intermediate to advanced mountain biker. There are many out-and-back and loop trails, all of which offer great technical challenges. Beginning riders can also find great riding here on the gravel and doubletrack Huckleberry Trail.

Start: Hardy Creek Trailhead. Other trail access points start about 1 mile before the Hardy Creek Trailhead on the east side of the road.

Length: Varies depending on trails selected.

Approximate riding time: Varies depending on rides selected.

Difficulty: Easy to difficult, depending on trails selected. Most of the rides are geared toward the intermediate rider.

Total climbing: Varies depending on trails selected.

Trail surface: Gravel roads, doubletrack, and singletrack.

Land status: Bureau of Land Management (BLM).

Seasons: May through October.

Nearest town: Estacada.

Other trail users: Hikers and equestrians.

Canine compatibility: Dogs permitted.

Wheels: A bike with front suspension is nice to have to handle the technical trails in this area.

Trail contacts: BLM, Salem District Office, 1717 Fabry Road SE, Salem, OR 97306; (503) 375-5646; www.or.blm.gov/salem/html/rec/mollalla.htm.

Fees and permits: No fees or permits are required.

Maps: Maptech maps: Wilhoit; Fernwood. The Molalla River Trails brochure is available online at www.or.blm.gov/salem/html/rec/moll_trails3.pdf or by calling (503) 375-5646.

Finding the Trailhead

From I-205 take the Park Place/Molalla exit onto Oregon Highway 213 and continue south toward Molalla. After 14.5 miles turn left on South Molalla Road. Continue 3 miles to the center of Molalla. At the red flashing light, turn left on Highway 211 (East Main Street) toward Estacada. Travel 0.7 mile and turn right on Mathias Road. Go 0.3 mile and turn left on Feyrer Park Road. Continue 1.7 miles and turn right on Dickey Prairie Road. Travel 5.4 miles to the Glen Avon Bridge. Cross the bridge and go 3.4 miles on south Molalla to the Hardy Creek Trailhead located on the right side of the road. *DeLorme: Oregon Atlas & Gazetteer:* Page 59 A7 and Page 61 D5.

The Ride

The colorful names of Oregon's cities, counties, parks, and natural landmarks depict a piece of the state's history that is truly unique. Many of the names in Oregon come from the Native Americans. In fact, the earliest record of the word "Oregon" is found in an excerpt from a journey proposal written in 1765 by an English officer named Major Robert Rogers: "The rout . . . is from the Great Lakes

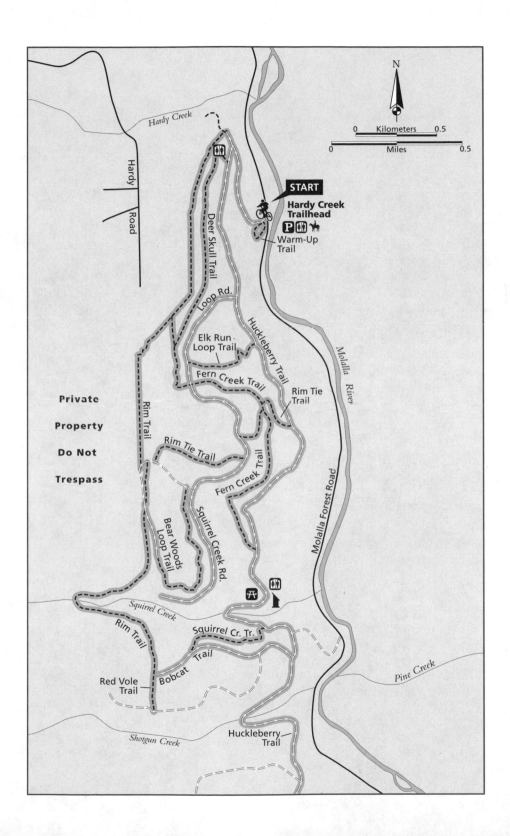

N

0 — Kilometers — 0.5

0 — Miles — 0.5

Hardy Creek

Hardy Road

START
Hardy Creek Trailhead

Warp-Up Trail

Deer Skull Trail

Loop Rd.

Huckleberry Trail

Elk Run Loop Trail

Fern Creek Trail

Rim Tie Trail

Molalla River

Rim Trail

Rim Tie Trail

Fern Creek Trail

Private

Property

Do Not

Trespass

Bear Woods Loop Trail

Squirrel Creek Rd.

Molalla Forest Road

Squirrel Creek

Rim Trail

Squirrel Cr. Tr.

Bobcat Trail

Red Vole Trail

Pine Creek

Shotgun Creek

Huckleberry Trail

toward the Head of the Mississippi, and from thence to the River called by the Indians Ouragen . . ."

Over the next century "Oregon" became a familiar term for explorers visiting the Northwest, and in 1848 the name was officially adopted when Oregon became a U.S. territory. In 1859 Oregon became the thirty-third state to join the Union.

During the great Oregon migration, which began in the 1840s and spanned the next thirty years, more than 50,000 immigrants traveled four to six months over 2,000 miles of open country to reach the Oregon territory. That they made it in one piece, despite suffering through the hardships of disease, scorching heat, storms, and starvation, can largely be attributed to the assistance of the Nez Perce, Cayuse, Umatilla, and Walla Walla Indians who often guided them across hazardous rivers and traded them salmon, vegetables, and fruit.

Many of these travelers ended their journey in Oregon City; they later established small towns throughout the Willamette Valley. One of these towns is called Molalla, founded in 1875 and named for the Molalla Indians. The word "Molalla" is thought to be a combination of two Chinookian words—"mulex" meaning elk and "olalla" meaning berry. The early settlers who lived in the Molalla River Valley called

HUH?

Is it molah-LA or mow-LA-la? Oregon is full of unique names that have been given to rivers, towns, landmarks, and groups of people. Visitors to the state who try to pronounce these names may get a raised eyebrow or two from the locals—but heck, it's fun to give it a try. Try to pronounce these tongue twisters:

Celilo (suh-LEYE-lo)

Champoeg (sham-POO-ee)

Chemeketa (Chem-MEH-keh-tah)

Coquille (koh-KEEL)

The Dalles (Dalz)

Deschutes (duh-SHOOTS)

Heceta (he-SEE-tuh)

Klamath (KLA-muth)

Malheur (mal-HOO-er)

Molalla (mow-LA-la)

Ochoco (OH-chuh-ko)

Oregon (OR-i-gen)

Owyhee (o-WEYE-hee)

Umpqua (UHMP-Kwaw)

Wallowa (Wahl-AH-Wah)

Willamette (wil-AM-uht)

Yachats (YAH-hahts)

◀ *Molalla River.*

the Indians who lived there the Molallies. The Molallies, or Molallas, were a warlike tribe who rode swift ponies and instigated numerous conflicts with settlers and other local Indian tribes. They gained a reputation as one of the fiercest tribes in the Oregon territory.

Close to the town of Molalla is the Molalla River Recreational Trail System, the brainchild of Mark Flint, a local bike advocate, and Bob Ratcliff of the Bureau of Land Management. Mark and Bob met at a local Bikeway project planning meeting in 1992 at which Bob mentioned a piece of land along the Molalla River Corridor that was available for development as a multiuse trail.

Trail construction began in 1993, and in 1994 local mountain bike groups called the Portland United Mountain Pedalers (PUMP) and the Molalla Saddle Club joined the effort in cooperation with the Bureau of Land Management. The BLM provided its engineering expertise, building materials, flags, bridges, and grant money to fund the project.

This trail system has several miles of technical singletrack geared toward intermediate to advanced cyclists. There are both out-and-back trails and loops that offer plenty of challenges. Local riders recommend the Rim Trail, which requires heart-pumping, leg-grinding, technical expertise. Another recommendation is the 1.9-mile Fern Creek Trail, offering adrenaline-rush downhills and drenching stream crossings. A more mellow trail, well suited to beginner riders, is the 6.6-mile Huckleberry Trail, which is mostly gravel road and doubletrack riding. This is a great trail for less experienced riders, as well as a good warm-up for more advanced cyclists wanting to tackle the more technical routes later in the day.

Miles and Directions

The Molalla River Recreational Trail System provides excellent singletrack and gravel road opportunities geared mostly toward intermediate riders. You can access the trails listed below from the Hardy Creek Trailhead or some of the other trail-access points starting about a mile before it on the east side of the road.

- Bear Woods Loop Trail: 1.5 mile; moderate
- Bobcat Trail: 0.2 mile; moderate
- Deer Skull Trail: 1.1 mile; difficult
- Elk Run Loop Trail: 0.5 mile; moderate
- Fern Creek Trail:
    Upper Section: 0.5 mile; moderate
    Middle Section: easy to moderate; 1.1 miles
    Lower Section: moderate to difficult; 0.3 mile
- Huckleberry Trail: 6.6 miles; easy to moderate
- Red Vole Trail: 0.3 mile; moderate
- Rim Tie Trail: 1 mile; moderate to difficult

- Rim Trail:
    - Upper Section: 1.8 miles; moderate
    - Lower Section: 2.3 miles; difficult
- Squirrel Creek Trail: 0.6 mile; moderate

Ride Information

Local Events and Attractions

The End of the Oregon Trail Interpretive Center, 1726 Washington Street, Oregon City, OR 97045; (503) 657-9336; www.endoftheoregontrail.org/index.html.

Organizations

Portland United Mountain Pedalers (PUMP), 818 SW Third, #228, Portland, OR 97204; (503) 690-5259; www.pumpclub.org. **Salem Merry Cranksters,** Salem, OR; (503) 365-8914; www.merrycranksters.org.

10 Banks-Vernonia State Park Trail

A fun ride located just a quick 30-minute drive west of Portland, this tour consists of an easy 21-mile biking, hiking, and equestrian route, which follows the old railway line from the city of Banks to the city of Vernonia. The route climbs a gentle grade, which winds through a mixed deciduous and fir forest before crossing a series of bubbling creeks. One of the trail's great highlights is the 80-foot-high, 600-foot-long Buxton train trestle.

Start: Manning Trailhead, located at the intersection of U.S Highway 26 and Pihl Road in the town of Manning (approximately 27 miles west of Portland).

Other starting locations: There are seven designated trailheads for the 21-mile Banks-Vernonia State Park Trail that travels along the old railway line between Banks and Vernonia. They are as follows (listed from north to south): Vernonia, Beaver Creek, Tophill, Buxton, Pongratz Road, Manning, and Banks.

Length: 14.6 miles out and back (with longer options).

Approximate riding time: 2 to 3 hours.

Difficulty: Easy, due to smooth paved trail and well-graded gravel road and small amount of elevation.

Total climbing: 900 feet.

Trail surface: Gravel road, paved road, paved trail.

Land status: State park.

Seasons: Open year-round (the driest times to ride are May through October).

Nearest town: Manning.

Other trail users: Hikers and equestrians.

Canine compatibility: Leashed dogs permitted.

Wheels: This ride is suitable for bikes without front suspensions due to the easy grade and smooth terrain.

Trail contacts: Oregon Parks and Recreation, 1115 Commercial Street NE, Suite 1, Salem OR 97301; (800) 551-6949 or (503) 324-0606; www.oregonstateparks.org/park_145.php.

Fees and permits: No fees or permits required.

Maps: Maptech map: Buxton.
The Banks-Vernonia State Trail Guide is available from Oregon Parks and Recreation, (800) 551-6949 or online at www.oregonstate parks.org/park_145.php.

Finding the Trailhead

Head approximately 27 miles west on U.S. Highway 26 toward the coast. You'll arrive at the small town of Manning, where you'll turn right on Pihl Road and then take an immediate right into a gravel parking lot. This is the Manning Trailhead. *DeLorme: Oregon Atlas & Gazetteer:* Page 65 B7 and C7.

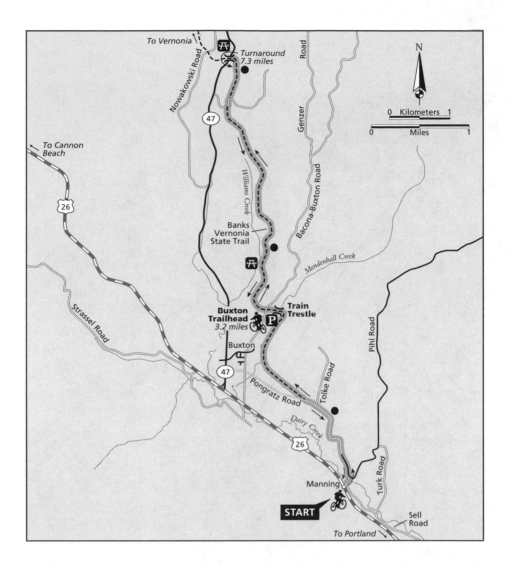

The Ride

There are seven access points along this 21-mile-long trail (starting in Banks and ending in Vernonia), allowing for many trail-riding options. The trail is built with an 8-foot-wide gravel-and-paved section for hikers and bicyclists and a 4-foot dirt trail for horseback riders. The section described here combines a 14.6-mile out-and-back section, starting at the Manning Trailhead.

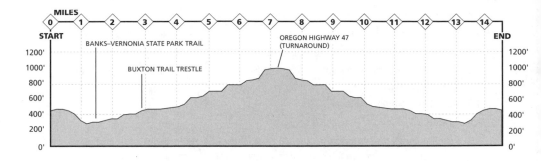

Starting in the 1920s, the original railway line carried lumber from the Oregon-American lumber mill in Vernonia to the city of Portland. The mill closed in 1957 and the railway line was subsequently forced to shut down. In 1974 the State Highway Department purchased the rights to use the land and officially transferred this right-of-way to the Oregon Parks and Recreation Department in 1990.

The beginning of this easy, scenic route winds along a gravel road through rural farmland in Washington County. Century-old farmhouses and old wooden barns are nestled within large fields of carefully tended crops.

Washington County rests on a bed of basalt lava on the western edge of the Columbia Plateau. Twenty million years ago this area was covered with lava that had flowed down the Columbia River basin from eastern Oregon. After the last Ice Age, water flooded the area, and upon receding deposited sand, gravel, and topsoil throughout the region. These rich deposits, combined with the region's fairly mild temperatures, are perfect for growing such specialty crops as grass seed, hazelnuts, berries, hops, wine grapes, and nursery products.

After riding along this rural road for about a mile and a half, you'll hook up with the Banks–Vernonia State Park Trail. After riding on the trail for about 3 miles, you'll pass the Buxton train trestle on your left. It's hard to believe this high, stilted, wood construction once supported loaded freight trains weighing many tons.

You may encounter horseback riders on this trail. If you see a horse, be sure to stop and pull your bike to the side and wait for the horse and rider to pass.

The trail is open year-round; but if you ride in the winter and spring, be prepared to wade through some muddy sections.

Miles and Directions

0.0 Starting from the Manning Trailhead parking lot, turn right on paved NW Pihl Road.

0.1 Cross a bridge over Dairy Creek, then turn left on NW Pongratz Road.

0.3 The road turns to gravel.

◀ *Buxton train trestle.*

1.5 Turn right on the paved Banks–Vernonia State Park Trail.

2.9 The paved path turns into gravel. You'll pass by the old Buxton train trestle on your left.

3.0 Cross a wood bridge over Mendenhall Creek.

3.2 You'll pass the Buxton Trailhead parking lot. (Note: This trailhead has a rest room and drinking water.)

4.3 Pass a picnic area on the left.

7.0 Cross a gravel road and continue straight.

7.3 Reach a bridge that crosses over Oregon Highway 47 (Nehalem Highway). This is your turnaround point. **Option:** You can continue straight for 13.7 miles to the end of the trail in Vernonia.

14.6 Arrive at the trailhead.

Ride Information

Local Information

Washington County Museum, 17677 NW Springville Road, Portland, OR 97229; (503) 645-5353.

Organizations

Portland United Mountain Pedalers (PUMP), 818 SW Third, #228, Portland, OR 97204; (503) 690-5259; www.pumpclub.org.

11 Tillamook State Forest

Located in the Tillamook State Forest, this fun route is a smorgasbord of roots, rocks, stump jumps, and rock gardens that will test your technical prowess. Thrown into this mix are many short, intense climbs that will thrill those craving a cardio workout. Additional highlights are short sections of creek riding and a view of University Falls.

Start: The route begins at the Rogers Camp Trailhead, located 39 miles west of Portland off Oregon Highway 6.
Length: 8.2-mile loop.
Approximate riding time: 2 to 3 hours.
Difficulty: Advanced, due to technical obstacles on the trail including stump jumps, drop-offs, rock gardens, and root bundles.
Total climbing: 775 feet.
Trail surface: Singletrack and doubletrack.
Land status: State forest.
Seasons: April through October.
Nearest town: Hillsboro.
Other trail users: Hikers.

Canine compatibility: Dogs permitted.
Wheels: A bike with a front suspension is nice to have to handle the numerous stump jumps, drop-offs, rock gardens, and root bundles on the route.
Trail contacts: Tillamook State Forest, Forest Grove District Office, 801 Gales Creek Road, Forest Grove, OR 97116; (503) 357-2191; www.odf.state.or.us/tsf/tsfhome.htm.
Fees and permits: None.
Maps: Maptech maps: Roaring Creek; Woods Point. Tillamook State Forest/Wilson River Highway Area map.

Finding the Trailhead

From I-405 and Highway 26 in Portland, head 20.5 miles west on U.S. Highway 26 to its junction with Highway 6. Head left (west) on Highway 6 toward Banks and Tillamook. Go 18.6 miles west and turn left at the intersection with Beaver Dam Road/Rogers Camp Trailhead. Go 0.1 mile to a T-intersection. Turn left toward the Rogers Camp Trailhead. Continue 0.2 mile to the parking area. *DeLorme: Oregon Atlas & Gazetteer:* Page 65 D5.

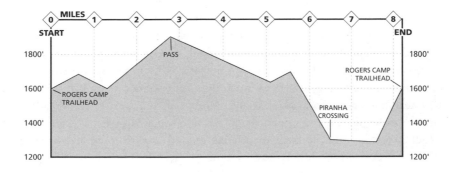

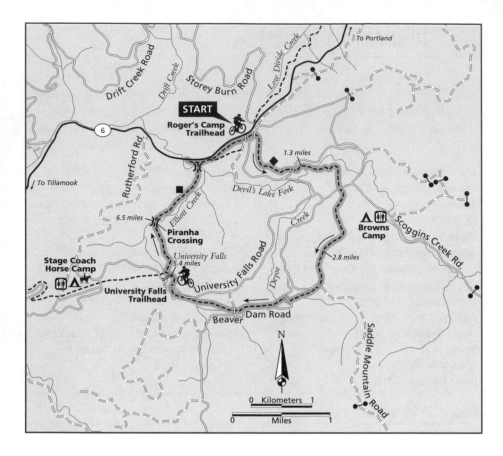

The Ride

The 364,000-acre Tillamook State Forest has fun technical trails that are a favorite after-work and weekend riding spot for local riders. Located in the northern Oregon Coast Range, this second-growth forest was literally charred when one of the largest fires in Oregon history swept through the area in August of 1933. Over the next eighteen years, major fires continued to plague this region, burning a total of 355,000 acres and 13.5 million board feet of timber. Logging virtually came to a halt, rivers filled with sediment and debris, and wildlife vanished. The area was so devastated it became known as the "Tillamook Burn." In 1948 Oregon voters authorized $12 million in bonds to replant the area. Work began the next year. Helicopters reseeded vast tracts of land by air and millions of trees were planted by hand. When this immense effort was finished, more than 72 million trees had been planted. A major fire prevention campaign was also initiated and new fire roads and fire lookouts were built. Today a productive second-growth forest has established itself and streams and wildlife have recovered.

The Tillamook State Forest offers some of the best technical singletrack close to Portland.

You can explore a scenic part of the forest on this loop route that combines the Nels Rogers Trail (also called the Historic Hiking Trail) and the Gravelle Brothers Trail into a power workout filled with stumps, roots, rocks, and drop-offs. You'll start the route by warming up on a steep uphill jaunt through a maze of quad-burning, arm-jarring roots. After 0.6 mile you'll begin a downhill surf on a singletrack trail gushing with technical teasers that will numb your brain and rack your body. At 1.2 miles you'll cross a bubbling creek whose banks are decorated with a green umbrella of bigleaf maple and red alder trees. Shortly thereafter you can do a brief detour to view University Falls. From here the route crosses several doubletrack roads and then climbs to the top of a small pass through a clear-cut area near the 2.8-mile mark. You'll sail down through rock and root gardens until you reach the 6.5-mile mark, where you'll cross Elliot Creek at Piranha Crossing. You'll complete the loop on a very steep uphill crank on a rocky doubletrack road until you meet up with Highway 6 at the 8-mile mark. From here it's an easy pedal back to your starting point.

Miles and Directions

0.0 From the parking area head south and uphill on the narrow doubletrack road.

0.1 Turn right on the singletrack trail marked HISTORICAL TRAIL. Begin a steep ascent through a maze of tree roots.

0.3 Go straight through a four-way intersection and continue the steep ascent.

0.6 Cross a doubletrack road and continue straight on a singletrack trail as it descends at a rapid pace filled with tight turns and gnarly roots.

1.0 Cross a gravel road and continue straight.

1.2 Turn right at the T-intersection marked MAIN TRAIL. Descend to a creek.

1.3 Turn left on a gravel road and cross a bridge, then turn left and continue on the single-track trail.

2.3 Cross a gravel road and continue straight on the singletrack trail.

2.4 Cross a doubletrack road and continue straight on the singletrack trail.

2.6 Cross a doubletrack road and continue straight on the singletrack trail. The route heads out of the trees through a clear-cut area.

2.8 Arrive at the top of a small pass and begin a fast downhill.

2.9 Cross a doubletrack road and continue straight on the singletrack trail. You'll reenter a shady forest corridor.

3.6 Cross a motorcycle trail. Go a short distance and arrive at T-intersection. Turn right on a doubletrack road.

3.8 Turn left and continue on the singletrack trail.

4.0 Cross a gravel road.

4.2 Cross a wood bridge over a creek.

4.7 Cross a gravel road.

5.0 Cross a doubletrack road.

5.4 Cross a gravel road and continue on the singletrack trail marked UNIVERSITY FALLS. Crank up the steep, rock-strewn trail.

5.6 Cross a doubletrack road and continue on the singletrack trail. The trail descends and meets up with a doubletrack road. Cross the road and continue on the singletrack trail.

5.8 Arrive at a three-way junction. Take a hard right and continue on the singletrack trail.

6.5 Turn right on a doubletrack road and ride over Elliot Creek on a wood bridge that is signed PIRANHA CROSSING. Continue riding on a rocky doubletrack road.

7.3 Turn right and cross a wood bridge over the creek and begin a steep ascent out of the creek canyon.

8.0 Arrive at the end of the doubletrack. Lift your bike over a concrete piling, ride next to Highway 6 for about a 100 yards, and then turn right on Beaver Dam Road at the Rogers Camp Trailhead sign. Ride uphill and turn left at a T-intersection.

8.2 Arrive at the trailhead.

Ride Information

Local Information
Washington County Visitors Association, 5075 SW Griffith Drive, Suite 120, Beaverton, OR 97005; (800) 537-3149; www.wcva.org.

Organizations
Portland United Mountain Pedalers (PUMP), 818 SW Third, #228, Portland, OR 97204; (503) 690-5259; www.pumpclub.org.

◀ *Taking a break at University Falls.*

12 Hagg Lake

The 15-mile Hagg Lake Trail offers cyclists some of the finest singletrack near the City of Roses. The route, following the contours of Henry Hagg Lake, offers all flavors of mountain bike terrain—twists, turns, open meadows, forest, stream crossings, fun rolling hills, and small sections of pavement. Rewards along the way include prime blackberry picking and awesome swimming holes.

Start: West Shore Drive at Scoggins Valley Park at Hagg Lake.
Length: 15.1-mile loop.
Approximate riding time: 3 to 4 hours.
Difficulty: Moderate, due to short, steep hill climbs and twisting, sometimes rough terrain.
Total climbing: 400 feet.
Trail surface: Singletrack, doubletrack, and paved road.
Land status: County park.
Seasons: April through October.
Nearest town: Forest Grove.
Other trail users: Hikers.
Canine compatibility: Leashed dogs permitted.

Wheels: A bike with a dual suspension is recommended to help avoid excessive jarring on some of the technical sections of the trail.
Trail contacts: Washington County Parks, 155 North First Avenue, Suite B-60, Hillsboro, OR 97124; (503) 846-3692; www.co. washington.or.us/deptmts/sup_serv/fac_mgt/parks/hagglake.htm.
Fees and permits: $4.00 day use fee.
Maps: Maptech map: Gaston; Gales Creek. You can download a map of the park by visiting www.co.washington.or.us/deptmts/sup_serv/fac_mgt/parks/hagglake.htm.

Finding the Trailhead

From Portland, head 21 miles west on U.S. Highway 26 to its junction with Oregon Highway 6. Turn left on Highway 6 (toward Banks, Forest Grove, and Tillamook) and go 2.5 miles to its intersection with Highway 47. Turn south and proceed 12.5 miles to the junction with Scoggins Valley Road. Turn right (west) and head 3.1 miles to the Henry Hagg Lake/Scoggins Valley Park entrance (there is an entrance fee of $4.00 during the summer). Go 0.3 mile past the entrance booth to the junction with West Shore Drive. Turn left and travel 0.9 mile to a gravel parking area with rest rooms (no water) on the right side of the road. *DeLorme: Oregon Atlas & Gazetteer:* Page 59 A7 and Page 65 D7.

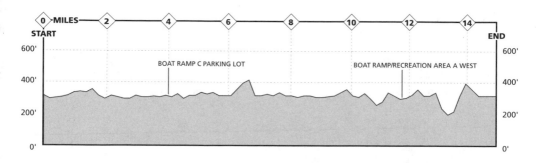

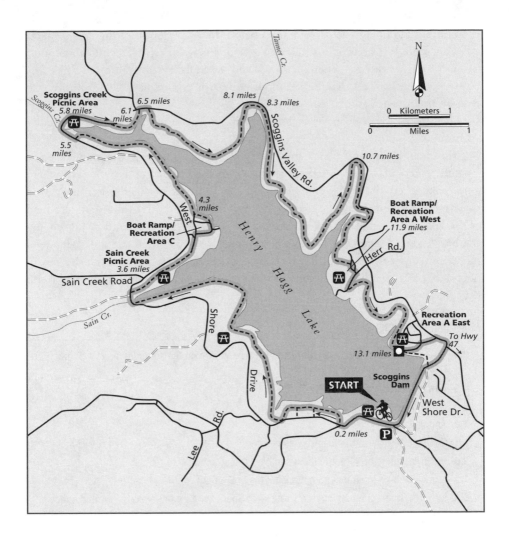

The Ride

Located just 40 miles from downtown Portland, Henry Hagg Lake and Scoggins Valley Park are a popular recreational spot for Tualatin Valley residents. The lake and park are maintained and operated by Washington County and owned by the U.S. Bureau of Reclamation. With 1,113 acres of surface area, the lake was constructed in the mid-1970s to provide supplemental water and flood control for the Tualatin Valley. The lake was named after Henry Hagg, a local dairy farmer who was one of the first people to suggest the reservoir project to the Bureau of Reclamation in 1959. Hagg was a member of the Tualatin Valley Irrigation District, the Agricultural Committee of the Portland Chamber of Commerce, and the Oregon State University Research

Committee. He died in 1979, four years before the completion of the lake project.

This route is a continuous roller coaster of fun with twisty, technical sections; smooth stretches through open meadows; and quiet, flat sections through thick forest. Hagg Lake Trail also has many bailout points for cyclists who want to finish the ride on the paved road that circles the lake.

Portions of the trail may be closed during winter months because of muddy conditions.

Mountain bikers and hikers aren't the only people enjoying this popular park. Boaters, water-skiers, and fishermen also use the lake. The east end of the lake, where a no-wake speed limit is not enforced, is used by motorboaters and water-skiers, and the west end is reserved for canoeing, sailing, and kayaking. Triathlons are also held at the lake, with the Hagg Lake Triathlon (held the second weekend in July) being the best known. Hagg Lake Trail is a city dweller's off-road mecca and is guaranteed to be crowded on weekends during the summer. The best time to ride here is in September and October when the summer crowds have dispersed and the trail is still dry.

Miles and Directions

0.0 From the gravel parking area, turn right (west) and ride on the shoulder of West Shore Drive.

0.2 Turn right on the dirt singletrack trail.

0.4 Continue on the main trail to the left.

1.0 Turn left.

1.1 Continue straight at the four-way intersection.

2.0 Continue straight (right). Continue another 20 feet and stay to the left.

2.2 A trail joins the main trail from the left. Stay to the right.

3.3 Turn right where the trail intersects with West Shore Drive and ride along the road shoulder.

3.4 Turn right on the signed singletrack trail.

3.5 The singletrack trail joins a doubletrack dirt road. Continue another 200 feet and arrive at a T-intersection with a gravel road. Turn right. The trail quickly turns back into singletrack.

3.6 The trail turns into a paved path and takes you through the Sain Creek Picnic Area. Water and rest rooms are available here. Continue riding through the picnic area on the paved path past an extravagant pavilion and continue on the signed singletrack trail.

4.0 Arrive at the paved parking area of the Boat Ramp–Recreation Area C. Continue through the long parking lot that parallels the lake and pick up the singletrack trail at the other side of the lot.

4.7 Turn left at a T-intersection. Ride ahead another 100 feet and then take a right and continue cruising on the singletrack trail.

5.0 Turn right and head downhill.

5.5 Continue straight (left). Go uphill to a paved road. Turn right at the paved road.

On the Hagg Lake Trail.

5.8 Pass the Scoggins Creek Picnic Area on your right. There are portable toilets but no water at this picnic area.

6.1 Arrive at a gravel parking area on your right. Pick up the signed singletrack trail at the far end of this parking lot.

6.5 Cross a small bridge and then take a quick right. (FYI: If you miss this turn, you'll end up at the paved road.)

6.6 Arrive at a T-intersection. Turn right on a wider trail.

8.1 Turn right on a paved road.

8.3 Turn right on a signed singletrack trail.

8.7 Turn right at the trail fork.

9.1 Turn right at the trail fork.

10.7 Arrive at the paved road. Turn right on the gravel shoulder and go about 100 feet and continue on the singletrack trail.

11.0 Turn left at the signed trail marker. (FYI: This trail sign is easy to miss!)

11.2 Turn left at the trail junction.

11.9 Arrive at Boat Ramp–Recreation Area A West. This recreation area has rest rooms and water. Ride across the parking lot and begin heading up the hill on the exit road. Look for a trail sign on your right.

12.1 Turn left at the T-intersection.

12.5 Continue straight across a faint trail intersection and start powering uphill.

12.8 Turn right and continue on the singletrack trail.

13.1 Arrive at a paved road, where you turn left and continue until you reach the intersection with Scoggins Valley Road.

13.3 Turn right on Scoggins Valley Road. Continue about 200 feet and then turn right on West Shore Drive and cross the dam.

15.1 Arrive back at the trailhead.

Ride Information

Local Information
Washington County Visitors Association, Beaverton, OR; (800) 537-3149; www.wcva.org.

Local Events and Attractions
Momokawa Saké Brewery, 820 Elm Street, Forest Grove; (800) 550-7253; www.momokawa.com.

Montinore Vineyards, 3663 SW Dilley Road, Forest Grove; (503) 359-5012.

Hagg Lake Triathlon, AA SPORTS, LTD, Beaverton; (503) 644-6822; www.racecenter.com/hagglake/index.htm.

Accommodations
McMenamins Grand Lodge, 3505 Pacific Avenue, Forest Grove; (503) 992-9533; www.mcmenamins.com/grandlodge/index.html.

Restaurants
The Yardhouse Pub at the Grand Lodge, 3505 Pacific Avenue, Forest Grove; (503) 992-3442.

Organizations
Portland United Mountain Pedalers (PUMP), 818 SW Third, #228, Portland, OR 97204; (503) 690-5259; www.pumpclub.org.

WORDS FROM THE WISE: OREGON PIONEER WISDOM AND FOLKLORE

- The nicest time of day is tomorrow about sunup.
- It's good luck to sing before breakfast.
- Never start sewing on Friday, because you will never finish the garment.
- Don't build a reputation when young that will be hard to keep when old.
- If the fire says "snow" with sparks popping out all over, it will snow shortly.
- Don't bring digging implements into the house, or there will be a death in the family.
- If you leave the house and forget something, you must return to the house and sit down before leaving again. Otherwise, you will have bad luck.
- Raw wool is good for corns. Get some wool from a fence that sheep have passed and place it on the corns.
- When horses are always tired and lathered in the morning, witches are riding them at night.
- To keep witches from the stable, put a broomstick crossways at the barn door.
- It is bad luck to walk a few feet into a cabin with one shoe off.

13 Silver Falls State Park

This hilly loop tour explores the forests and creeks in Silver Falls State Park. You'll have many options to vary your route on the park's 25 miles of multiuse trails.

Start: The route starts at the 214 Trailhead off Oregon Highway 214 in Silver Falls State Park.
Length: 8.1-mile loop.
Approximate riding time: 1.5 to 2 hours.
Difficulty: Moderate, due to elevation gain and occasional technical sections.
Total climbing: 900 feet.
Trail surface: Singletrack, doubletrack, gravel road, and paved path.
Land status: State park.
Seasons: May through October.
Nearest town: Silverton.
Other trail users: Hikers and equestrians.
Canine compatibility: Leashed dogs permitted.

Wheels: A bike with front suspension comes in handy for the creek crossings and one rock-garden section.
Trail contacts: Silver Falls State Park, Oregon Parks and Recreation, 1115 Commercial Street NE, Salem OR 97301; (800) 551-6949; www.oregonstateparks.org/park_211.php.
Fees and permits: $3.00 day use fee.
Maps: Maptech maps: Stout Mountain. The Silver Falls State Park Map is available from Oregon Parks and Recreation by calling (800) 551-6949 or online at www.oregonstateparks.org/park_211.php.

Finding the Trailhead

From Portland travel about 25 miles south on I-5 to Woodburn. Take exit 271 toward Woodburn and Silverton. At the end of the off-ramp, turn left on Highway 214 East toward Woodburn/Mount Angel/Silverton. Go 2.5 miles through downtown Woodburn and then turn right at a stoplight and continue south on Highway 99E/Highway 214 toward Mount Angel. Travel 1.1 miles and then turn left and continue on Highway 214 south toward Mount Angel and Silverton. Stay on Highway 214 for 27.9 miles to its junction with Lookout Mountain Road at the EQUESTRIAN AREA TRAILHEAD PARKING sign in Silver Falls State Park (this road is easy to miss!). Turn left on Lookout Mountain Road and continue 0.1 mile to a large gravel parking area on the right side of the road.
From I-5 in Salem turn east on Highway 22 toward North Santiam Highway–Stayton–Detroit Lake. Travel 5 miles east and take exit 7 on Highway 214 toward Silver Falls State Park. At the end of the off-ramp, turn left on Highway 214 and continue 4.5 miles to a stop sign. Turn left, staying on Highway 214, and travel 12.2 miles east to the entrance to Silver Falls State Park. After entering the park turn right at an easy-to-miss turn marked EQUESTRIAN AREA TRAILHEAD PARKING. Go 0.1 mile to a large gravel parking area on the right side of the road. *DeLorme: Oregon Atlas & Gazetteer:* Page 54 A3.

The Ride

Silver Falls State Park—at 8,700 acres, Oregon's largest state park—is best known for its Trail of Ten Falls that traipses past many waterfalls in a spectacular canyon carved by the North Fork and South Fork of Silver Creek. Although mountain biking isn't

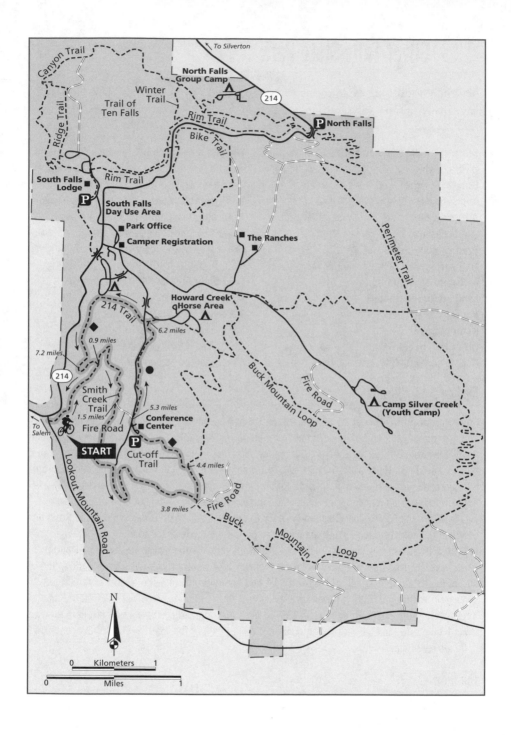

To Silverton

Canyon Trail

North Falls
Group Camp

Winter
Trail

Trail of
Ten Falls

214

Ridge Trail

Rim Trail

Bike Trail

P North Falls

South Falls
Lodge

Rim Trail

P

South Falls
Day Use Area

Park Office

Camper Registration

The Ranches

Perimeter Trail

214 Trail

Howard Creek
Horse Area

6.2 miles

7.2 miles

0.9 miles

214

Smith
Creek
Trail

Buck Mountain Loop

Fire Road

Camp Silver Creek
(Youth Camp)

5.3 miles

To
Salem

1.5 miles

Fire Road

Conference
Center

START

Cut-off
Trail

4.4 miles

P

Lookout Mountain Road

3.8 miles

Fire Road

Buck

Mountain

Loop

N

0   Kilometers   1

0   Miles   1

allowed on this trail, you can ride on 25 miles of multiuse trails in the surrounding hills.

In the 1880s a community called Silver Falls was established in this area, which consisted of nothing more than a sawmill, a hotel, and several hunting lodges. The land was overzealously logged for its timber until the late 1920s, when the state considered turning the area into a national park. The logging stopped, but unfortunately the national park status was never realized. Ironically, the land had been subjected to too much logging and farming and didn't pass muster with the National Park Service. The federal government purchased the land during the Great Depression and designated it a Recreational Demonstration Area. It now features recreational facilities, multiuse trails, and the South Falls Lodge.

This cycling trek begins at the southern end of the park on a singletrack trail that descends a ridge through an impressive Douglas fir and western hemlock forest carpeted with Oregon grape, salal, sword fern, and the showy purple stalks of foxglove. After 0.9 mile you'll turn on the Smith Creek Trail and ride on fun ups and downs through a shady forest until you cross rambling Smith Creek at 2.5 miles. From here you'll crank 550 feet on a steep ascent to the junction with the Buck Mountain Loop Trail at 3.8 miles. You'll be rewarded for all your hard work on a fun descent for another 1.3 miles. Watch your speed at the 4.8-mile mark—you'll have to contend with a rock garden that will test your technical expertise. At 5.1 miles you'll turn on a civil jogging path that winds through a large conference center and travels on flat terrain through a green forest corridor until you reach the junction with the 214 Trail at the 6.2-mile mark. From here get ready to crank over 350 feet on a steep uphill jaunt back to the trailhead.

Miles and Directions

0.0 Start the route by crossing Lookout Mountain Road and riding on the 214 Trail, marked with a brown multiuse sign.

0.4 The singletrack trail intersects with a gravel fire road. Continue straight on a rough gravel road. The road turns into a dirt doubletrack road after 0.4 mile and begins to descend.

0.9 Turn right on a doubletrack road marked with a small yellow trail sign. You are now riding on the Smith Creek Trail.

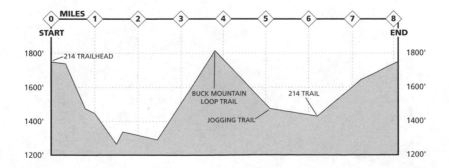

1.2 The route turns into a wide singletrack and continues to descend.

1.5 Take a very sharp right at the small yellow Trail marker. (FYI: A fire road heads left.) Begin a steep ascent.

1.8 You'll begin descending.

2.2 Turn right at the trail fork. Continue 100 yards and turn right on a singletrack trail at a T-intersection.

2.5 The trail crosses Smith Creek. From here you'll begin a steep climb.

3.8 Arrive at the top of a small hill. Turn left on the unsigned Buck Mountain Loop Trail (a doubletrack road) and begin descending. **Option:** You have the option of turning right here and completing the 6.1-mile Buck Mountain Loop Trail.

4.4 Take a sharp left on the unsigned "Cut-off Trail" and continue your fast descent on a singletrack trail.

4.8 You may have to walk your bike through a huge rock garden for 0.1 mile.

5.1 Turn left at the JOGGING TRAIL/CONFERENCE CENTER sign. Descend to a footbridge and cross a creek.

5.2 Turn right on a paved trail that winds through the Conference Center. Follow the paved trail toward the Lower Parking Area.

5.3 Arrive at the parking area. Ride across the large gravel parking lot. Turn left on the singletrack trail at a large trailhead sign. Go 20 feet and then turn right on the Jogging Trail as it parallels the paved entrance road to the Conference Center.

6.2 Go left at the T-intersection and cross a paved road. Continue on the unsigned 214 Trail on the other side. Begin a very steep ascent up a forested ridge. Eventually the single-track turns to a doubletrack road.

6.5 Ignore a side trail on the right.

7.2 Turn right at the T-intersection.

8.1 Arrive at the trailhead.

Ride Information

Local Information

Silverton Chamber of Commerce, Silverton; (503) 873-5615; www.silverton.or.us/chamber.

Local Events and Attractions

Mount Angel Oktoberfest, held in mid-September in downtown Mount Angel; (503) 845-9440; www.oktoberfest.org.

Oregon Gardens, 879 West Main Street, Silverton; (503) 874-8100; www.oregongarden.org.

Accommodations

Abiqua Creek Farms B&B, 16672 Nusom Road, Silverton; (503) 873-6878.

Silver Falls State Park Campground, Silver Falls State Park, Silver Falls; (800) 551-6949; www.oregonstateparks.org/park_211.php.

Towering Douglas fir trees in Silver Falls State Park.

14 Minto-Brown Island Park

This easy loop route explores Minto–Brown Island Park in Salem. It features views of the Willamette River, cool shady forest, open sunny pastures, and opportunities to view amazing bird life.

Start: First trailhead parking area at Minto–Brown Island Park in Salem.
Length: 5.8-mile loop.
Approximate riding time: 1 hour.
Difficulty: Easy due to smooth trail surface and flat terrain.
Total climbing: 5 feet. Elevation profiles are not provided for rides with little or no elevation gain.
Trail surface: Paved bike path and wood-chip trail.
Land status: County park.
Seasons: Open year-round. Some sections of the route may be muddy during the winter months.

Nearest town: Salem.
Other trail users: Hikers and joggers.
Canine compatibility: Leashed dogs permitted.
Wheels: A hybrid bike or mountain bike without front suspension will work fine because of this ride's flat, smooth surface.
Trail contacts: Salem Parks Operations Division, 1460 Twentieth Street SE, Salem, OR 97302; (503) 588–6261; www.open.org/~parks/minto_brown.htm.
Fees and permits: No fees or permits are required.
Maps: Maptech map: West Salem.

Finding the Trailhead

From I–5 in south Salem, take exit 252 at Kuebler Boulevard. Turn west on Kuebler Boulevard and travel 2 miles. Turn right (north) on Commercial Street and continue north for 3.5 miles (after 3 miles it turns into Liberty Street). Turn left on Bush Street. Go 1 block and then turn left on Commercial Street heading south. Proceed to the next light and turn right on Owens Street. Go 1.2 miles on Owens Street (this turns into River Road) and then turn right on Minto Island Road. Go 0.2 mile and turn right into a paved parking area at the trailhead. *DeLorme: Oregon Atlas & Gazetteer:* Page 53 A8.

The Ride

You'll love pedaling through this 835-acre park covered with orchards, large open fields, and pockets of forest, sloughs, and waterways. Originally there were two islands in the Willamette River. After a catastrophic flood in 1861, an abundance of topsoil was left behind, causing the two islands to join. The original homesteader on Brown Island was Isaac Whiskey Brown, who grew tobacco and raised livestock. John Minto, an early homesteader and legislator, purchased 247 acres and settled on the neighboring Minto Island in 1867.

Currently the park is managed by the Salem Regional Park and Recreation Agency as a wildlife and recreation area with more than 20 miles of paved and

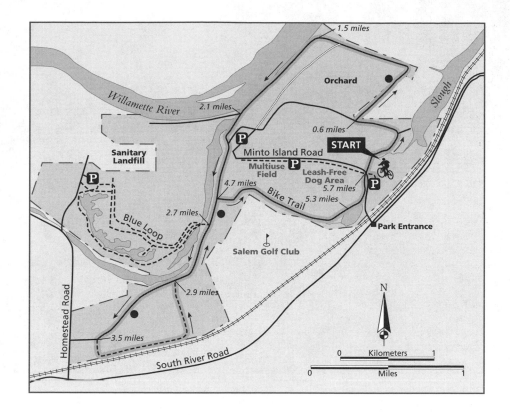

unpaved pathways. It is an important wintering area for dusky Canada geese that arrive in mid-October and stay through mid-April. Look for them in the open fields and waterways in the park. Commercial agriculture crops are still grown on the island. More than 244 acres are planted each year; crops include potatoes, sweet corn, snap beans, and wheat.

This easy 5.8-mile loop route is a combination of paved and dirt paths that take you to the Willamette River, through shady wooded areas past sloughs and ponds, and through large, sunny pastures and fields. Your canine partner will be glad to know the park also has a twenty-acre leash-free area in a large grassy field surrounded by deciduous trees. Rover will never grow tired of playing Frisbee or fetch in this huge outdoor playground. To get to the leash-free area, turn right on Minto Island Road and travel 0.5 mile to a gravel parking area on the left side of the road.

The ride described here is only one of dozens of possible routes you can explore. You can try this route or create your own.

Miles and Directions

0.0 Start riding on the paved trail that starts to the left of the rest rooms at the far end of the parking area.

Cruising next to the Willamette River in Minto-Brown Island Park.

0.1 Ride over a wood bridge and arrive at an intersection with a paved road. Turn right and continue on the paved route marked by a BIKE ROUTE sign.

0.3 Turn left at the trail junction and continue pedaling on the paved trail.

0.6 Turn right at the trail junction and continue cruising on the flat paved path. Enter a shady corridor of stately cottonwood trees. (FYI: This is a yummy blackberry area. They ripen starting in mid-August.)

1.3 Veer right at the trail junction (a dirt path heads left at this junction) and continue on the paved path that passes through a large grove of cottonwoods.

1.5 The paved path begins paralleling the Willamette River. (FYI: Watch for dusky Canada geese, blue herons, and other birds along this section of the route.)

2.1 Turn left (away from the river) and continue riding on the paved trail. A dirt trail heads right.

2.2 Arrive at a T-intersection with a paved trail. Veer right and continue on the paved path. After this turn there is a parking area on the left and rest rooms on the right side of the trail.

2.3 Arrive at a trail junction. Go right on the paved path as it skirts the right side of the picnic area.

2.4 Turn right on a paved path.

2.5 Turn right at the trail junction and continue riding on the paved path. The trail parallels a slough on the right.

2.7 Turn left at the trail junction and continue riding on the paved path.

2.9 Turn right and continue pedaling on the paved path.

3.0 Veer right and continue on the paved path.

3.3 Continue straight (left). A side trail heading right crosses a bridge.

3.5 Turn left onto a dirt path. The paved trail heads right at this junction.

4.1 You'll ride past the Salem Golf Course on your right.

4.3 Turn right on a paved path.

4.7 Turn right on a paved path.

4.8 Turn right on a paved path.

5.3 You'll pedal past a large lily pond on your right.

5.7 The paved path intersects with Minto Island Road. Cross the road and then turn right on the paved path on the other side.

5.8 Turn left into the parking area and the trailhead.

Ride Information

Local Information

Salem Chamber of Commerce, 1110 Commercial Street NE, Salem, OR 97301; (503) 581-1466; www.salemchamber.org.

Organizations

Salem Merry Cranksters, P.O. Box 17564, Salem, OR 97305; (503) 365-8914; www.merrycranksters.org

Honorable Mentions

Compiled here is an index of great rides within a two-hour drive of Portland. Check them out and let us know what you think. You may decide that one or more of these rides deserves higher status in future editions, or perhaps you have a ride of your own that merits some attention.

A Larch Mountain

This 15-mile, advanced-level loop tests your technical skills and cardio capacity as it climbs over 2,700 feet in the Yacolt Burn State Forest in southwest Washington.

To get there from the intersection of I–205 and I–84 West in Portland, head 9.5 miles north on I 205 to the Washington State Route 500 East exit 30. Go 1.5 miles to a stoplight at NE Fourth Plain Road. Continue straight (north) on SR 503 toward Battleground. Continue 14 miles north on SR 503 (you'll pass through Battleground after 8 miles) and turn right on Rock Creek Road. Go 2.8 miles to a stop sign where the road name changes to Lucia Falls Road. Continue straight another 5.9 miles to the junction with Sunset Falls Road. Turn right and continue 2.1 miles to the junction with Dole Valley Road. Turn right (eventually this turns into Forest Road L–1000) and travel 5.1 miles to Rock Creek Campground. Turn left into the campground entrance road and go 0.1 mile to a brown pump house and parking area on the right side of the road.

From the campground you'll ride out the entrance road and turn left on FR L–1000. At 0.3 mile turn left on FR L–1200. At 0.9 mile continue straight (right) on FR L–1200 and follow it to Grouse Point at 5.5 miles. At Grouse Point turn right on the Larch Mountain Trail and begin a steep climb over technical terrain until you reach the 7.8-mile mark. From here turn right (toward Cold Creek Campground) and begin an exciting technical descent as the route careens down the side of Larch Mountain until you reach FR L–1000 at 12.5 miles. Cross FR L–1000 and crank on the singletrack trail for another 1.5 miles to Cold Creek Campground, where the trail intersects with FR L–1300. Turn left on L–1300, pedal a short distance, and then turn right on the singletrack trail. Follow the singletrack for another 0.8 mile to the junction with FR L–1000. Cross the road and ride into Rock Creek Campground and your starting point. If you want to check out other trails in this area, be sure to ride the inspiring Tarbell Trail that also starts from Rock Creek Campground. The best time to ride this route is May through October.

For more information contact the Washington Department of Natural Resources, Southwest Region, 601 Bond Road, Castle Rock, WA 98611; (360) 577–2025; www.parks.wa.gov/ada-rec. The Yacolt Burn State Forest Map is a good reference map for this area and is available from the Bureau of Land Management, P.O. Box 2965, Portland, OR 97208; (503) 808–6001; www.or.blm.gov/lo/index.htm. *DeLorme: Washington Atlas & Gazetteer:* Page 23 B6.

B Lewis River

Located in the Gifford Pinchot National Forest in Washington, this 19.2-mile, out-and-back, intermediate ride follows the contours of the scenic Lewis River. It's a classic river trail with a good mix of steep ups and downs, cliff riding, numerous rock gardens, and creek crossings. To get there from Portland, follow I–5 north for 21 miles to its junction with Washington State Route 503. Turn east on Route 503 (which turns into Forest Road 90 east of Cougar) and travel 52.5 miles to the junction with FR 9039. Turn left and continue 0.8 mile to the parking area on the left. From the parking area, ride across the river and start riding on the singletrack trail on the right. Follow the trail for 9.6 miles until it arrives at a junction with FR 90. From here, turn around and retrace the route back to the trailhead. The best time to ride this route is late May through October.

This ride requires a $5.00 Northwest Forest Pass. You can purchase it online at www.naturenw.org or by calling (800) 270–7504.

For more information contact the Gifford Pinchot National Forest, Wind River Information Center, 1262 Hemlock Road, Carson, WA 98610; (509) 427–3200; www.fs.fed.us/gpnf. *DeLorme: Washington Atlas & Gazetteer:* Page 34 C1.

C Siouxan Creek–Horseshoe Creek Falls–Chinook Falls

This 12.5-mile out-and-back intermediate tour follows the contours of picturesque Siouxan Creek in the Gifford Pinchot National Forest in southwest Washington.

From Portland head north on I–5 for 9 miles to the exit for Washington State Route 502. Travel east on Washington Route 502 for 7 miles to the junction with Washington Route 503. Turn left (north) on Washington Route 503 and go 17 miles. Turn right on Forest Road 54 and go 8 miles to FR 5701. Turn left on FR 5701 and follow it about 4 miles to the road's end and the trailhead.

Start riding on a trail that heads downhill toward the creek. At a T-intersection turn right. At 1.1 miles continue straight at the trail junction. After 1.7 miles head left to a viewpoint of Horseshoe Creek Falls. Return to the main trail and continue climbing. At 3.2 miles go straight on Trail 130. At 4 miles you have the option of turning left on Trail 130A and riding 0.5 mile out and back to a viewpoint of Chinook Falls. From here continue on Trail 130 as it parallels the creek. After 6.5 miles you'll arrive at your turnaround point, where the trail crosses the Siouxan Creek. Return on the same route back to your starting point. The best time to ride this route is May through October.

This ride requires a $5.00 Northwest Forest Pass. You can purchase it online at www.naturenw.org or by calling (800) 270–7504.

For more information contact the Gifford Pinchot National Forest, Wind River Information Center, 1262 Hemlock Road, Carson, WA 98610; (509) 427–3200; www.fs.fed.us/gpnf. *DeLorme: Washington Atlas & Gazetteer:* Page 23 A7.

D Gales Creek

This 4.2-mile, out-and-back, intermediate trail travels through a second growth forest of Douglas fir, red alder, and stately cottonwood trees in the Tillamook State Forest. A combination of singletrack and some doubletrack, it climbs for 632 feet along the banks of Low Divide Creek. It is very technical in sections and tests your cardio fitness.

To get there from I–405 and U.S. Highway 26 in Portland, head 20.5 miles west on U.S. Highway 26 to the junction with Oregon Highway 6. Head left (west) on Highway 6 toward Banks and Tillamook to just before milepost 37, where you'll turn right toward Gales Creek Campground. Continue 1.5 miles to the second day use parking area on the left side of the road.

Start riding on the trail located on the far left side of the parking area. At 2.1 miles you'll reach a gravel parking area and your turnaround point. You can complete a longer route by combining this trail with one of the many fire roads in the Tillamook State Forest. You can also combine this trail with Tillamook State Forest (Ride 11). The time to ride this route is late May through October.

For more information contact Tillamook State Forest, Forest Grove, OR; (503) 357–2191; www.odf.state.or.us/tsf/tsfhome.htm. Before you ride this trail, it is highly recommended that you obtain a Tillamook State Forest/Wilson River Highway Area Map from the Tillamook State Forest. *DeLorme: Oregon Atlas & Gazetteer:* Page 65 C6.

E Champoeg State Heritage Area

Established in 1901, Champoeg State Park is located on the banks of the Willamette River and features white oak woodlands, open grassy meadows, a large campground, hiking and biking trails, historic buildings, and a large visitor center. This easy, 6.4-mile, out-and-back ride explores the park's bike path that sails along the shores of the Willamette River through a shady, forested setting.

Champoeg State Heritage Area is between Portland and Salem, just west of Wilsonville. From I–5 take Donald/Aurora/Champoeg State Park exit 278. Turn west and drive 3.5 miles on Ehlen Road/Yergen Road. Turn right on Case Road and continue for 1.3 miles to Champoeg Road. Turn left and proceed 0.8 miles on Champoeg Road to the entrance. Turn right on the entrance road, pass the visitor center, and keep left at all intersections until you reach the Riverside Day Use Parking Area.

From the parking area, ride east on the paved path for 3.2 miles to the intersection with Schuler Road (your turnaround point). You can pedal this route year-round.

This park requires a $3.00 day use pass, which you can purchase at the visitor center.

For more information contact Oregon State Parks and Recreation, 1115 Commercial Street NE, Suite 1, Salem OR 97301; (800) 551–6949; www. oregonstateparks.org/park_113.php. *DeLorme: Oregon Atlas & Gazetteer:* Page 60 B1.

F Willamette Mission State Park

This easy, 2.3-mile loop takes you on a tour of Willamette Mission State Park past the scenic Willamette River, Mission Lake, and what is thought to be the world's biggest black cottonwood tree at 26 feet in circumference and 155 feet tall.

From I–5 take exit 263 toward Brooks and Gervais. (This exit is approximately 8 miles south of Woodburn and 9 miles north of Salem.) At the end of the off-ramp, change your mileage indicator to zero. Turn west on Brooklake Road and go 1.6 miles to the intersection with Wheatland Road. Turn right and drive 2.4 miles to the entrance road to Willamette Mission State Park. Turn left into the park and drive 0.6 mile to the pay booth for the park. (You'll need to pay a $3.00 day use fee. If an attendant is not in the booth, you can purchase a permit from the self-pay machine.) Continue 1.2 miles (staying to the left at each road junction) to the Filbert Grove Day Use Area.

You can follow the route cues described here or design your own route on the many trails in the park. Start the tour on the trail adjacent to the rest rooms at the far northwest corner of the parking area. At 0.2 mile turn right on the paved bike path that parallels the wide, lazy Willamette River. At 1.2 miles turn right on a grassy doubletrack road. Soon you'll pass Mission Lake on your left. As you continue through a walnut orchard, stay to the left at all trail junctions. At 1.9 miles arrive at a paved road and a sign that points to the world's largest black cottonwood tree. Continue pedaling on the paved road for 0.4 mile (at the first road junction go left and at the second road junction go right). At 2.3 miles arrive back at your starting point. You can pedal this route year-round.

For more information contact Oregon State Parks and Recreation, 1115 Commercial Street NE, Suite 1, Salem OR 97301–1002; (800) 551–6949; www. oregonstateparks.org/park_139.php. *DeLorme: Oregon Atlas & Gazetteer:* Page 59 D8.

G Dan's Trail–Dimple Hill

This 8.2-mile out-and-back intermediate tour takes you to the top of 1,495-foot Dimple Hill in the McDonald Dunn Research Forest. The route starts in Chip Ross Park and climbs 785 feet through a scenic forest to the summit, where you'll have awesome views (on a clear day) of Corvallis and the surrounding Coast Mountain Range.

To get there, travel about 20 miles south of Salem on I–5 to exit 234B. At the end of the off-ramp, follow Pacific Boulevard SE for a mile until it turns into U.S. Highway 20. Follow U.S. Highway 20 west toward Corvallis. After about 10 miles turn right on Conifer Boulevard and drive 1.4 miles to Oregon Highway 99 West. Turn left and go 0.3 mile to the intersection with Walnut Boulevard. Turn right and travel 1.1 miles to NW Highland Drive. Turn right and proceed 0.9 mile to Lester Avenue. Turn left and go 0.9 mile to the trailhead at the road's end at Chip Ross Park.

From the parking area at Chip Ross Park, start riding toward the yellow gate. Head north past the gate and continue on the old road that heads right. At the next trail fork, head right. You'll immediately begin climbing. Ignore a trail on the left and then another on the right. At 0.5 mile the trail levels off a bit. As you continue, ignore paths that head left off the main trail. At 0.8 mile turn right on a singletrack trail and begin a fast downhill. At 1 mile arrive at a four-way intersection. Turn right and continue to the next trail intersection, where you'll head right on Dan's Trail. At 1.1 miles ignore a trail that heads left. At 1.2 miles the route takes you under some ugly power lines. Ignore a trail that heads left as you begin a fast downhill. At 1.6 miles ignore a trail that heads right. At the next intersection, head left to continue your quest to reach the summit of Dimple Hill. Go across a gravel road and continue on Dan's Trail. At 2.1 miles ignore a trail that heads left. At 2.3 miles arrive at the intersection with a doubletrack road. Continue to the left on the singletrack trail and get ready for some tough climbing. At 2.8 miles arrive at a four-way intersection. Go straight. At 4.1 miles arrive at the summit of Dimple Hill, where the trail intersects with a gravel road. Enjoy the summit views and then retrace the route back to the trailhead. The best time to ride this route is May through October.

For more information contact Oregon State University, College of Forests, 8692 Peavey Arboretum Road, Corvallis, OR 97330; (541) 737–6702, (541) 737–4434 (recorded message); www.cof.orst.edu/resfor/rec/purpose.sht. You can obtain a map online at www.cof.orst.edu/resfor/rec/smcdfor.sht. *DeLorme: Oregon Atlas & Gazetteer:* Page 53 D6.

H Marys Peak

This is an advanced, 13-mile, out-and-back, singletrack ride that climbs over 2,300 feet to the summit of Marys Peak, the highest point in the coastal range.

To get there from Corvallis, drive west on U.S. Highway 20/Oregon Highway 34 to Philomath. Go through Philomath and stay on U.S. Highway 20 toward Toledo/Newport. Soon after you cross Marys River, you'll turn left on Forest Road 2005 (Woods Creek Road). Drive on Woods Creek Road for approximately 7.5 miles. At the intersection with FR 112, park in the pullout on the left.

Begin the ride by going around a gate and cranking uphill on FR 2005. After about 3.5 miles you'll reach another gate. Ride around this gate, then bear right on East Ridge Trail. At the next intersection bear left and continue on East Ridge Trail. Eventually the trail intersects with a gravel road. Turn left on the gravel road and ride to the summit of Marys Peak. Follow the same route back to the trailhead. The best time to ride this route is late May through October.

For more information contact the Alsea Ranger District, Siuslaw National Forest, 18591 Alsea Highway, Alsea, OR 97324; (541) 487–5811. *DeLorme: Oregon Atlas & Gazetteer:* Page 52 C4.

Columbia River Gorge, Hood River, and Mount Hood

E stablished in 1986, the Columbia River Gorge National Scenic Area is home to one of the highest concentrations of waterfalls in North America. It stretches for 60 miles on both sides of the river, from Troutdale to The Dalles, Oregon, on the south, and from Camas to Lyle, Washington, on the north. Carved by the immense Columbia River, this national treasure is well known for its hiking trails but also offers mountain bikers trails with technical challenges and great gorge scenery. If you want some singletrack action, check out Gorge Trail 400 or Larch Mountain. If you want a mellower ride with great gorge views, pedal the Historic Columbia River Highway State Trail.

The Columbia River Gorge is also home to Hood River, best known for its world-class sailboarding. Hood River is also the gateway to great singletrack action in the Hood River Valley and on Mount Hood. The Mount Hood National Forest features spectacular forested trails that take you along beautiful rivers, to the top of scenic vistas, and around high alpine lakes. Rides that should not be missed around Hood River and Mount Hood include: East Fork Hood River, Surveyor's Ridge, Fifteen Mile Creek, Gunsight Ridge, Timothy Lake, Crosstown–Pioneer Bridle–Still Creek Loop, and Old Salmon River Trail.

A quick 15 miles east of Hood River on I–84 is the small community of The Dalles. Established in 1857, it was for years the center of trade for goods transported up and down the Columbia River between western and eastern Oregon. Fur trappers congregated here before shipping their furs to Fort Vancouver, and The Dalles was the put-in for pioneers who braved the Columbia's once fierce rapids on their trek to the Willamette Valley. A short drive east from The Dalles is the Deschutes River State Park–Harris Ranch ride that explores the Deschutes River Canyon and the old Harris Ranch homestead. This is an excellent route for bicycle camping. If you don't want to rough it out on the trail, the Deschutes River State Park also offers more civilized camping options.

15 Gorge Trail 400

Waterfalls, misty clouds, and mossy forest entice thousands of people to visit the Columbia River Gorge each year. Known more as a hiker's paradise, this beloved piece of northwest Oregon also has trails open to mountain bikes. Gorge Trail 400 is the mountain biker's red carpet, providing tantalizing views of this area's mesmerizing scenic beauty.

Start: Wahclella Falls Trailhead is located 40 miles east of Portland off I-84 in the Columbia River Gorge.

Other starting locations: Dodson/Warrendale, Eagle Creek, and Cascade Locks off I-84 in the Columbia River Gorge.

Length: 6 miles out and back.

Approximate riding time: 1 to 2 hours.

Difficulty: Moderate, due to steep climbs, some drop-offs, trail erosion, roots, and rocks.

Total climbing: 1,000 feet.

Trail surface: Singletrack and doubletrack.

Land status: National scenic area.

Seasons: April through October.

Nearest town: Portland.

Other trail users: Hikers.

Canine compatibility: Leashed dogs permitted.

Wheels: A bike with front suspension recommended for this moderately technical trail.

Trail contacts: USDA Forest Service, Columbia River Gorge National Scenic Area, 902 Wasco Avenue, Suite 200, Hood River, OR 97031; (541) 386-2333; www.fs.fed.us/r6/columbia.

Fees and permits: Requires a $5.00 Northwest Forest Pass or a $30.00 annual pass. You can purchase it online at www.nature nw.org or by calling (800) 270-7504.

Maps: Maptech maps: Bonneville Dam; Tanner Butte.

Finding the Trailhead

From Portland head east on I-84 for approximately 40 miles, to Bonneville Dam (exit 40). At the stop sign, turn right and pull into the gravel parking lot at the Wahclella Falls Trailhead. *DeLorme: Oregon Atlas & Gazetteer:* Page 68 C1.

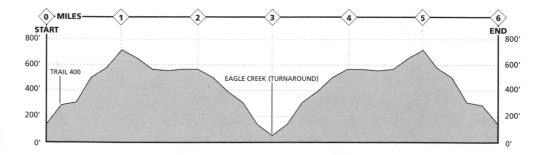

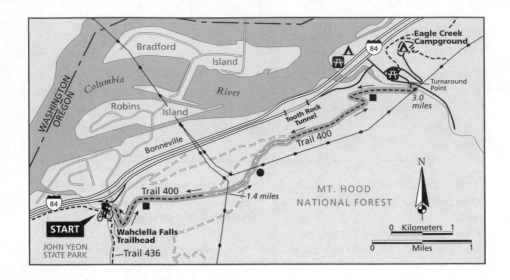

The Ride

Oregon's amazing cascading waterfalls and beautiful greenery await those who visit the Columbia River Gorge. The Columbia River courses through a 3,000-foot tree-lined gorge, whose steep cliff walls are lush with a variety of ferns, shrubs, and mosses. The beauty of this area has long been appreciated, but at the turn of the century those interested in accessing the Columbia River Gorge found it quite a difficult passage. It became the charge of two visionaries, Samuel Lancaster and Sam Hill, to build a highway through the gorge, to make it more accessible to the public. These two men imagined building a scenic highway that would complement and blend into the natural landscape, and they looked to roads that wound through the mountains of Germany, Italy, and Switzerland for inspiration.

▶ "The Columbia River Gorge is many things to many people. Its beauty can be observed not only on a grand scale of cliffs, waterfalls, and cloud-capped vistas, but also the world-in-miniature of its animal and plant life." – Kenton L. Chambers, botanist, 1988

Lancaster and Hill convinced the state government to build the Columbia River Highway. It was completed in 1922, running 196 miles from Astoria to The Dalles at an estimated cost to the state of $11 million. Even though this was an enormous expense at the time, the artistry of the stone bridges and walls that lined the highway was well worth the many public dollars spent. Locally quarried basalt was used to construct the eye-pleasing bridges, walls, and public buildings, which still exist today along a stretch of the highway running between Troutdale and Warrendale. One of the biggest attractions along this section of the old highway is 642-foot Multnomah

Bonneville Dam on the Columbia River.

Falls. These spectacular falls were a popular stopping point when the highway was first opened and today are one of the most popular sightseeing destinations in Oregon. Multnomah Falls Lodge sits at the base of the falls as a classic example of the artistic stonework present along the highway.

Although many of the trails in the Columbia Gorge are open only for hiking, there is an excellent singletrack trail that provides mountain bikers the opportunity to experience this unique area. Gorge Trail 400 runs for 35 miles in an east-west direction through the Columbia Gorge. The trail described here is a 6-mile out-and-back ride beginning at the Bonneville Dam exit off I-84 at the Wahclella Falls Trailhead and traveling to Eagle Creek. This section of Trail 400 is great for cyclists looking for a short, steep, scenic ride.

The ride starts with a very steep, 2-mile climb up a forested ridge filled with dark evergreens, maples, and red cedars. Bright green, moss-coated logs and rocks add contrast to the variety of trees that cover this steep ridge. Sections of this trail have eroded and can be slippery and muddy after a heavy rainfall. After about 2 miles, you'll begin a fun descent to Eagle Creek—your turnaround point. If you have time, stash your bike (bikes not allowed) and hike along the Eagle Creek Trail, one of the most scenic trails in the Gorge. This somewhat precipitous trail winds along a steep canyon of rough-patterned rock walls, tumbling side creeks, and spectacular views of waterfalls (Metlako Falls at 1.5 miles, Punch Bowl Falls at 2.1 miles, and High Bridge at 3.3 miles). If you don't have time to hike the Eagle Creek Trail, but still want to hit the footpath, try the short hike to Wahclella Falls, which is accessible from the parking area at the start of the ride. The only major drawback to Trail 400 is the noise of automobile traffic rising intrusively from of I–84. If you can ignore the twentieth century, this trail is well worth a visit!

Miles and Directions

0.0 Starting from the parking lot, look for the large Wahclella Falls Trailhead sign. The start of Trail 400 is just to the left of the sign. You'll begin climbing right away as the trail winds up a steep ridge.

1.2 The trail turns to doubletrack.

1.4 Cross beneath a large group of power lines. Veer left at the road junction. In a short distance you'll arrive at another road junction. Turn left.

1.6 Turn left at the road junction.

1.8 The road forks. Turn right on a singletrack trail.

2.1 Turn left toward Eagle Creek and continue on Trail 400. Trail 402 heads right toward Wauna Viewpoint.

2.7 There's a good view here of the Columbia River and Bonneville Dam.

3.0 The trail comes to a T at Eagle Creek. At this point, reverse the directions back to your starting point. **Side trip:** If you have time, stash your bike and hike along the Eagle Creek Trail.

6.0 Arrive at the trailhead.

Ride Information

Local Information
Portland Visitors Information and Service Center, 701 SW Sixth Avenue, Portland, OR 97204; (877) 678-5263; www.pova.com/visitor/index.html.

Accommodations
McMenamins Edgefield, 2126 SW Halsey Street, Troutdale; (503) 669-8610; www.mcmenamins.com.

Organizations
Friends of the Columbia Gorge, 522 SW Fifth Avenue, Suite 820, Portland, OR 97204; (503) 241-3762; www.gorgefriends.org.

16 Historic Columbia River Highway State Trail

Relive the historic past by touring a section of the restored Columbia River Highway. On this easy, paved route you'll wind along the edge of the scenic Columbia River Gorge for over 9 miles on an out-and-back route between Hood River and Mosier. Along the way you'll be able to stop at many spectacular viewpoints and pass through the historic Mosier Twin Tunnels.

Start: The ride begins at the Mark O. Hatfield West Trailhead in Hood River. An alternative starting point is the Mark O. Hatfield East Trailhead in Mosier.

Length: 9.2 miles out and back.

Approximate riding time: 1.5 to 2 hours.

Difficulty: Easy, due to the smooth paved surface.

Total climbing: 675 feet.

Trail surface: Paved multiuse trail.

Land status: State park.

Seasons: Open year-round (can be icy during the winter months).

Nearest town: Hood River.

Other trail users: Hikers and in-line skaters.

Canine compatibility: Leashed dogs permitted.

Wheels: A hybrid bike or bike without suspension will do fine on this route due to the smooth, paved surface.

Trail contacts: Oregon Parks and Recreation, Salem, OR; (800) 551-6949; www. oregonstateparks.org/park_155.php.

Fees and permits: Requires a $3.00 Oregon State Park day pass or a $25.00 annual pass. You purchase a day pass from the self-pay station at the Hood River and Mosier Trailheads. The annual pass can be bought at the visitor center at the Hood River Trailhead.

Maps: Maptech map: White Salmon. A Columbia River Gorge bicycle map is available in the visitor center at the Hood River Trailhead or is available online at www.odot.state.or.us/region1/f_hcrh/news_111400.htm.

Finding the Trailhead

Mark O. Hatfield West Trailhead in Hood River: From the intersection of I-205 and I-84 in Portland, go 54 miles east on I-84 toward Hood River and The Dalles. Turn off the highway at exit 64 where a sign indicates HOOD RIVER HIGHWAY 35/WHITE SALMON/GOVERNMENT CAMP. At the end of the off-ramp, turn right (south) toward Hood River. Continue 0.3 mile to a stop sign and a four-way intersection. Turn left (east) on the Old Columbia River Highway. You'll also see a sign indicating HISTORIC STATE PARK TRAIL. Travel 1.3 miles on the Old Columbia River Highway until you reach a parking area, visitor center, and the Mark O. Hatfield West Trailhead on the left side of the road.

Mark O. Hatfield East Trailhead in Mosier: From Hood River go 5 miles east on I-84 to Mosier exit 69. At the end of the off-ramp, turn right. Go 0.2 mile and then take a sharp left on Rock Creek Road at the HISTORIC STATE PARK TRAIL sign. Continue 0.6 mile on Rock Creek Road to the Mark O. Hatfield East Trailhead on the left side of the road. *DeLorme: Oregon Atlas & Gazetteer:* Page 68 C4, Page 69 C5.

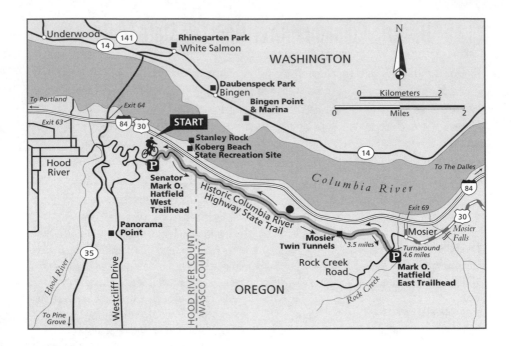

The Ride

The Historic Columbia River Highway State Trail takes you on a tour along a historic section of the Columbia River Highway. This fun, easy route is a favorite hiker-biker trail that travels for 4.6 miles between the sailboarding capital of Hood River and the small, cozy town of Mosier. The trail is part of the Columbia River Highway built between 1913 and 1922. The Mosier Twin Tunnels, which were originally designed by Conde B. McCullough, a well-known state bridge engineer for the Oregon Highway Department, are a main feature of the trail. The tunnels were built in 1921 and were lined with timbers for extra support and finished with handcrafted stonework. They had viewing portals and a mesmerizing walk built right into the cliff outside.

In addition to the Mosier Twin Tunnels, two other tunnels, Oneonta and Mitchell Point, were built along the Columbia River Highway between 1914 and 1921. When the original highway was relocated in the 1950s, the Oneonta and Mitchell Point tunnels were filled with rock and abandoned.

In May of 2000 Secretary of the Interior Bruce Babbitt announced that 51 of the original 55 miles of road of the Columbia River Highway between Troutdale and The Dalles were designated a National Historic Landmark, one of about 2,300 National Historic Landmarks across the country. An employee of the Oregon Department of Transportation, Robert W. Hadlow, Ph.D., nominated the highway for this special designation and wrote, "It is an outstanding example of modern highway development in twentieth-century America for its pioneering advances in road design. The road, and its associated designed landscape, was a technical and civic achievement of its time, successfully mixing ambitious engineering with sensitivity to the magnificent landscape."

The Mosier Twin Tunnels section is one of many sites along the highway that have been restored and reopened for the public to enjoy. This spectacular 4.6-mile section of the trail was opened to the public in July of 2000 and cost a hefty $5.6 million to build—think of what kind of mountain bike inventory you could accumulate with that type of budget! A large percentage of the project was funded with federal dollars and the remainder was paid for with private donations. Why did it cost so much? Rockfall at the west tunnel entrance has always been a huge danger and it was up to the Oregon Department of Transportation to come up with a viable solution. The solution chosen was a concrete deck structure made up of foam and cement that rests on concrete pillars. It is anchored to the cliff with 25-foot anchor bars and is designed to support the impact of a 5,000-pound rock falling from a height of 200 feet. To be sure the structure blended into the natural surroundings, the concrete was tinted a very dark gray to blend in with the surrounding basalt cliff. This amazing project took five years to complete; you will understand why when you ride under the concrete deck and explore the inside of the tunnels.

Before you start zipping down this fast paved route, be sure to stop in the visitor center and check out the interpretive displays describing the restoration process of this historic route. The friendly folks manning the desk inside can fill your head with dozens of other things to see and do while you are in the area.

Miles and Directions

0.0 Start riding east on the paved trail adjacent to the visitor center where a trail sign reads SENATOR MARK O. HATFIELD WEST TRAILHEAD. (FYI: On the first part of the route, you'll pedal through a wet ecosystem of fir trees mixed with bigleaf maple and other deciduous tree species. In the spring, bright purple lupine and bright yellow balsamroot add splashes of color next to the trail.)

0.2 You'll pass an interpretive sign on your right that describes the different ecosystems along the route.

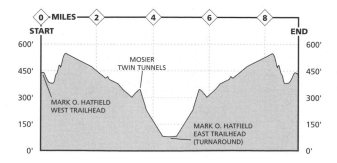

The dramatic Columbia River Gorge.

2.7 You'll pass a viewpoint on your left of the Columbia River and cliff-lined gorge.

3.5 Enter the Mosier Twin Tunnels. (FYI: From inside the tunnels you'll have opportunities to stop and soak in more stunning views of the gorge.)

3.7 Exit the Mosier Twin Tunnels.

3.8 You'll pass a side trail on the left leading to a viewpoint where you may catch glimpses to the north (on a clear day) of Mount St. Helens and Mount Adams.

4.4 At the T-intersection and stop sign, turn right and head uphill to the Mark O. Hatfield East Trailhead.

4.6 Arrive at the Mark O. Hatfield East Trailhead and your turnaround point. This trailhead also has water, rest rooms, and a phone. **Option:** You can also complete this ride from this trailhead by reversing the trail directions.

9.2 You'll arrive back at the Hood River Trailhead and your vehicle.

Ride Information

Local Information

Hood River Chamber of Commerce, 405 Portway Avenue, Hood River, OR 97031; (800) 366-3530; www.hoodriver.org.

Local Events and Attractions

Gorge Games begin in mid-July, Hood River; (541) 386-7774; www.gorgegames.com.

Hood River Blossom Festival, held the third week in April, Hood River; (541) 354-2865.

Hood River Harvest Festival, held the third week in October at the Hood River Expo on the Waterfront, Hood River; (800) 366-3530.

Hood River Vineyards, 4693 Westwood Drive, Hood River; (541) 386-3772.

Mount Hood Scenic Railroad, 110 Railroad Avenue, Hood River; (800) 872-4661; www.mthoodrr.com.

Accommodations

Columbia Gorge Hotel, 4000 Westcliff Drive, Hood River; (800) 345-1921; www.columbiagorgehotel.com.

Mosier House B&B, 704 Third Avenue, Mosier; (541) 478-3640; www.mosierhouse.com.

Memaloose State Park, located 11 miles west of The Dalles (westbound exit only), Oregon State Parks, Salem; (800) 551-6949; www.oregonstateparks.org.

Organizations

Friends of the Columbia Gorge, 522 SW Fifth Avenue, Suite 820, Portland, OR 97030; (503) 241-3762; www.gorgefriends.org.

KNOW THE LINGO ...

Chinook Jargon

The Northwest Indian tribes developed a universal language to use when trading and speaking with trappers, farmers, explorers, and passers-through. This universal language developed into Chinook jargon, which borrowed heavily from the English and French languages. Here is a sampling of some common words:

- **Bos-ton:** American
- **Cul-tus:** Worthless
- **Huy-huy:** To barter or trade
- **Kam-ooks:** Dog
- **Kla-how-ya:** Hello or goodbye
- **Klootch-man:** Woman
- **Mam-ook:** To make, to work

- **Mem-a-loose:** To die, dead
- **Mow-ich:** Deer
- **O-lal-lie:** Berries
- **Si-wash:** Indian
- **Skoo-kum:** Strong, powerful
- **Tal-a-pus:** Coyote
- **Ty-ee:** Chief

17 Surveyor's Ridge

This trail is one of the classic singletrack Oregon rides that has everything an avid cyclist could ever want—creek crossings, rocks, roots, gravel, steep ascents, and a gut-wrenching, arm-aching descent. You'll also have phenomenal views of Mount Hood.

Start: The intersection of Forest Road 630 and FR 17 (Pine Mont Drive).
Other starting locations: Surveyor's Ridge Trail 688 trailhead off Forest Road 620 accessible from Forest Road 44 (Dufur Mill Road).
Length: 24.4-mile loop.
Approximate riding time: 3 to 5 hours.
Difficulty: Difficult, due to steep ascents and descents and roots, rocks, and a stream crossing.
Total climbing: 2,200 feet.
Trail surface: Singletrack, gravel roads, and paved roads.
Land status: National forest.

Seasons: June through October.
Nearest town: Hood River.
Other trail users: Hikers and equestrians.
Canine compatibility: Dogs permitted.
Wheels: A bike with front suspension is nice to have to handle the occasional technical sections on this route.
Trail contacts: Mount Hood National Forest, Hood River Ranger District, 6780 Highway 35, Mount Hood-Parkdale, OR 97041; (541) 352-6002; www.fs.fed.us/r6/mthood.
Fees and permits: No fees or permits required.
Maps: Maptech maps: Dog River; Parkdale.

Finding the Trailhead

From I-84 east in Hood River, take exit 64 to Mount Hood/ Oregon Highway 35/White Salmon/Government Camp. Travel south on Highway 35 for 11 miles to Pine Mont Drive (FR 17). Turn left and continue 6.3 miles to its intersection with FR 630. Turn right and park your car on the right side of the road. *DeLorme: Oregon Atlas & Gazetteer:* Page 68 D4.

The Ride

From Surveyor's Ridge Trail 688, cyclists will get a bird's-eye view of Mount Hood and the surrounding ridges and extensive valleys. This grand view makes up only a small portion of the 189,000-acre Mount Hood National Forest, which stretches more than 60 miles from the Columbia River Gorge south to the Olallie Scenic Area at the base of Mount Jefferson in the Central Cascades. Mount Hood is the centerpiece of this national forest and has been an indelible landmark for residents and visitors alike for centuries.

In 1792 William Broughton, commissioned by Royal Navy Captain George Vancouver, rowed up the Columbia River and saw Mount Hood for the first time. He named this majestic peak after Lord Samuel Hood of the British navy. Several other notable explorers, including Lewis and Clark who traveled through the area in 1805, appeared equally impressed with Mount Hood.

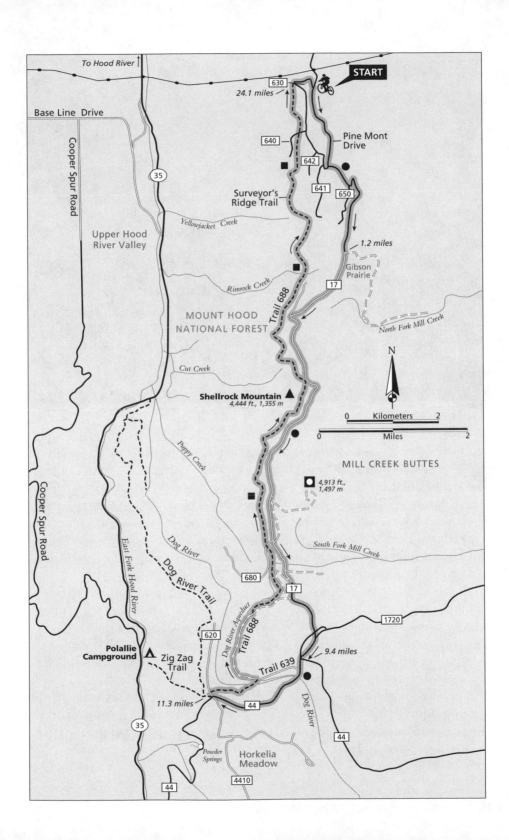

To Hood River

START

630
24.1 miles

Pine Mont Drive

Base Line Drive

640
642
641
650

Cooper Spur Road

35

Surveyor's Ridge Trail

Yellowjacket Creek

Upper Hood River Valley

1.2 miles

Gibson Prairie

Rimrock Creek

17

North Fork Mill Creek

MOUNT HOOD NATIONAL FOREST

Trail 688

Cut Creek

N

Shellrock Mountain
4,444 ft., 1,355 m

Kilometers
0   2

Miles
0   2

Puppy Creek

MILL CREEK BUTTES

4,913 ft.,
1,497 m

Cooper Spur Road

South Fork Mill Creek

Dog River

East Fork Hood River

Dog River Trail

680

17

1720

Dog River Aqueduct

Trail 688

9.4 miles

Polallie Campground

620

Zig Zag Trail

Trail 639

Dog River

11.3 miles

44

35

44

Powder Springs

Horkelia Meadow

44

4410

Majestic Mount Hood.

Up to this point, settlers traveling west toward the Willamette Valley had no other choice but to transport their wagons and stock by boat from The Dalles to Oregon City via the Columbia River. At the time, this was the only way settlers coming from eastern Oregon could travel to the Willamette Valley. With no competition, transport companies charged outrageous fees for the dangerous trip down the Columbia River. By the early 1800s, settlers began to protest the fees, eventually sparking the idea in a determined man named Samuel Barlow to establish a less-expensive wagon route over land to take settlers to the Willamette Valley.

In September of 1845, Barlow led seven wagons from The Dalles and began to establish a wagon route past Dufur, proceeded through the Tygh Valley, then continued over a pass located not far from today's Government Camp. In October of the same year, another settler named Joel Palmer decided to follow Barlow's lead. He led twenty-three wagons to meet Barlow and his party, and together they helped build a crude mountain road now known as Barlow Road.

The road was not without its own set of problems. Laurel Hill, located just west of Government Camp, was so steep that wagons had to be lowered down the hill using ropes and winches. Despite this, the road was used until 1919, when the state finally built a paved road that connected with the Columbia River Highway.

Today hundreds of miles of forest service roads and singletrack trails traverse some of the same forest and mountain terrain that the first settlers were forced to travel. The 24.4-mile Surveyor's Ridge Trail is a great route over a ridge that separates the East Fork of Hood River and the West Fork of Neal Creek. This ridge is thought to be named after Newton Clark, a surveyor who first charted the area in the spring of 1884.

▶ **Hood River County Facts**
Established: June 23, 1908
Area: 522 square miles
Average temperature: 33.6 degrees Fahrenheit in
**   January, 66.7 degrees Fahrenheit in July**
Population (2001): 20,439
Annual precipitation: 30.85 inches
Principal industries: Agriculture, food processing,
**   lumber, recreation and tourism, electronics**
**   and electronics manufacturing**

This route starts out along a somewhat grueling, yet uneventful 10-mile climb on gravel and paved forest service roads. All of the climbing is worth the effort, however. Once you reach the singletrack Surveyor's Ridge Trail, you are whisked downhill through pine forests and exposed ridges offering some of the grandest views of Mount Hood in the entire state. This trail is one of the most popular cycling trails in Oregon and can be crowded on the weekends. It definitely lives up to its reputation as you'll see and is worth checking out.

Miles and Directions

0.0 Start by riding a short distance on FR 630 to the junction with paved FR 17. Turn right and begin a long uphill climb.

1.2 The road comes to a fork. Stay to the left and keep riding on paved FR 17.

1.6 Go left at the road fork and continue on FR 17.

2.8 You'll come to a three-way intersection. Continue straight on FR 17. The road turns to gravel here.

8.4 Turn right at the road fork.

8.5 FR 17 turns back into pavement.

9.2 The road comes to a T. Turn right and continue riding on FR 17 toward FR 44 and Highway 35.

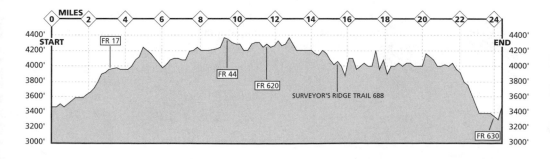

9.4 You'll come to the intersection of FR 44 (Dufur Mill Road). Turn right on the paved FR 44.

11.3 Turn right on FR 620 at the Surveyor's Ridge Trail 688 sign. Almost immediately you'll see the Surveyor's Ridge Trail 688 trailhead sign on your right. Turn right and start riding on the singletrack Trail 688.

12.8 Turn left at the trail fork. The Cook Meadows Trail 639 heads right. Cross a stream.

13.0 The trail turns into doubletrack and parallels the Dog River Aqueduct.

15.3 Very important! Just as the doubletrack dirt road turns to gravel, make a sharp left and continue riding on Surveyor's Ridge Trail 688.

16.2 Cross a gravel road and continue straight on the Trail 688.

17.8 (FYI: Walk out to a good viewpoint on your left of the Hood River Valley.)

18.9 Turn left at the trail fork and continue on Surveyor's Ridge Trail 688.

20.2 Turn left at the T-intersection and continue on Trail 688. The trail going right heads toward Gibson Prairie Horse Camp.

21.0 Cross a gravel road and continue straight.

21.4 Cross another gravel road and continue straight.

22.1 Reach a very poorly marked trail intersection. Turn right and continue on Trail 688.

23.1 Turn right at the trail fork and continue riding on Trail 688 toward Bald Butte.

23.2 Cross a gravel road and continue straight.

24.0 Arrive at a large section of power lines. Turn right on a dirt road.

24.1 Turn left at the T-intersection on unsigned FR 630.

24.4 Arrive back at your starting point.

Ride Information

Local Information
Hood River Chamber of Commerce, 405 Portway Avenue, Hood River, OR 97031; (800) 366-3530; www.hoodriver.org.

Local Events and Attractions
Gorge Games begin in mid-July, Hood River; (541) 386-7774; www.gorgegames.com.
Hood River Blossom Festival, held the third week in April, Hood River; (541) 354-2865.
Hood River Harvest Festival, held the third week in October at the Hood River Expo on the Waterfront, Hood River; (800) 366-3530.
Hood River Vineyards, 4693 Westwood Drive, Hood River; (541) 386-3772.

Mount Hood Scenic Railroad, 110 Railroad Avenue, Hood River; (800) 872-4661; www.mthoodrr.com.

Accommodations
Columbia Gorge Hotel, 4000 Westcliff Drive, Hood River; (800) 345-1921; www.columbiagorgehotel.com.
Mosier House B&B, 704 Third Avenue, Mosier; (541) 478-3640; www.mosierhouse.com.
Memaloose State Park, located 11 miles west of The Dalles (westbound exit only), Oregon State Parks, Salem; (800) 551-6949; www.oregonstateparks.org.

18 Fifteen Mile Creek

This technical singletrack ride is one of the best in the Hood River Valley. Highlights include and exhilarating 5-mile descent, stunning views of Mount Hood, and a tough climb back to your starting point.

Start: Fifteen Mile Campground off Forest Road 2730 in the Mount Hood National Forest.
Length: 11.1-mile loop.
Approximate riding time: 2.5 to 3.5 hours.
Difficulty: Difficult, due to steep ascents and rocky descents and other technical obstacles.
Total climbing: 1,800 feet.
Trail surface: Singletrack.
Land status: National forest.
Seasons: June through October.
Nearest town: Hood River.
Other trail users: Hikers.
Canine compatibility: Dogs permitted.

Wheels: A bike with front suspension is nice to have to handle the many technical sections on this route.
Trail contacts: Mount Hood National Forest, Hood River Ranger District, 6780 Highway 35, Mount Hood–Parkdale, OR 97041; (541) 352-6002; www.fs.fed.us/r6/mthood.
Fees and permits: Requires a $5.00 Northwest Forest Pass or a $30.00 annual pass. You can purchase one online at www.naturenw.org or by calling (800) 270-7504.
Maps: Maptech maps: Fivemile Butte; Flagpoint.

Finding the Trailhead

From I-84 east in Hood River, take exit 64 for Oregon Highway 35/White Salmon and Government Camp. At the end of the off-ramp, turn right (south) toward Government Camp. Continue 26.6 miles on Highway 35 to FR 44 (Dufur Mill Road). Turn left and continue 8.8 miles to FR 4420. Turn right and continue 2.2 miles. At the road junction, turn left on FR 2730. Proceed 2 miles to the Fifteen Mile Campground on the left side of the road. *DeLorme: Oregon Atlas & Gazetteer:* Page 63 A5.

The Ride

One of the most scenic areas in Oregon (not to mention most popular; it's visited by thousands each year) is the 3,000-foot-deep Columbia River Gorge, declared a National Scenic Area in 1986. This picturesque gorge, flanked with evergreen and deciduous forests, is brimming with bubbling creeks, cascading waterfalls, and lush hiking trails.

The mile-wide Columbia River is the dividing line between Oregon and Washington. Its present-day course through the Columbia River Gorge was carved by catastrophic floods that occurred during the last Ice Age over 15,000 years ago. The source of the floods was 3,000-square-mile glacial Lake Missoula, which formed when massive glaciers blocked drainage-ways in western Montana. Over a period of

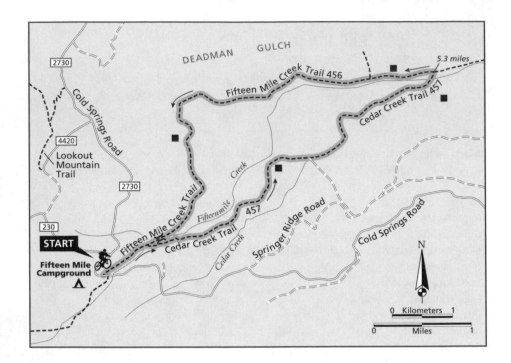

2,000 years, the glaciers holding back the lake gradually gave way to the enormous pressure created by the large volume of water. When the glaciers broke, a huge wall of water was sent careening through the Columbia basin. Billions of gallons of water flowed in a swift rage, carving out the steep canyon walls of what is now the Columbia River Gorge.

Since this corridor is the only transportation route available at sea-level between California and Canada, travelers have gratefully used the Columbia River for hundreds of years. Lewis and Clark traveled the Columbia River in 1805, and it served as a transportation route during the great Oregon migration in the mid-1800s. Settlers had the choice of braving the large rapids at Cascade Locks or traveling over Mount Hood on the Barlow Trail to the Willamette Valley. Many chose the locks.

When the Northern Pacific Railroad established a route through the Columbia River Gorge in 1883, agriculture began to really develop in the fertile valleys flanking the river. The Hood River Valley in the gorge is now famous for its apple, cherry, and pear orchards. More recently it has also become a place renowned for its great sailboarding, as a unique combination of wind and river currents attracts sailboarders from all over the world.

Today a popular place to gather is in the town of Hood River. This youth-oriented town is full of coffee houses, microbrew pubs, sailboarding shops, and bike shops. Folks into microbrews should check out Hood River's own microbrewery, the

Full Sail Brewpub. This great little watering hole has a strong following, and its Amber Ale is potentially the best in the state.

People from around the globe come to this part of the gorge to play on the wind-whipped waves of the Columbia River and to ride some of the best single-track in the state. Situated at the foot of the Mount Hood National Forest, Hood River is the gateway to this diverse national forest, crisscrossed with hundreds of miles of forest service roads and singletrack trails. Budget-minded visitors often camp for free in the Mount Hood National Forest.

An excellent introduction to mountain biking in the Mount Hood National Forest is the 11.1-mile-long Fifteen Mile Creek Loop Trail. This intermediate-level trail starts off with a rip-roaring 5-mile downhill that sweeps along ridges; bounces down some technical, rocky sections; and offers incredible views of Mount Hood and the Hood River Valley. After you finish the fun downhill, you'll ride along Fifteen Mile Creek, dodging several sections of roots and rocks that will further test your balance and skill. The last half of the trail promises to be a great workout, with over 1,800 vertical feet of elevation gain. Another great attraction to this trail is that most of the time you'll have it all to yourself.

Miles and Directions

0.0 Start riding on Trail 456.

0.5 Turn right on Cedar Creek Trail 457 and cross Fifteen Mile Creek.

3.3 Cross a gravel road and continue straight on Cedar Creek Trail 457.

5.3 Cross a creek and turn left on Fifteen Mile Creek Trail 456.

7.2 Cross a creek.

8.2 Turn left at the trail fork.

8.5 Cross a stream.

8.7 Turn left at a T-intersection.

10.0 Cross Foster Creek.

10.5 Cross a wooden bridge.

10.6 Continue riding straight on Trail 456.

11.1 Arrive back at your starting point.

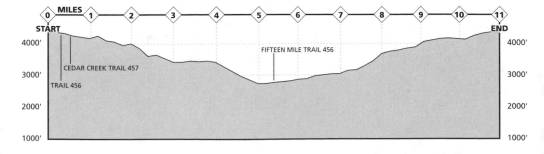

Great singletrack riding on the Fifteen Mile Creek Trail in the Mount Hood National Forest.

Ride Information

Local Information

Hood River Chamber of Commerce, 405 Portway Avenue, Hood River, OR 97031; (800) 366-3530; www.hoodriver.org.

Local Events and Attractions

Gorge Games begin in mid-July, Hood River; (541) 386-7774; www.gorgegames.com.

Hood River Blossom Festival, held the third week in April, Hood River; (541) 354-2865.

Hood River Harvest Festival, held the third week in October at the Hood River Expo on the Waterfront, Hood River; (800) 366-3530.

Hood River Vineyards, 4693 Westwood Drive, Hood River; (541) 386-3772.

Mount Hood Scenic Railroad, 110 Railroad Avenue, Hood River; (800) 872-4661; www.mthoodrr.com.

Accommodations

Columbia Gorge Hotel, 4000 Westcliff Drive, Hood River; (800) 345-1921; www.columbiagorgehotel.com.

Mosier House B&B, 704 Third Avenue, Mosier; (541) 478-3640; www.mosierhouse.com.

Memaloose State Park, located 11 miles west of The Dalles (westbound exit only), Oregon State Parks, Salem; (800) 551-6949; www.oregonstateparks.org.

19 East Fork Hood River

This route is a swift singletrack ride that takes you to the tumbling rapids of the East Fork of Hood River. The route is packed with long fast stretches, short intense hills, and tight switchbacks. A great intermediate ride close to Hood River, it is a great afternoon escape.

Start: The trailhead is 25.2 miles south of Hood River on Oregon Highway 35.
Length: 10.8 miles out and back.
Approximate riding time: 2 to 3 hours.
Difficulty: Moderate, due to soft sandy stretches and steep, twisty ascents and descents.
Total climbing: 500 feet.
Trail surface: Singletrack, wood ramps, and bridges.
Land status: National forest.
Seasons: May through October.
Nearest town: Hood River.
Other trail users: Hikers.

Canine compatibility: Dogs permitted.
Wheels: A bike with front suspension is useful for a few rough obstacles, but overall a rigid fork will do fine.
Trail contacts: Mount Hood National Forest, Hood River Ranger District, 6780 Highway 35, Mount Hood, OR 97031; (541) 352-6002; www.fs.fed.us/r6/mthood.
Fees and permits: Requires a $5.00 North-west Forest Pass or a $30.00 annual pass. It can be purchased online at www.naturenw.org or by calling (800) 270-7504.
Maps: Maptech maps: Dog River; Badger Lake. Green Trails Mount Hood.

Finding the Trailhead

From I-84 east in Hood River, take exit 64. Turn south on Highway 35 and travel 25.2 miles to a gravel parking area for the East Fork Trailhead and Tamanawas Falls, located on the right side of the road.
From Portland go approximately 55 miles east on U.S. Highway 26 to the intersection with Highway 35. Turn north on Highway 35 and travel about 15 miles to a gravel parking area for the East Fork Trailhead and Tamanawas Falls, on the left side of the road (0.2 mile north of Sherwood Campground). *DeLorme: Oregon Atlas & Gazetteer:* Page 62 A4.

The Ride

The Hood River Valley, gateway to the Mount Hood National Forest, is one of Oregon's mountain biking hotspots. Challenging terrain and high mountain scenery lure singletrack junkies to explore the endless maze of trails in this immense 1.2-million-acre national forest. The centerpiece is 11,235-foot Mount Hood. In October of 1792, Royal Navy Lt. William E. Broughton named the mountain after a famed British naval officer (and later, admiral), Alexander Arthur Hood (who never saw the mountain). This snowcapped peak is the highest mountain in Oregon and the second-most climbed mountain in the world (second to Japan's Mount Fuji).

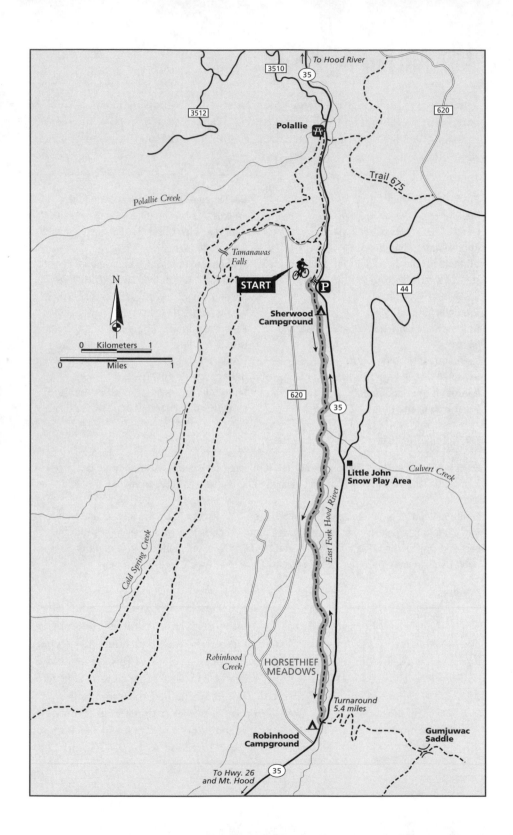

To Hood River

3510

35

3512

620

Polallie

Trail 675

Polallie Creek

Tamanawas
Falls

N

START

P

44

Sherwood
Campground

0 Kilometers 1
0   Miles   1

620

35

Little John
Snow Play Area

Culvert Creek

East Fork Hood River

Cold Spring Creek

Robinhood
Creek

HORSETHIEF
MEADOWS

Turnaround
5.4 miles

Gumjuwac
Saddle

Robinhood
Campground

To Hwy. 26
and Mt. Hood

35

Different historical records show that the first person to summit this lofty peak did so in either 1845 or 1857; the first woman summited in 1867.

At about 780,000 years old, Mount Hood is young compared to other Cascade peaks. Classified as a stratovolcano, the mountain has had four eruptive periods over the last 15,000 years. Evidence of recent volcanic activity is present at Crater Rock, a volcanic lava dome believed by geologists to be only 200 years old. It is located south of the summit and emits a steady outflow of sulfur gas and steam. The mountain's twelve glaciers and winter snowpack provide runoff for many streams and rivers that flow into the Hood River Valley.

The East Fork Hood River rushes down the southeast slopes of Mount Hood for over 20 miles to where it joins the main river near the small community of Dee. This fantastic singletrack tour follows the contours of this bouldery river starting just north of Sherwood Campground and traveling south to its ending point at Robinhood Campground. You'll begin by crossing a skinny footbridge over the river and then heading south on Trail 650. The route has many fun twists and turns and short, intense ups and downs as it follows the contours of a ridge above the river. After 3.9 miles watch out for some soft sandy spots as the trail gets closer to the river. The last 0.3-mile of the route you'll cross a series of wood ramps through a marshy area until you reach Robinhood Campground. From here you'll have a blast riding the same route back to the trailhead.

Miles and Directions

0.0 Start by crossing a skinny wood bridge over the East Fork Hood River. After you cross the bridge, turn left (south) on Trail 650.

3.9 (FYI: The trail is close to the river at this point and can be very sandy and soft in spots.)

5.4 Arrive at Robinhood Campground (your turnaround point). Retrace the route back to the trailhead.

10.8 Arrive at the trailhead.

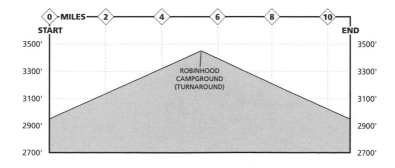

East Fork Hood River.

Ride Information

Local Information

Hood River Chamber of Commerce, 405 Portway Avenue, Hood River, OR 97031; (800) 366-3530; www.hoodriver.org.

Local Events and Attractions

Gorge Games begin in mid-July, Hood River; (541) 386-7774; www.gorgegames.com.
Hood River Blossom Festival, held the third week in April, Hood River; (541) 354-2865.
Hood River Harvest Festival, held the third week in October at the Hood River Expo on the Waterfront, Hood River; (800) 366-3530.
Hood River Vineyards, 4693 Westwood Drive, Hood River; (541) 386-3772.

Mount Hood Scenic Railroad, 110 Railroad Avenue, Hood River; (800) 872-4661; www.mthoodrr.com.

Accommodations

Columbia Gorge Hotel, 4000 Westcliff Drive, Hood River; (800) 345-1921; www.columbiagorgehotel.com.
Sherwood Campground and Robinhood Campground, Mount Hood National Forest, Hood River Ranger District, Mount Hood; (541) 352-6002; www.fs.fed.us/r6/mthood.

20 Crosstown-Wally's Tie-Skiway Trail

This smooth and fast singletrack route races through a shady forest in the Mount Hood National Forest. The route combines three popular cross-country ski trails—Crosstown, Wally's Tie, and Skiway. You can try this route or get creative and make up your own route on this fun maze of trails.

Start: Summit Ski Area located about 47 miles east of Portland off U.S. Highway 26.
Length: 6.1 miles out and back with a short loop.
Approximate riding time: 1 to 1.5 hours.
Difficulty: Easy, due to smooth trail surface and small elevation gain.
Total climbing: 465 feet.
Trail surface: 5.7 miles singletrack; 0.4 mile doubletrack.
Land status: National forest.
Seasons: June through October.
Nearest town: Sandy.

Other trail users: Hikers and equestrians.
Canine compatibility: Dogs permitted.
Wheels: A bike without front suspension will work fine due to the smooth trail surface and few trail obstacles.
Trail contacts: Mount Hood Information Center, 65000 East Highway 26, Welches, OR 97067; (503) 622-7674; www.fs.fed.us/r6/mthood.
Fees and permits: No fees or permits are required.
Maps: Maptech maps: Government Camp.

Finding the Trailhead

From the intersection of I-205 and I-84 in Portland, head 6.3 miles east on I-84 to exit 13, for 238th Drive/Wood Village. Turn right and proceed 2.8 miles. Turn left on Burnside Road. Continue about 0.6 mile and turn left (east) on U.S. Highway 26. Continue 37.6 miles to the Summit Ski Area/Government Camp turnoff. Turn left and then take a quick right into a large paved parking area in front of the Summit Ski Lodge. *DeLorme: Oregon Atlas & Gazetteer:* Page 62 B2.

The Ride

This entertaining ride starts at the Summit Ski Area at Government Camp. Established in 1927, this is the oldest ski area in the Pacific Northwest and the first one

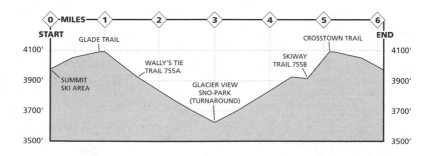

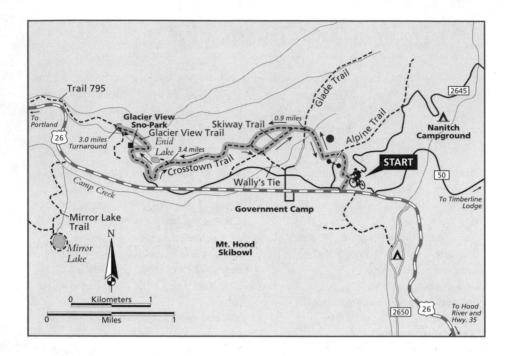

built on Mount Hood. Mount Hood is also host to Mt. Hood Skibowl, Timberline, Mount Hood Meadows, and Cooper Spur. While skiers flock to the mountain to explore trails in the winter, mountain bikers can explore many of the trails during the dry, summer months.

At the start of the ride don't be deterred by two signs to the right of the Summit Ski Lodge that say NO DOGS and NO MOUNTAIN BIKES. They refer to the ski lodge property and not to this trail. Begin the ride on Crosstown Trail 755, located on the left side of the Summit Ski Lodge. Warm up by cranking up a short ascent on a singletrack trail with great views of Mount Hood. After 0.2 mile you'll enter a cool Douglas fir and red cedar forest. If you have your canine cycling partner with you, he'll appreciate the fact that in the first mile you'll cross multiple small creeks, which provide plenty of opportunities for him to cool off. Over the next 2 miles, the trail races through a fern-filled forest with wild rhododendrons, salal, and sword fern. After 2.8 miles look for a large open meadow and small pond on the right side of the trail. Occasional roots, rocks, and ruts caused by horses provide some mellow technical sections. After 3 miles you'll arrive at Glacier Sno-Park, which is your turnaround point.

From here retrace the route to the junction with Wally's Tie Trail 755A. You'll have a short spin on Wally's Tie Trail and then you'll turn onto the Skiway Trail, where you'll

Smooth singletrack on the Crosstown Trail.

have a short steep climb up a rough doubletrack road. At 5.1 miles you'll turn back on the zippy Crosstown Trail and follow it back to the trailhead. If you are looking for a longer route, check out the Crosstown–Pioneer Bridle–Still Creek Loop.

Miles and Directions

0.0 Start riding uphill on Crosstown Trail 755, a singletrack trail located to the left of the blue Summit Ski Area Lodge. (FYI: As you climb you'll have a gorgeous view of Mount Hood.)

0.1 Turn right on a narrower singletrack trail marked by a brown HIKER/BIKER sign.

0.2 The trail curves sharply to the left and crosses a wide, doubletrack road and then enters a deep forest corridor.

0.3 Continue straight at the four-way junction where a sign reads CROSSTOWN TRAIL .75/WALLY'S TIE 1.5/GLACIER VIEW SNO-PARK 2.5. The Alpine Trail heads right.

0.4 Cross a wood bridge over a small rushing creek and begin to descend slightly. Over the next 0.5 mile, you'll cross multiple wood bridges over small creeks.

0.9 Continue straight at the four-way junction on the signed Crosstown Trail. You'll cross the Glade Trail.

1.0 Continue straight at the four-way junction on the signed Crosstown Trail. You'll cross Ski-way Trail 755B.

1.6 Turn right at the T-junction toward the signed Crosstown Trail. Wally's Tie Trail 755A heads left.

2.6 Turn left at the T-junction and continue on the Crosstown Trail. Enid Lake Loop Trail 792A heads right.

2.9 Turn left at the T-junction.

3.0 The Crosstown Trail ends at the Glacier View Sno-Park. Turn around and head back toward the Summit Ski Area on the Crosstown Trail. **Option:** You have the option of continuing west on the Pioneer Bridle Trail, which is part of the Crosstown–Pioneer Bridle–Still Creek Loop honorable mention route.

3.4 Turn right and continue riding on the Crosstown Trail. Enid Lake Loop Trail 792A goes straight.

4.5 Turn right on Wally's Tie Trail 755A.

4.7 Turn left at the T-junction on Skiway Trail 755B. Begin a steep ascent on a rocky, rutted doubletrack road.

5.1 Turn right on the Crosstown Trail at a four-way junction.

5.2 Continue straight on the Crosstown Trail at the four-way junction. You'll cross the Glade Trail.

6.1 Arrive back at the trailhead.

Ride Information

Local Information
Mount Hood Area Chamber of Commerce,
65000 East Highway 26, Welches, OR 97067;
(503) 622-3017; www.mthood.org.

21 Timothy Lake

This gorgeous lake ride is a great introduction to riding singletrack. The ride meanders around the great expanse of Timothy Lake, situated in the Mount Hood National Forest. You'll have multiple opportunities to gaze at majestic Mount Hood in the distance and cool off in Timothy Lake.

Start: Timothy Lake Trailhead 28 at Timothy Lake in the Mount Hood National Forest.
Length: 13.8-mile loop.
Approximate riding time: 3 to 4 hours.
Difficulty: Easy, due to smooth trail surface and minimal elevation gain.
Total climbing: 70 feet. Elevation profiles are not provided for rides with little or no elevation gain.
Trail surface: Singletrack, doubletrack, and paved road.
Land status: National forest.
Seasons: June through October.
Nearest town: Sandy.

Other trail users: Hikers and equestrians.
Canine compatibility: Dogs permitted.
Wheels: A bike with a front suspension is nice to have because of short sections of rocky doubletrack road and small technical obstacles.
Trail contacts: Hood Information Center, 65000 East Highway 26, Welches, OR 97067; (503) 622-7674; www.fs.fed.us/r6/mthood.
Fees and permits: No fees or permits are required.
Maps: Maptech maps: Timothy Lake; Wolf Peak.

Finding the Trailhead

From the intersection of I-205 and I-84 in Portland head east for 7.2 miles on I-84 to exit 13, for 238th Drive/Wood Village. At the end of the off-ramp, turn right on 238th Avenue and proceed 2.9 miles to the intersection with Burnside Road. Turn left (east) and continue to the intersection with U.S. Highway 26. Turn left (east) and go 51.4 miles to the junction with Forest Road 42 (Skyline Road). Turn right and continue 8.3 miles to the junction with FR 57. Turn right and continue 3.6 miles (passing four campgrounds on your right) and cross over the dam. Turn right and continue 0.1 mile to a road intersection. Turn right on a gravel road and travel 0.1 mile to the Timothy Lake Trail 528 Trailhead parking area. *DeLorme: Oregon Atlas & Gazetteer:* Page 62 C2.

The Ride

Timothy Lake is a shimmering oasis in the immense Mount Hood National Forest. The 1,400-acre reservoir was created when the Oak Grove Fork of the Clackamas River was dammed in 1956 for a PGE hydroelectric plant. The lake was named after the timothy seed that sheepherders once planted in the meadows it now covers. Located at an elevation of 3,227 feet, the lake is host to five large developed campgrounds and four boat ramps. Fishing enthusiasts flock here to catch brook trout, cutthroat trout, rainbow trout, and kokanee (landlocked salmon). The lake also supports a healthy population of crawdads that can be trapped just offshore.

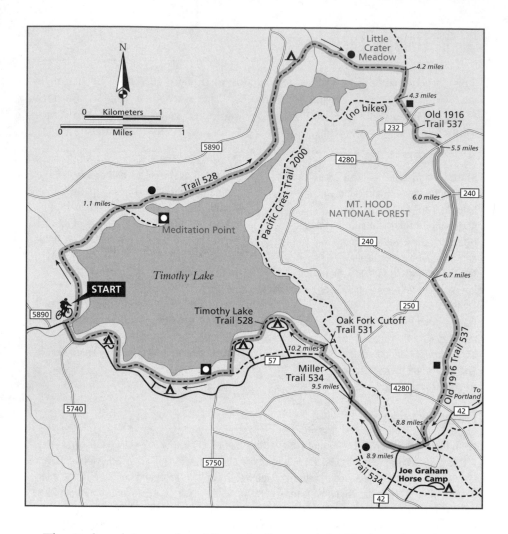

The singletrack is smooth and fast and sails around the lakeshore through a cool Douglas fir and cedar forest. After 5.5 miles of soaring, you'll have to gear down to grind on a rough doubletrack for a little over a mile before you pounce back on the singletrack and start heading south for 3 miles on a mix of singletrack and double-track. At 8.8 miles you'll begin a short 0.7-mile of paved road riding, but soon enough you're back riding on zippy singletrack. After 10.2 miles you'll sail around the south end of the lake past four campgrounds and boat ramps. (Watch out for kids and folks fishing on this section of the route.) From here you can admire the snowy peak of 11,235-foot Mount Hood towering above the lake. This peak is the tallest in Oregon and is covered with twelve glaciers and five unique ridges. It's the sec-ond-most climbed mountain in the world after Japan's Mount Fuji. Evidence of recent volcanic activity is present at Crater Rock, a lava dome located south of the

Timothy Lake is a great summer ride in the Mount Hood National Forest.

summit. A lava dome is created when lava slowly erupts and accumulates above a volcanic vent. Geologists believe this dome is only about 200 years old.

After finishing your ride, it's tradition to wash off the trail dust by diving into the cool waters of the lake. Better yet, nab a campsite at one of the lake's campgrounds and spend the weekend riding the trails and swimming in the lake. A recommended campground is Gone Creek, which has primo lakeside sites with striking views of Mount Hood. The Timothy Lake Trail can be accessed from this campground's lakeshore sites. Due to its close proximity to Portland, this route can be crowded on summer weekends and campgrounds fill up fast. To avoid the weekend crowds, plan to visit on a weekday.

Miles and Directions

0.0 Start riding in a clockwise direction on Timothy Lake Trail 528 where a sign indicates MEDI-TATION POINT 1½ MILES–PACIFIC CREST TRAIL 4½ MILES.

1.1 Continue riding straight on Timothy Lake Trail 528. Meditation Point Trail 526 heads right.

3.3 You'll reach a junction with a gravel road. Turn left and ride about 100 yards. Turn right and continue riding on Timothy Lake Trail 528.

4.2 Turn right and continue on Timothy Lake Trail 528. A sign indicates BICYCLISTS DISMOUNT FOR 600 FEET TO OLD 1916 TRAIL 537.

4.3 Turn left on signed Old 1916 Trail 537. The sign indicates you'll reach FR 42 in 4 miles. (FYI: No bikes are allowed on the Pacific Crest Trail 2000, which continues straight.)

4.8 Cross a gravel road and continue on the singletrack trail.

5.5 Cross FR 4280 and continue riding on Old 1916 Trail 537. The trail turns from singletrack to a rough doubletrack road.

6.0 Arrive at a trail junction. Turn right on the signed Old 1916 Trail 537. The sign also indicates you'll reach Joe Graham Horse Camp in 3 miles.

6.7 Turn left on Old 1916 Trail 537. The sign reads SKYLINE ROAD 2 MILES. The trail turns to singletrack. This junction is easy to miss!

8.3 Cross a gravel road and continue riding on the singletrack trail.

8.4 Turn right on a doubletrack road where a sign indicates TRAIL 537.

8.5 Turn left on signed Old 1916 Trail 537. This sign is difficult to see! After this junction the trail turns back to fun singletrack.

8.8 Turn right on the unmarked paved FR 42.

8.9 Turn right on paved FR 57 toward Timothy Lake.

9.5 Turn right on the singletrack Miller Trail 534.

10.0 Turn right on the signed Oak Fork Cutoff Trail 531.

10.2 Arrive at a T-intersection. Turn left on Timothy Lake Trail 528. Over the next 3 miles, you will follow this trail as it winds next to the lakeshore and passes through four campgrounds and boat ramps. Ignore side trails going left.

13.4 You'll pass by a fishing dock on your right and then the trail turns to pavement. Ride about 100 yards on the paved trail and then turn right on the paved road that crosses the dam.

13.5 After crossing the dam turn right on a paved road.

13.7 Turn right on a gravel road.

13.8 You'll arrive at the trailhead parking area and your vehicle.

Ride Information

Local Information

Mount Hood Area Chamber of Commerce,
65000 East Highway 26, Welches, OR 97067;
(503) 622–3017; www.mthood.org.

22 Gunsight Ridge

This ride gives you everything: steep climbs, scree, narrow openings between boulders, roots, rocks, drop-offs, and precipitous switchbacks. Its highlight is the 5-mile singletrack portion along Gunsight Trail where cyclists climb up the spine of a ridge with great views of the magnificent Mount Hood. Once you reach the summit, a fast, switchback descent careens down the backside of Gunsight Ridge to Gumjuwac Saddle.

Start: The Bennett Pass Sno-Park off Oregon Highway 35.
Length: 19.2 miles out and back with a loop combination.
Approximate riding time: 3 to 5 hours.
Difficulty: Difficult, due a large amount of elevation gain and technical terrain.
Total climbing: 2,400 feet.
Trail surface: Singletrack and gravel road.
Land status: National forest.
Seasons: June through October.
Nearest town: Hood River.

Other trail users: Hikers and equestrians.
Canine compatibility: Dogs permitted.
Wheels: A bike with front suspension is recommended due to the steep ascent and technical terrain.
Trail contacts: Hood Information Center, 65000 East Highway 26, Welches, OR 97067; (503) 622-7674; www.fs.fed.us/r6/mthood.
Fees and permits: No fees or permits are required.
Maps: Maptech maps: Badger Lake; Mount Hood South.

Finding the Trailhead

From Hood River, travel 34 miles south on Highway 35 to Bennett Pass. Turn left on Forest Road 3550 and park in the gravel parking lot on the right side of the road.
From the intersection of U.S. Highway 26 and Highway 35 (coming from Portland and Government Camp), turn left (north) on Highway 35 and travel 6 miles to Bennett Pass. Turn right on FR 3550 and park in the gravel lot on the right side of the road. *DeLorme: Oregon Atlas & Gazetteer:* Page 62 B3.

The Ride

Mount Hood's glacial peak rises majestically above the Hood and Columbia River Valleys to the north, the Willamette Valley to the west, and Oregon's high desert plains to the east. This impressive snowcapped volcano is one of the most famous mountains in the Cascade range, inspiring countless stories and legends.

Mount Hood is a major character in the many different versions of the Native American fire legend of the mid-Columbia region. These characters include the spirit of Mount Hood, known as "Yi-east" (also spelled "Wy'east"), a passionate warrior, and the spirit of Mount Adams, known as "Pa-toe," a well-meaning giant.

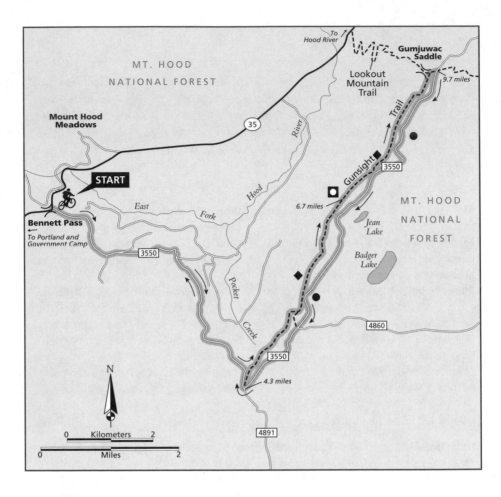

One version of these fire legends tells of a time when thick forests were filled with game, meadows brimmed with camas (a sweet bulb plant that is a favorite food of the western Indians), and waters teemed with salmon and other fish. Yi-east and Pa-toe, who lived on the western edge of a great sea, were sons of the Great Spirit and often came to Koyoda Spielei (the high priest who brought wisdom and law to the people and the animals) with their troubles. When a lovely maiden mountain spirit moved to the valley between the Great Spirit's two sons, a great conflict began. The lovely maiden flirted with Pa-toe but, in truth, loved Yi-east. When the two sons declared their love for the young maiden, quarrels erupted between them. Yi-east and Pa-toe spewed smoke, fire, and lava over all the land, destroying the forests, killing the animals, and darkening the sky.

With this firestorm, the inland sea disappeared and a great hole developed in the earth between the two mountains. Water flowed through this hole until a natural bridge formed with a tunnel of water running beneath it. The people who lived in the area, including the young maiden spirit, fled the chaos to hide in caves. Koyoda tried to stop the two sons from fighting but had no luck. Finally, Koyoda went to the Great Spirit to end the battle. The Great Spirit told the brothers that as a result of their terrible quarrel, the young maiden (Squaw Mountain) would remain forever hidden and the new bridge would stand as a token of peace between them. He warned that if the brothers began fighting again the bridge would fall. As a reminder of their foolishness and that beauty does not last forever, the Great Spirit left an ugly old woman named Loo-Wit in the form of a mountain (Mount St. Helens) to guard this bridge.

The 19.2-mile Gunsight Ridge Loop Trail is such a trail to inspire similar legends, combining great views of Mount Hood with 5 miles of challenging singletrack and 14 miles of gravel road. It throws everything at you—steep climbs and switchbacks, scree, narrow passages, roots, rocks, and drop-offs. This ride starts 34 miles south of Hood River on Bennett Pass Road off Oregon Highway 35. Bennett Pass Road (FR 3550) is also a popular cross-country ski trail in the winter. The road climbs steadily for several miles. At the 2.5-mile mark is a section called "the terrible traverse." In the winter it is piled high with snow and the slope becomes very icy and steep. The road turns into a single, narrow path, feared by many skiers who cross it.

You'll continue climbing until you intersect with the 5-mile, singletrack portion of the ride on Gunsight Trail, where you'll climb up the spine of a ridge with great views of Mount Hood. Once you reach the summit, you'll catch a fast, switchback descent down to the other side of Gunsight Ridge to Gumjuwac Saddle. Apparently, Gumjuwac Saddle is a phonetic translation of a turn-of-the-century sheepherder, named Gum Shoe Jack, with a fetish for wearing rubber boots. The last section of the ride is along a bumpy, rocky, eroded gravel road that will surely test the toughness of your backside. If you want the exercise of a strenuous ride coupled with great views of majestic Mount Hood, Gunsight Ridge Loop Trail is a route worth experiencing.

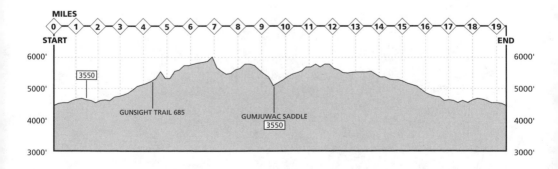

Miles and Directions

0.0 From the parking lot, turn right and start riding on FR 3550 (Bennett Pass Road).

1.1 Turn left at the road fork.

1.4 Turn right at the road fork.

1.9 Turn left at the road fork. (FYI: There is a great viewpoint of Mount Hood on your left.)

2.5 (FYI: Look behind you to see another spectacular view of Mount Hood.)

4.3 Make a sharp left turn to begin the singletrack section of the ride on Gunsight Trail 685. (FYI: If you continue straight, FR 3550 comes to a T. If you turn right, you'll reach Bonnie Meadows in 1 mile. If you turn left, you'll reach Badger Lake in 7 miles.)

4.7 You may have to push your bike across a rocky section of the trail.

5.4 Turn left at the trail fork.

6.7 Climb up a rock outcropping on your left to see a spectacular view of Mount Hood. The trail begins to descend here.

7.3 You may have to push your bike across another rocky section of the trail.

7.7 Turn left on FR 3550.

MOUNT HOOD

The lone giant. Sitting quietly and etched starkly along the Portland skyline, Mount Hood with its perfect cone and cool, glacier-clad slopes belies its purpose—to blow up. It is, after all, a volcano. You need only to look to the northeast, to the scarred, headless, and now considerably shorter Mount St. Helens, for a reminder of what volcanoes do. Mount Hood isn't necessarily all that quiet, either. Earthquakes (on a scale you can register with your feet) occur here on average every two years, generally on the south side of the summit. Though short in duration, they're nonetheless indicators of a mountain in flux. A seismic rash in July of 1980, during which nearly sixty earthquakes occurred in a five-day span, prompted the development of a localized emergency response plan, should the mountain decide to shed.

Despite its seemingly pristine form, Mount Hood has been erupting for hundreds of thousands of years. The last eruptive episode ended within a few years of the arrival of Lewis and Clark in 1805. Their journal entries describe the Sandy River, just east of Portland, as curiously choked with debris— in contrast to the river we see today. For the last 200 years, though, aside from a little hissing and rumbling, the mountain has been fairly quiet.

◀ *Pedaling hard on the Gunsight Ridge route.*

7.9 Turn left, returning to the singletrack Gunsight Trail 685.

9.7 You'll intersect with FR 3550 at Gumjuwac Saddle. Turn right on FR 3550 and begin a steep climb.

13.9 Arrive at an intersection with FR 4860 on your left, stay to the right, and continue riding on FR 3550.

15.0 At this point you have completed the loop portion of the ride and are back at the trailhead of Gunsight Trail 685. The road forks here. Turn right and continue down a rocky descent on FR 3550 back toward your vehicle.

19.3 Arrive at the trailhead.

Ride Information

Local Information

Mount Hood Area Chamber of Commerce, 65000 East Highway 26, Welches, OR 97067; (503) 622–3017; www.mthood.org.

Local Events and Attractions

Gorge Games, begin in mid-July, Hood River; (541) 386–7774; www.gorgegames.com.
Hood River Blossom Festival, held the third week in April, Hood River; (541) 354–2865.
Hood River Harvest Festival, held the third week in October at the Hood River Expo on the Waterfront, Hood River; (800) 366–3530.

Hood River Vineyards, 4693 Westwood Drive, Hood River; (541) 386–3772.
Mount Hood Scenic Railroad, 110 Railroad Avenue, Hood River; (800) 872–4661; www.mthoodrr.com.

Accommodations

Columbia Gorge Hotel, 4000 Westcliff Drive, Hood River; (800) 345–1921; www.columbiagorgehotel.com.

23 Deschutes River State Park-Harris Ranch

Sagebrush-covered hills, red mesas, and gray lava cliffs are backdrops to this easy but scenic ride that winds along the Deschutes River through the Deschutes River Canyon. One of the highlights of this ride is the old Harris Ranch homestead, built at the turn of the century. The weather-beaten house tells a story of tough pioneers and simpler times.

Start: The entrance to Deschutes River State Park.

Length: 22.8 miles out and back (with longer options).

Approximate riding time: 3 to 5 hours.

Difficulty: Easy, due to the mostly flat terrain and the well-graded, doubletrack road.

Total climbing: 115 feet.

Trail surface: Doubletrack road.

Land status: State park.

Seasons: Year-round.

Nearest town: The Dalles.

Other trail users: Hikers and equestrians.

Canine compatibility: Leashed dogs permitted.

Wheels: A bike with suspension is recommended to avoid arm jarring on the doubletrack road.

Trail contacts: Oregon State Parks and Recreation, 1115 Commercial Street NE, Salem, OR 97301; (800) 551-6949; www.oregonstateparks.org/park_37.php.

Fees and permits: $5.00 parking fee.

Maps: Maptech maps: Wishram; Emerson; Locust Grove.

Finding the Trailhead

From The Dalles travel 14 miles east on I-84 to exit 97 for Oregon Highway 206/Celilo Park/Deschutes River State Park. Turn right at the end of the off-ramp and then take an immediate left on Highway 206. Head east for 3.1 miles and turn right into the entrance for Deschutes River State Park. Park in the gravel lot on the left just after you turn into the park entrance. *DeLorme: Oregon Atlas & Gazetteer:* Page 84 B1.

The Ride

This is an old railroad grade now converted into a multiuse trail for mountain bikers, hikers, and equestrians. The 22.8-mile trail begins at Deschutes River State Park, 13 miles east of The Dalles at the confluence of the Deschutes and Columbia Rivers. Overnight camping, rest rooms, and day use facilities are available. While visiting the park, be sure to look for the signs throughout the area that describe what life was like for Native Americans and early settlers living and traveling through this region many years ago.

The ride begins at the gravel parking lot to the left of the park entrance. You will ride up a short, steep incline and then continue around a metal gate. Continue riding on a doubletrack dirt and gravel road for 11.4 miles all the way to the abandoned Harris Ranch homestead.

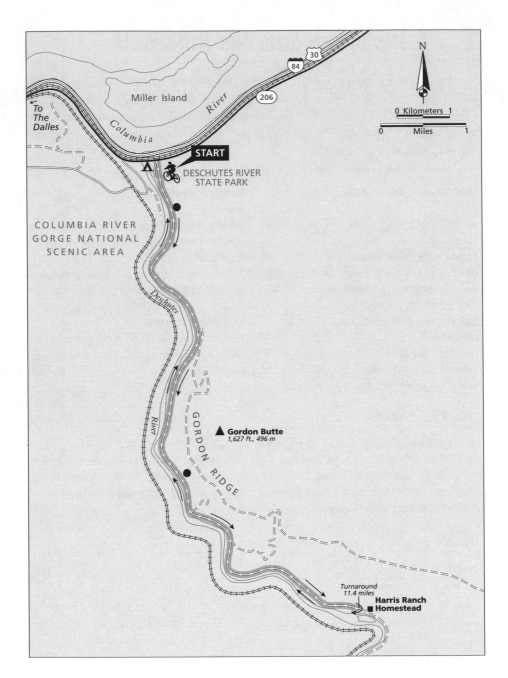

The trail winds through the Deschutes River Canyon, a prodigious chasm averaging over 2,000 feet deep and filled with interesting geological history. Forty million years ago this canyon was part of a flat, semitropical plain suspected of receiving more than 240 inches of rain per year. Thirty million years ago the Continental Plate

Harris Ranch Homestead.

collided with the Pacific Plate, lifting the land upward to form the Coastal and Cascade Mountain Ranges. This cataclysmic event caused the earth's crust to fracture, and hot molten magma rose to the surface, creating gigantic basalt flows. As you pedal through this deep canyon, steep, eroding basalt walls speak their own stories. Curved layers bend and push against one another, creating bulges, breaks, and unique columns.

At mile 6 and again at mile 8.2, the trail takes you past wildlife observation areas (converted old railroad cars). The high walls of the canyon provide an excellent habitat for red-tailed hawks and other birds of prey, and the well-stocked Deschutes River attracts plenty of osprey and blue herons. The river's abundant aquatic vegetation and grassy banks also attract Canada geese, mallard ducks, and a variety of other waterfowl.

At mile 11.4 you will reach the Harris Ranch homestead. The worn, weather-beaten boards of this old house tell stories of rugged pioneers and simpler times. The walls inside the house are lined with old newspaper and magazines. An ad from the *Scientific American* boasts "Tribune Bicycles for 1899—The Best Wheels in the World.

Made by The Black Manufacturing Company, Erie, Pennsylvania." Old mattress springs, worn shoes, and a rusting potbelly stove are silent reminders of a different way of life and a different time.

The corrals and barn nearby are made of thick, wide, pine planks from old-growth juniper. The tightly planked fences and small pens were once used to work sheep. Explore the old barn and you'll discover a sheep-shearing machine with stations for several workers. When it was used, the metal arms of this machine were held by men who probably sheared over a hundred head a day.

The Harris Ranch homestead is your turnaround point. But you also have the option to continue riding on the trail for several more miles and doing some overnight camping (be sure to stock up on water at the campground before you head out). If you don't want to camp in the wilds, you can camp in the Deschutes State Park Campground at the start of the ride. This trail is technically easy, but the scenery, wildlife, and history of the gorge make it a very rewarding ride for almost anyone.

Miles and Directions

0.0 Start at the gravel parking lot at the Deschutes River State Park entrance. Look for the trail sign. Ride up a small dirt incline to the start of the doubletrack road.

0.1 Ride around a metal gate. Over the next 2 miles ignore side trails going right.

3.6 (FYI: To the right of the trail is an outhouse and a good rest stop if needed.)

5.8 (FYI: To the right is another outhouse.)

6.0 (FYI: On the right side of the trail is an old railroad car—a good place to stop and view some of the wildlife.)

8.1 Cross a cattle guard.

8.2 (FYI: Pass another old railroad car that serves as a wildlife viewing area.)

8.3 Cross a cattle guard

10.3 Cross a cattle guard

11.4 Reach the Harris Ranch homestead. This is your turnaround point and a fun place to do some exploring. **Option:** From here you can continue another 5.6 miles into the canyon.

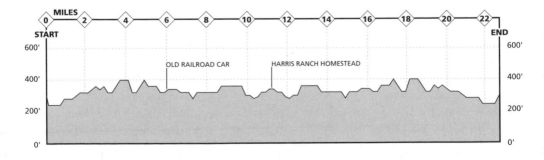

Ride Information

Local Information

The Dalles Chamber of Commerce, 404 West Second Street, The Dalles, OR 97058; (800) 255-3385; www.thedalleschamber.com.

Local Events and Attractions

Fort Dalles Museum, West Fifteenth Street and Garrison Street, The Dalles; (541) 296-4547.

Columbia Gorge Discovery Center & Wasco County Historical Museum, 4500 Discovery Drive, The Dalles; (541) 296-8600; www.gorgediscovery.org.

Accommodations

Deschutes River State Park Campground, Deschutes River State Park; (800) 551-6949; www.oregonstateparks.org/park_37.php.

Captain Gray's Guest House, 210 West Fourth Street, The Dalles; (541) 298-8222.

In Addition

Mountain Bike Camping

If you consider your mountain bike saddle the most comfortable seat in the house and crave an opportunity to prove your self-sufficiency, try bicycle camping. It requires more planning and preparation than a standard day trip, but the satisfaction gained from reaching a campground or a remote outdoor destination on two wheels, knowing you're ready for a cozy night outdoors, makes the extra effort worthwhile.

If you plan on doing a lot of bicycle camping/touring, it's a good idea to invest in quality equipment. Everyone should have a pair of medium-to-large panniers that can be mounted on a rear rack (if you are planning a long trip, you might consider a front rack). A lightweight backpacking tent, sleeping pad, and sleeping bag can be attached to the rear rack using two or three bungee cords. We all have a tendency to overpack, but the extra weight of unnecessary equipment may cause you to tire more easily. Here are some tips to help you find the appropriate amount of gear:

- Bring a multipurpose tool that has a can opener, bottle opener, scissors, knife, and screwdriver.
- Pack only one extra change of clothes, plus any necessary layers such as a polypropylene shirt and tights, polar fleece, wool socks, and rain gear. If you are on a multiday trip, bring extra shorts and T-shirts, and if it's winter, bring an extra pair of polypropylene tights and shirt, as well as a few extra pairs of wool socks.
- Bring a tin cup and spoon for eating and drinking and a lightweight pot for cooking.
- Invest in a lightweight backpacking stove, tent, and sleeping bag.
- Bring along freeze-dried food. You can buy many prepackaged rice and noodle mixes in the grocery store for half of what you'll pay at outdoor stores.
- Bring the minimum amount of water needed for your intended route. Anticipate if there will be water available. Invest in a water filter that can be used along the trail.

Equipment List

Use the checklist of equipment below when you are planning for a single or multiday trip. You can develop your own equipment list based on the length of your trip, the time of year, weather conditions, and difficulty of the trail.

Essentials
Bungee cords
Compass
Day panniers
Duct tape
Fenders
Pocket knife or multipurpose tool
Rear rack
Front rack
Trail map
Water bottles
Water filter
Tool kit
Patch kit
Crescent wrench
Tire levers
Spoke wrench
Extra spokes
Chain rivet tool
Extra tube
Tire pump

Clothing
Rain jacket/pants
Polar fleece jacket
Wool sweater
Helmet liner
Bicycle tights
T-shirts/shorts
Sturdy bicycle shoes/boots
Swimsuit
Underwear
Bike gloves
Eye protection
Bike helmet/liner

First-Aid Kit
Bandages (various sizes)
Gauze pads
Surgical tape

Antibiotic ointment
Hydrogen peroxide or iodine
Gauze roll
Ace bandage
Aspirin
Moleskin
Sunscreen
Insect repellent

Personal Items
Towel
Toothbrush/toothpaste
Soap
Comb
Shampoo

Camping Items
Backpacking stove
Tent
Sleeping bag
Foam pad
Cooking and eating utensils
Can opener
Flashlight/batteries
Candle lantern
Touring panniers
Pannier rain covers
Zip-locked bags
Large heavy-duty plastic garbage bags
Small duffels to organize gear

Miscellaneous Items
Camera/film/batteries
Notebook/pen
Paperback book

Honorable Mentions

Compiled here is an index of great rides located in the Columbia River Gorge, Hood River Valley, and Mount Hood. Check them out and let us know what you think. You may decide that one or more of these rides deserves higher status in future editions, or perhaps you have a ride of your own that merits some attention.

I Larch Mountain

An advanced, 6.2-mile ride in the Columbia River Gorge, the Larch Mountain Loop has over 1,000 feet of elevation gain and a few unridable sections. This trail is renowned for its roots, rocks, and water bars.

Drive 36 miles east of Portland on I–84 to Corbett, exit 22. Turn right and drive up Corbett Hill Road. Turn left on the Columbia River Highway at the Crown Point/Multnomah Falls sign. Turn right at the intersection of East Larch Mountain Road. You will eventually see a sign that reads DANGER. ROAD NOT PATROLLED IN WINTER. Drive approximately 1.5 miles past this sign until you reach a hairpin curve with a gated dirt road. Park here.

From the gate, ride up the hill for about a half mile and turn left on Trail 441. Ride for almost 1 mile, and then turn right on Trail 446. Turn left at the next intersection. Keep riding on Trail 446 until it ends at the intersection with Trail 424. Turn right and ride on Trail 424 until you reach the junction with East Larch Mountain Road. Turn right and ride to the end of the road at the summit of Larch Mountain. From the summit, ride back down the hill on Trail 441 (located behind the rest room) until you intersect with a dirt road. Turn left and ride back to your starting point. The best time to ride this route is June through October.

For more information contact the Columbia River Gorge National Scenic Area, 902 Wasco Avenue, Suite 200, Hood River, OR 97031; (541) 386–2333; www.fs. fed.us/r6/columbia/home.htm. A good reference map for this area is the Green Trails Map of Bridal Veil Falls. *DeLorme: Oregon Atlas & Gazetteer:* Page 67 D8.

J Post Canyon Loop

Post Canyon Loop is an advanced, technical, 6-mile ride located 4 miles from the town of Hood River. It is filled with ultranarrow bridge crossings and expert-level technical test pieces. To get there from the intersection of Fifth and Oak Streets in Hood River, drive west on Oak Street (turns into West Cascade Street) for 1.8 miles to Country Club Road. Turn left, then drive 1.5 miles before turning right on Post Canyon Road. Go about 0.5 miles on Post Canyon Road until the pavement ends and park on the shoulder.

Ride a little over a mile along the gravel road until reaching a singletrack trail on your left. Enjoy a loop ride on singletrack and doubletrack roads until you intersect with Post Canyon Road again. Ride back to your car. This trail has many unsigned intersections and is an easy place to get lost. Stop by a bike shop in Hood River to get the latest information on trail updates. The best time to ride this route is April through October.

For more information contact Hood River County Forestry Department, 918 Eighteenth Street, Hood River, OR 97031; (541) 387–6888. *DeLorme: Oregon Atlas & Gazetteer:* Page 68 C4.

K Knebal Springs Loop

This 9.2-mile, intermediate, singletrack loop has over 1,300 feet of elevation gain and is located approximately 35 miles south of Hood River.

Travel about 26 miles south of Hood River on Oregon Highway 35 to Forest Road 44 (Dufur Mill Road). Turn left and go 5.4 miles to the junction with FR 17. Stay to the right on FR 44 and continue 2.4 miles and turn left on FR 120. Turn left and park on the shoulder

Start the loop by riding on signed Trail 455 for 3.5 miles to the junction with Knebal Springs Trail 474. After about 5.5 miles the trail intersects with FR 1720. Turn left on FR 1720 and ride 1.3 miles to Knebal Springs Trail 474 on the left. Turn left on Knebal Springs Trail 474 and ride back to your starting point at 9.2 miles. The best time of year to ride this route is May through October.

This ride requires a $5.00 Northwest Forest Pass, which can be purchased online at www.naturenw.org or by calling (800) 270–7504.

For more information, contact the Mount Hood National Forest, Hood River Ranger District, 6780 Highway 35, Mount Hood Parkdale, OR 97041; (541) 352–6002; www.fs.fed.us/r6/mthood. A great reference map for this area is the *Mountain Biking & Cross-Country Skiing Guide/Map Greater Portland, Hood River, & Mount Hood* available from Adventure Maps, (800) 849–6589; www.adventuremaps.com. *DeLorme: Oregon Atlas & Gazetteer:* Page 63 A5.

L Eightmile Creek

This 6.2-mile, intermediate loop combines a good mix of climbing and trail obstacles and scenic views of Eightmile Creek.

To get there from Hood River, head about 26 miles south on Oregon Highway 35 to Forest Road 44 (Dufur Mill Road). Turn left, and go approximately 11 miles, and turn left on FR 4430. Continue 0.3 mile and turn right on FR 150 toward Eightmile Campground. Park at the campground.

Start the ride by heading out on the signed Eightmile Loop Trail 459 and follow it for the entire loop. If you're looking for a longer ride, combine this loop with the Knebal Springs Loop. The best time of year to ride this route is May through October.

This ride requires a $5.00 Northwest Forest Pass, which can be purchased online at www.naturenw.org or by calling (800) 270–7504.

For more information, contact the Mount Hood National Forest, Hood River Ranger District, 6780 Highway 35, Mount Hood–Parkdale, OR 97041; (541) 352–6002; www.fs.fed.us/r6/mthood. A great reference map for this area is the *Mountain Biking & Cross-Country Skiing Guide/Map Greater Portland, Hood River, & Mount Hood* available from Adventure Maps, (800) 849–6589; www.adventuremaps.com. *DeLorme: Oregon Atlas & Gazetteer:* Page 63 A5.

M   Old Salmon River Trail

This easy, 5.4-mile, out-and-back tour parallels the banks of the bouldery Salmon River and takes you through a stunning old growth red cedar forest.

To get there from the intersection of I–205 and I–84 in Portland, head 6.3 miles east on I–84 to exit 13, at 238th Drive/Wood Village. Turn right on 238th Drive and proceed 2.8 miles. Turn left on Burnside Road. Continue about 0.6 mile and turn left (east) on U.S. Highway 26. Drive approximately 28 miles to the small town of Welches and the junction with Old Salmon River Road (Forest Road 2618). Turn right and go 2.3 miles to the signed North Trailhead on the right side of the road.

Start riding south on the signed singletrack trail. Follow it as it winds along the river and periodically rejoins the road until you reach your turnaround point at the South Trailhead at 2.7 miles. Turn around and retrace the route back to the North Trailhead. The best time of year to ride this route is May through October.

This ride requires a $5.00 Northwest Forest Pass, which can be purchased online at www.naturenw.org or by calling (800) 270–7504.

For more information contact the Mount Hood Information Center, 65000 East Highway 26, Welches, OR 97067; (503) 622–7674; www.fs.fed.us/r6/mthood. A great reference map for this area is the *Mountain Biking & Cross-Country Skiing Guide/Map Greater Portland, Hood River, & Mount Hood* available from Adventure Maps, (800) 849–6589; www.adventuremaps.com. *DeLorme: Oregon Atlas & Gazetteer:* Page 62 B1.

N   Skibowl

Get ready to crank over 40 miles of advanced singletrack at Mt. Hood Skibowl. You can explore the trails on the mountain by your own pedal power, or you can ride the ski lift to the top with your bike and then ride down. An all-day lift ticket is $16. In addition to the lift ticket, you'll also have to purchase a $5.00 Northwest Forest Pass. Mt. Hood Skibowl also rents mountain bikes for $10 per hour, $25 for a half day, or $32 for a whole day.

To get there from the intersection of I–205 and I–84 in Portland, head 6.3 miles east on I–84 to exit 13, at 238th Drive/Wood Village. Turn right on 238th Drive and proceed 2.8 miles. Turn left on Burnside Road. Continue about 0.6 mile and turn left (east) on U.S. Highway 26. Continue 36 miles to the Skibowl turnoff. Turn right and go to a large paved parking area.

The ski area is open for mountain biking from June through September.

For more information contact Mt. Hood Skibowl, 87000 East Highway 26, Government Camp, OR 97208; (800) 754–2695; www.skibowl.com. *DeLorme: Oregon Atlas & Gazetteer:* Page 62 B2.

O Crosstown-Pioneer Bridle-Still Creek Loop

This 19.6-mile, advanced loop combines a great mix of technical singletrack and doubletrack riding on the Crosstown, Pioneer Bridle, and Still Creek Trails.

To get there from the intersection of I–205 and I–84 in Portland, head 6.3 miles east on I–84 to exit 13, at 238th Drive/Wood Village. Turn right on 238th Drive and proceed 2.8 miles. Turn left on Burnside Road. Continue about 0.6 mile and turn left (east) on U.S. Highway 26. Drive 37.6 miles to the Summit Ski Area/Government Camp turnoff. Turn left and then take a quick right into a large paved parking area in front of the Summit Ski Lodge.

From the Summit Ski Area, you'll follow the Crosstown Trail for 3 miles to Glacier Sno-Park. From there you'll start riding on the more technical Pioneer Bridle singletrack trail for about 5.4 miles until it intersects with Forest Road 2632. Turn left, follow the paved road for 0.5 mile, and then turn left on Still Creek Trail 780. Follow the trail for about 1.1 miles to its junction with Still Creek Road and turn left. You'll have a very steep ascent for the next 7.5 miles until the road's junction with FR 2612/126. Turn left and go about 0.4 mile to the junction with FR 131. Turn left and continue 0.4 mile to the junction with FR 2650. Turn right and go 0.7 mile (stay right at road junctions) to U.S. Highway 26. Turn left and ride 0.6 mile back to the Summit Ski Area on the right side of the highway. This route is open June through October.

For more information contact the Mount Hood Information Center, 65000 East Highway 26, Welches, OR 97067; (503) 622–7674; www.fs.fed.us/r6/mthood. A great reference map for this area is the *Mountain Biking & Cross-Country Skiing Guide/Map Greater Portland, Hood River, & Mount Hood* available from Adventure Maps, (800) 849–6589; www.adventuremaps.com. *DeLorme: Oregon Atlas & Gazetteer:* Page 62 B2.

P Umbrella Falls-Sahalie Falls Loop

This advanced, 4.9-mile loop takes you on a tricky singletrack tour to view Umbrella and Sahalie Falls in the Mount Hood National Forest.

To get there from the intersection of I–205 and I–84 in Portland, head east 6.3 miles on I–84 to exit 13, at 238th Drive/Wood Village. Turn right on 238th Drive and proceed 2.8 miles. Turn left on Burnside Road. Continue about 0.6 mile and turn left (east) on U.S. Highway 26. Continue 39.6 miles to the junction with Highway 35. Turn north and continue 8.3 miles to the turnoff for the Mount Hood Meadows Ski Area on the left. Turn left and proceed to the trailhead parking area.

Start climbing on the trail signed for Elk Meadows. Turn left at 0.3 mile. At 2.2 miles go right toward Umbrella Falls. At 2.6 miles admire the charming cascade of the falls. Turn around and head back to a trail junction, where you'll turn right and descend toward Sahalie Falls. At 4.3 miles enjoy views of Sahalie Falls. Cross a paved road at 4.8 miles and continue on the singletrack trail. Arrive back at the trailhead at 4.9 miles. The route is open June through October.

This ride requires a $5.00 Northwest Forest Pass. It can be purchased online at www.naturenw.org or by calling (800) 270–7504.

For more information contact the Mount Hood Information Center, 65000 East Highway 26, Welches, OR 97067; (503) 622–7674; www.fs.fed.us/r6/mthood. A great reference map for this area is the *Mountain Biking & Cross-Country Skiing Guide/Map Greater Portland, Hood River, & Mount Hood* available from Adventure Maps, (800) 849–6589; www.adventuremaps.com. *DeLorme: Oregon Atlas & Gazetteer:* Page 62 B3.

Q Clear Creek-Camas Trail

This intermediate, 9.6-mile, out-and-back ride travels for 1.9 miles on Clear Creek Trail 487 as it parallels Clear Creek and then hooks into Camas Trail 490A for 2.9 miles as it parallels Camas and Clear Creeks and offers spectacular views of White River Canyon and Mount Hood.

To get there from the intersection of I–205 and I–84 in Portland, head east 6.3 miles on I–84 to exit 13, 238th Drive/Wood Village. Turn right on 238th Drive and proceed 2.8 miles. Turn left on Burnside Road. In about 0.6 mile turn left (east) on U.S. Highway 26. Continue approximately 55 miles to the junction with Highway 216. Turn left (east) and go 2 miles to the junction with paved Forest Road 2130. Turn left (north) for 3 miles to Clear Creek Campground and park. The trailhead is directly across the bridge over Clear Creek. This ride is open June through October.

For more information contact the Mount Hood Information Center, 65000 East Highway 26, Welches, OR 97067; (503) 622–7674; www.fs.fed.us/r6/mthood. *DeLorme: Oregon Atlas & Gazetteer:* Page 62 C4.

Eugene and Oakridge

Located at the southern end of the Willamette Valley, Eugene is about 60 miles east of the Oregon coast. East of Eugene on Highway 126 is the inspiring McKenzie River Trail. This classic 26-mile singletrack winds along the spring-fed waters of the McKenzie River past waterfalls and spectacular lava flows. The small community of Oakridge, about 36 miles southeast of Eugene on Highway 58, is another mountain biking destination that features a wide variety of inspiring singletrack rides geared toward all levels of riders. Located on the southwest slopes of the Cascade Mountains, Oakridge is surrounded on all sides by the immense Willamette National Forest. A recommended old-growth ride is the Larison Creek Trail. Other superb singletrack rides in this area include Goodman, Hardesty, Middle Fork Willamette, and Moon Point–Youngs Rock. Farther east on Highway 58, you'll find pristine Waldo Lake—Oregon's second-deepest freshwater lake. You can explore this pristine, high mountain lake on the epic 21-mile Waldo Lake Trail. Just outside of Cottage Grove, about 18 miles south of Eugene on I–5, are a great family ride on the Row River Trail and a great singletrack tour along picturesque Brice Creek.

24 Salmon Creek

You'll love this fast, easy route, which sweeps through an attractive forest along the banks of cheery Salmon Creek. If you are pedaling the route during school hours, you'll likely see the local high school cross-country team in action. This fun forest route is green and cool in the summer and golden in the fall. As an added bonus you'll get to check out a picturesque wood bridge that spans the creek at your turn-around point.

Start: The trailhead is located off Fish Hatchery Road about 2.5 miles east of Oakridge.
Length: 7.6 miles out and back.
Approximate riding time: 1 to 1.5 hours.
Difficulty: Easy, due to smooth trail surface and minimal elevation gain.
Total climbing: 140 feet. Elevation profiles are not provided for rides with little or no elevation gain.
Trail surface: Singletrack and doubletrack.
Land status: National forest.
Seasons: Open year-round.
Nearest town: Oakridge.

Other trail users: Hikers.
Canine compatibility: Dogs permitted.
Wheels: A bike without front suspension will work fine on this easy route due to the smooth trail surface and minimal elevation gain.
Trail contacts: Willamette National Forest, Middle Fork Ranger District, Lowell Office, 60 South Pioneer Street, Lowell, OR 97452; (541) 937-2129; www.fs.fed.us/r6/willamette.
Fees and permits: No fees or permits are required.
Maps: Maptech maps: Oakridge; Westfir East.

Finding the Trailhead

From I-5 in Eugene take exit 188A for Oregon Highway 58/Oakridge/Klamath Falls. Head east on Highway 58 for about 36 miles to Oakridge. After crossing Salmon Creek in Oakridge, travel 1.2 miles more on Highway 58 to Fish Hatchery Road. Turn left, go 1.3 miles, and turn right on an obscure dirt lane that takes you to the trailhead. (You'll reach this turnoff area immediately after you cross a bridge over Salmon Creek.) *DeLorme: Oregon Atlas & Gazetteer:* Page 43 B5.

The Ride

Thirty-six miles east of Eugene on Highway 58 is the small community of Oakridge, another mountain biking hotspot with a wide variety of golden singletrack rides geared toward all levels of riders. Located on the southwest slopes of the Cascade Mountains, Oakridge is surrounded on all sides by the extensive Willamette National Forest. The town celebrates its love of mountain biking at the annual Cascade Fat Tire Festival in mid-July. The festival features a series of mountain bike races (for kids, novices, and pros), mountain bike tours, and fun contests such as the fastest tire change and best bunny hop.

One of the singletrack tours featured at this festival is a ride on the fun Salmon Creek Trail. This easy route follows the twists and turns of lively Salmon Creek for

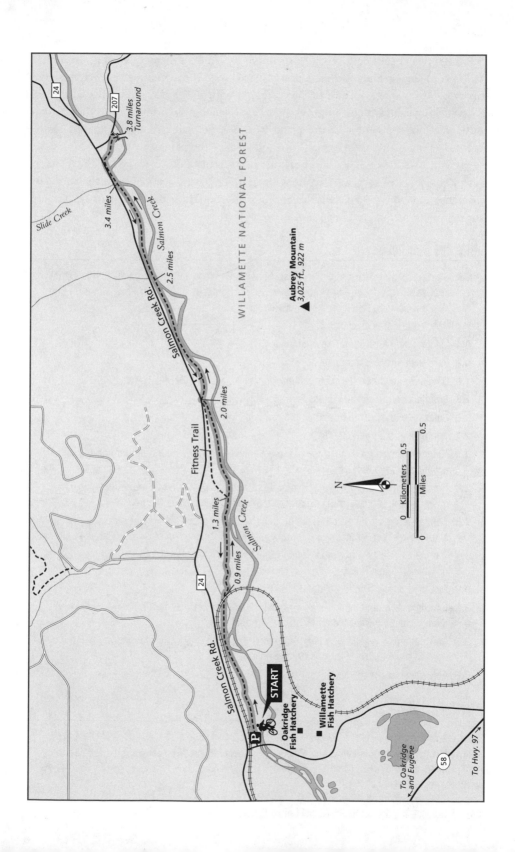

WILLAMETTE NATIONAL FOREST

24

207

3.8 miles
Turnaround

3.4 miles

Slide Creek

Salmon Creek

2.5 miles

Aubrey Mountain
3,025 ft., 922 m

Salmon Creek Rd.

2.0 miles

Fitness Trail

1.3 miles

Salmon Creek

N

Kilometers   0.5

Miles   0.5

0

0

0.9 miles

24

Salmon Creek Rd.

START

P

Oakridge
Fish Hatchery

Willamette
Fish Hatchery

58

To Oakridge
and Eugene

To Hwy. 97

3.8 miles to a charming footbridge spanning the creek. The route is a mix of single-track, doubletrack, and a short section of paved road through a forest corridor made up of bigleaf maple, oak, and fir and carpeted with the feathery fans of sword fern. This striking fern, which can grow to be 5 feet tall, has swordlike fronds that extend outward from the center of the plant. Native American tribes used the fronds to build sleeping platforms. They also roasted and ate the plant's roots.

If you love creek rides, another tour that should not be missed is the Larison Creek route (see Larison Creek, Ride 25). This advanced ride takes you past immense old-growth red cedar trees along the bouldery banks of Larison Creek, through bold terrain and beautiful scenery.

Miles and Directions

0.0 Start on the dirt path on a short downhill and then cross a wood bridge. (FYI: It is virtually impossible to get lost on this route because it's bordered by Salmon Creek Road on one side and Salmon Creek on the other side.)

0.1 Veer left at a trail junction.

0.4 Ignore a doubletrack road that heads left.

0.9 Pass underneath a train trestle.

1.0 Continue straight on the main trail and ignore a spur trail that heads left.

1.3 Turn right on the signed Fitness Trail.

2.0 Cross a doubletrack road and continue straight on the singletrack trail.

2.1 Turn right at the trail junction.

2.5 The trail narrows on a steep bank above the creek. Ignore a spur trail that heads left toward a paved road.

2.6 The trail turns into a doubletrack road. Go 200 yards and arrive at a road junction. Continue straight and ignore the doubletrack road that peels off to the right.

3.3 Turn left at the trail junction. (FYI: The trail that goes right dead-ends at a primitive campsite.) Go another 30 feet and then take a sharp right on an unmarked singletrack trail.

3.4 The trail intersects with paved Salmon Creek Road (Forest Road 24). Turn right and pedal on Salmon Creek Road.

3.6 Turn right on the signed Salmon Creek Trail 4365.

3.7 Turn right on a doubletrack road and follow this road 0.1 mile to a primitive camping area. Continue toward the creek on a singletrack trail.

3.8 Arrive at a picturesque wood bridge spanning Salmon Creek (your turnaround point). Retrace the route back to your starting point.

7.6 Arrive back at the trailhead.

Ride Information

Local Information
Oakridge Chamber of Commerce, P.O. Box 217, Oakridge, OR 97463; (541) 782-4146; www.oakridgechamber.com.

Local Events and Attractions
Cascade Fat Tire Festival, held the second weekend in July, Oakridge; (541) 782-4146.

25 Larison Creek

Have a day filled with adventure on this old-growth trail that sweeps up Larison Creek Canyon. Moss-coated logs, trees, and rocks create a glistening green canvas, and the soothing sounds of the creek make you want the trail to never end. This trail will challenge you with its many sections of roots, rocks, and creek crossings.

Start: The trailhead is located on Diamond Drive about 4.3 miles east of Oakridge.
Length: 12.4 miles out and back (with an 18.8-mile loop option).
Approximate riding time: 3 to 6 hours.
Difficulty: Difficult, due to many technical obstacles on the trail.
Total climbing: 1,320 feet.
Trail surface: Technical singletrack.
Land status: National forest.
Seasons: May through October.
Nearest town: Oakridge.
Other trail users: Hikers.

Canine compatibility: Dogs permitted.
Wheels: A bike with front suspension will help smooth out the abundant rock and root sections present on the trail.
Trail contacts: Middle Fork Ranger District, Lowell Office, 60 South Pioneer Street, Lowell, OR 97452; (541) 937-2129; www.fs.fed.us/r6/willamette.
Fees and permits: $5.00 Northwest Forest Pass, which you can purchase by calling (800) 270-7504 or online at www.naturenw.org.
Maps: Maptech maps: USGS Oakridge; Holland Point.

Finding the Trailhead

From I-5 in Eugene take exit 188A for Oregon Highway 58/Oakridge/Klamath Falls. Head east on Highway 58 for about 36 miles to Oakridge. From the bridge over Salmon Creek in Oakridge, travel 1.4 more miles on Highway 58 to Kitson Springs Road (Forest Road 23) at the Hills Creek Dam sign. Turn right and travel 0.5 mile to Diamond Drive (FR 21). Turn right and go 2.4 miles to a dirt parking lot and trailhead on the right side of the road. The trailhead is marked with a brown hiker sign. *DeLorme: Oregon Atlas & Gazetteer:* Page 43 C5.

The Ride

This ride tantalizes you with its vast old-growth forest and taunts you with its technical sections that are fun for advanced riders and very challenging for intermediate riders. You can ride the trail out and back as described here or complete an 18.8-mile loop by riding up forest service roads to the top of the Larison Creek Trail and riding down the technical singletrack.

The ride starts by following the shores of Larison Cove, an arm of the Hills Creek Reservoir. This quiet reservoir is popular for swimming and boating. Periodically it is closed due to high concentrations of toxic algae that show up as blue-green surface scum resembling thick pea soup. These algae can cause skin irritation, diarrhea, nausea, cramps, dizziness, and fainting. If you're tempted to swim in the

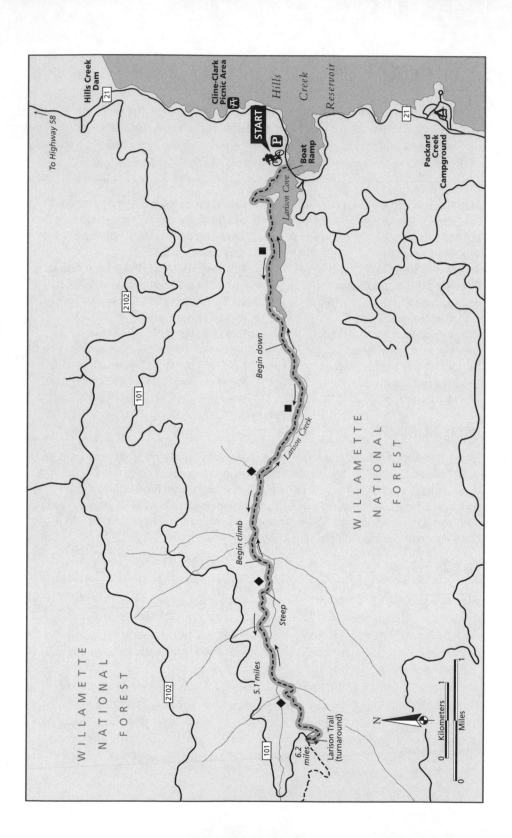

reservoir, always check ahead to be sure it is open for swimming. If you have your canine cycling partner with you, make sure he isn't tempted to take a dip in the reservoir while you aren't looking.

As you continue on the winding singletrack, you'll catch glimpses of wild rhododendrons that start flowering in April and the delicate, three-petaled trillium that begin blooming in March. After 1.5 miles the trail parallels the banks of Larison Creek and weaves around immense old-growth red cedar and Douglas fir trees. Larison Creek was named for George Larison, a homesteader who lived in the valley during the 1880s.

As you pedal next to the creek, moss-coated rocks and logs create a mystical backdrop to the sounds of the swirling water. While the beauty of the surrounding forest may distract you, the many tangled roots and rock gardens on the trail demand your attention. At 3.1 and 5.1 miles, you'll have to negotiate bridgeless creek crossings. After the 5.1-mile mark, the trail becomes very steep and tough and is often overgrown with blackberries and manzanita. After 5.8 miles the route passes through a clear-cut area and at 6.2 miles you'll arrive at Forest Road 100 and your turnaround point. From here, blast back down the technical trail for many more hours of fun. You also have the option of riding back to the trailhead on forest service roads.

Miles and Directions

0.0 Start pedaling on the singletrack Larison Creek Trail. **Option:** If you don't want to ride out and back on this trail, you can ride on forest service roads to the top of the trail and then ride down the singletrack. To do this, turn left out of the parking area on FR 21. After 2.3 miles turn left on paved Larison Rock Road (FR 2102). Continue climbing on this road for 1.9 miles to the junction with FR 101. Turn left (the road turns to gravel) and continue 8.4 miles to the junction with Larison Creek Trail 3646 on the left side of the road.

0.5 Pass a rest room on your left. Go 50 yards, cross a wood bridge over the creek, and then pass a campsite on your right.

3.1 You'll have to negotiate a bridgeless creek crossing.

5.1 Ford the creek and continue on a steep ascent. You'll continue riding through a shady forest for the next 0.6 mile and then the trail passes through an overgrown clear-cut area for 0.5 mile until it intersects with FR 101.

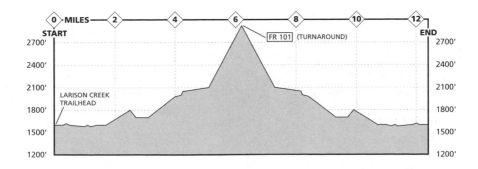

Immense red cedars on the Larison Creek Trail.

6.2 Arrive at the junction with FR 101 (your turnaround point). **Option:** If you want a faster way back to the trailhead, you can turn right on FR 101 and ride 8.4 miles to the junction with paved Larison Rock Road (FR 2102). Turn right and continue 1.9 miles to the junction with paved FR 21. Turn right and continue 2.3 miles to the trailhead parking area located on the right side of the road.

12.4 Arrive back at the trailhead.

Ride Information

Local Information
Oakridge Chamber of Commerce, P.O. Box 217, Oakridge, OR 97463; (541) 782-4146; www.oakridgechamber.com.

Local Events and Attractions
Cascade Fat Tire Festival, held the second weekend in July, Oakridge, OR; (541) 782-4146.

26 McKenzie River

Winding along the crystal-clear, fast-flowing McKenzie River, this classic singletrack trail twists its way through a forested ecosystem characterized by majestic stands of old-growth Douglas fir and a mix of younger trees with a spongy forest floor carpeted in green, glowing ferns and moss-coated logs. The trail is well maintained and full of bridges, stream crossings, waterfalls, and fast twisty sections. If you love to ride forever on singletrack, this trail is sure to please.

Start: McKenzie Bridge Trailhead.
Other starting locations: The main trail access points include Paradise Campground, Trailbridge Reservoir, and Santiam Wagon Road Trailhead.
Length: 19.6 miles out and back (with a 26.5-mile shuttle option).
Approximate riding time: 3 to 5 hours; 5 to 9 hours for the 26.5-mile route.
Difficulty: Moderate, due to some technical obstacles and elevation gain. Difficult, if you complete the entire 26.5-mile trail.
Total climbing: 400 feet; 1,800 feet if you complete the entire 26.5-mile trail.
Trail surface: Singletrack, doubletrack, and bridges.
Land status: National forest.
Seasons: May through October.

Nearest town: McKenzie Bridge.
Other trail users: Hikers.
Canine compatibility: Leashed dogs permitted.
Wheels: A bike with dual suspension is recommended to tackle the technical sections on the singletrack section of this route.
Trail contacts: McKenzie River Ranger District, 57600 McKenzie Highway, McKenzie Bridge, OR 97413; (541) 822-3381; www.fs.fed.us/r6/Willamette.
Fees and permits: $5.00 Northwest Forest Pass required. You can purchase it by calling (800) 270-7504 or online at www.naturenw.org.
Maps: Maptech maps: McKenzie Bridge; Belknap Springs; Tamolitch Falls.

Finding the Trailhead

From Eugene travel approximately 50 miles east on Oregon Highway 126 to the community of McKenzie Bridge. Continue east another 1.8 miles to the McKenzie Bridge Trailhead located on the left side of the road. **Shuttle option:** If you want to complete the entire 26.5-mile trail as a bike or car shuttle, continue another 25.5 miles east on Oregon Highway 126 to the intersection with a dirt road. Turn right and follow signs for MCKENZIE RIVER. *DeLorme: Oregon Atlas & Gazetteer:* Page 49 C7.

The Ride

The Model T Ford, Hupmobile, Overland, and Maxwell were some of the first automobiles to ramble over the twisty McKenzie Pass highway that was adopted into the Oregon State Highway System in 1917. This scenic highway originates in Eugene in the Willamette Valley, crosses over the Cascade Mountains, and ends in

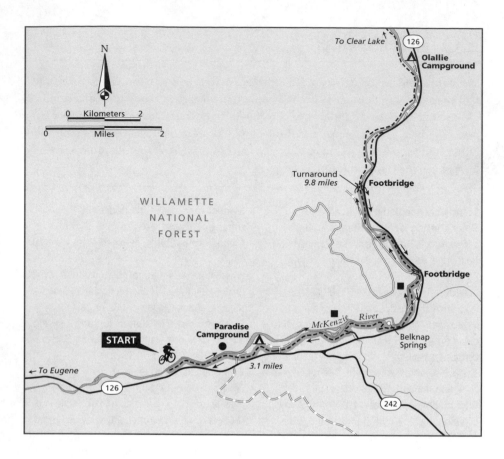

central Oregon at the small town of Sisters. Its moniker comes from a man named Donald McKenzie, a fur trapper who in 1812 led an exploration party commissioned by the Pacific Fur Trading Company from Astoria in search of rich fur-trapping grounds. His party was unsuccessful in their quest and what would be called the McKenzie corridor was left virtually untouched.

As the population of the Willamette Valley grew in the mid–1800s, there was increased pressure to build a road over Santiam Pass for settlers wanting to relocate to eastern Oregon and for those seeking gold in Idaho. After the first attempt to build a road over the pass failed in 1846, a crude road was finally built in 1862 by Felix and Marion Scott. Building what came to be known as the Scott Trail was a monumental task. Forty men, nine freight wagons, sixty yoke of oxen, and 900 head of horses and cattle were used in its construction. Even after this crude trail was in place, it still took up to five days to travel from Eugene to Sisters.

In the fall of 1872, John Craig, president of the incorporated McKenzie Salt Spring and Deschutes Wagon Road Company, considerably improved Scott Trail and began charging tolls—5 cents for sheep, 10 cents for horses and cattle, $1.00 for a horse and rider, and $2.00 per wagon. Thanks to these improvements, Scott Trail became a mail route to eastern Oregon. In the summer months mail was carried over the pass on horseback, but during the winter the route had to be traversed by foot using snowshoes. This difficult mail route began at McKenzie Bridge and ended at Camp Polk just outside Sisters on the eastern side of the Cascades.

Despite continued improvements over the years, travel over McKenzie Pass still proved to be quite an adventure. In 1919 the *Bend Bulletin* issued the following warning: "Unless auto tourists are well equipped with ropes, pulleys, boards, shovels, and every device needed in conquering the most obstinate snowdrifts, they are advised against trying the McKenzie Pass." Snowdrifts and sharp lava rocks scattered along the road continued to plague travelers over the next several years. Today, however, the McKenzie Highway (Oregon Highway 126) is the gateway to the McKenzie River National Recreation Area, said to be one of the most beautiful places in the state. Lava flows, snow-covered peaks, and the crystal-clear waters of the McKenzie River are just a few of the attractions along this scenic stretch of highway.

One attraction not to miss is the 26-mile McKenzie River National Recreation Trail, which winds along the fast-flowing McKenzie River. If you love to ride along endless and picturesque singletrack, you'll love this trail.

Miles and Directions

0.0 Start at the Southern Trailhead on the left side of the road 1.8 miles west of McKenzie Bridge on Highway 126.

2.2 Cross a gravel road and continue straight.

3.1 Cross a paved road, which is the entrance to Paradise Campground. Continue straight.

4.1 Cross a gravel road and continue straight.

4.8 The trail forks. Continue straight. (FYI: If you turn right you can exit to Highway 126.)

5.6 Cross a paved road and continue straight.

6.2 Cross a bridge.

6.4 Cross a bridge. Continue straight and look for a trail sign. The trail comes to a fork. Turn right.

6.7 Cross a road.

7.0 Cross a stream.

7.1 Turn left at the trail fork.

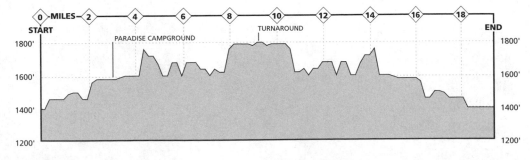

7.3 Cross a bridge.

7.4 Make a sharp left turn and cross a concrete bridge. Ride a short distance and look to your right for the trail sign. Turn right.

7.3 Cross a bridge.

8.8 Continue straight and ride around a metal gate. The trail turns into a doubletrack road.

9.1 Turn right to continue on the singletrack trail.

9.8 Arrive at a wood bridge. This is your turnaround point. Retrace the route back to the trailhead. **Option:** You can continue on the trail for another 16.7 miles to the upper trailhead.

19.6 Arrive back at the trailhead.

Ride Information

Local Information

McKenzie Bridge Chamber of Commerce,
McKenzie Bridge, OR 97413; (541)
896–3330.

◀ *Negotiating a bridge crossing on the McKenzie River Trail.*

27 Row River

This fun and easy tour starts in Cottage Grove adjacent to rambling Mosby Creek. The multiuse trail follows the course of the Row River to Dorena Lake. The route has many trailheads and places to stop to enjoy the views of the lake and the surrounding farming country. As an added bonus you can see the historic Mosby Creek Covered Bridge and the Dorena Covered Bridge.

Start: The Mosby Creek Trailhead in Cottage Grove, about 18 miles south of Eugene and 50 miles north of Roseburg off I-5.
Length: 25.2 miles out and back.
Approximate riding time: 3 to 4 hours.
Difficulty: Easy, due to smooth paved surface and minimal elevation gain.
Total climbing: 120 feet. Elevation profiles are not provided for rides with little or no elevation gain.
Trail surface: Paved multiuse trail.
Land status: Bureau of Land Management.
Seasons: Open year-round.
Nearest town: Cottage Grove.

Other trail users: Hikers.
Canine compatibility: Leashed dogs permitted.
Wheels: A hybrid bike will work fine due to the smooth paved surface.
Trail contacts: Bureau of Land Management, 2890 Chad Drive, Eugene District, Eugene, OR 97440; (541) 683-6600; www.edo.or.blm.gov/Rec/Row_Trail.htm.
Fees and permits: No fees or permits required.
Maps: Maptech maps: Cottage Grove; Dorena Lake; Culp Creek.

Finding the Trailhead

From I-5 in Cottage Grove take exit 174 toward Dorena Lake. At the end of the off-ramp, turn east on Row River Road and drive 1 mile east. Turn right on Currin Conn Road, then take a quick left on Mosby Creek Road. Go 2 miles southeast on Mosby Creek Road and then turn left on Layng Road. Take a quick left into the Mosby Creek Trailhead parking lot. *DeLorme: Oregon Atlas & Gazetteer:* Page 41 B8 and Page 42 B1.

The Ride

This unique rail-trail is owned and managed by the Bureau of Land Management (BLM). The original rail line was started in 1902, and steam engines carried logs, ore, supplies, and passengers along the route that stretched to the town of Disston. This tour starts at the Mosby Creek Trailhead, which has rest rooms and water. From the parking area this paved trail heads to the northeast. Just before crossing a picturesque bridge over Mosby Creek, check out the covered bridge just off the trail on the right. This bright white bridge was built in 1920 and extensive restoration work was completed in 1990. After 1.3 miles you'll cross the swift-moving Row River, which once was used to float logs to more than twenty mills that operated along its

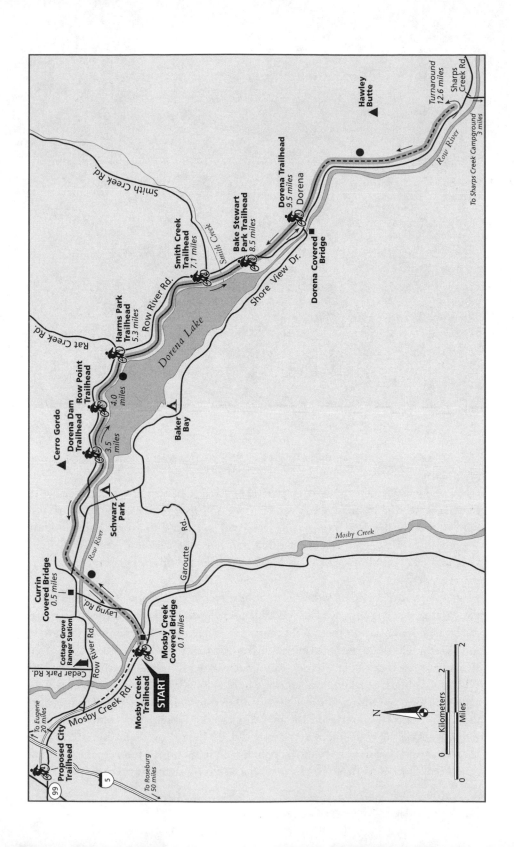

Scenic farming country on the Row River Trail.

banks. The route turns southeast and takes you past oak woodlands, wetlands, and small farms.

At 3.4 miles you'll arrive at Dorena Dam Trailhead, on the northwest edge of Dorena Reservoir. From here you can view the 150-foot-high earthen dam that was built to prevent floods and to provide irrigation and recreation for the surrounding communities. Over the next 5 miles, the trail hugs the northern shore of Dorena Lake and takes you through a shady Douglas fir forest with many open areas where you can view the lake.

A variety of creeks, including Rat, Smith, Teeter, Cedar, and King, empty into the Dorena Lake. These wetland ecosystems provide food and shelter for geese, ducks, blue herons, and osprey. Wild camas (an edible blue-flowered lily) also grows in this area. The root of this plant was a major part of the Native Americans' diet. When you reach the Bake Stewart Park Trailhead at 8.3 miles, you'll leave the lake behind. Continue pedaling through oak woodlands and past many small farms with cattle and horses. Once you reach the small town of Dorena at 9.5 miles, you have the option of turning right off the trail to view the Dorena Covered Bridge over the Row River. It was built in 1949, retired in 1973, and overhauled in 1996.

As the route continues, look for songbirds and listen for the loud croaking sounds of resident frogs. Red-tailed hawks are also a common sight. This section of the trail is thick with blackberries that ripen in mid- to late August. At 11 miles you'll reach the Hawley Butte Trailhead, where you have the option of getting drinks and snacks at the River Store across the road. From this point you'll pedal another 2.1 miles to the trail's end. Turn around and retrace the route back to your starting point at the Mosby Creek Trailhead.

Miles and Directions

0.0 Start by riding northeast on the paved path from the Mosby Creek Trailhead.

0.1 Stop and check out the Mosby Creek Covered Bridge located about 200 yards to the right of the paved path. Cross Mosby Creek after viewing the bridge.

0.5 Cross Layng Road.

1.3 Cross the Row River.

1.4 Cross Row River Road.

2.8 Cross Row River Road.

3.5 Dorena Dam Trailhead. Enjoy the views of Dorena Dam and Dorena Lake. (FYI: Rest rooms [no water] are here.)

4.0 Row Point Trailhead.

5.3 Harms Park. (FYI: Rest rooms (no water) and picnic tables are present here.)

7.1 Smith Creek Trailhead.

7.7 Pass a rest room on the right (no water).

8.5 Bake Stewart Park Trailhead. Just after the trailhead cross Row River Road.

9.5 Dorena Dam Trailhead. **Side trip:** You have the option of turning right on a dirt road and then turning right on Row River Road to view the Dorena Covered Bridge.

11.0 Hawley Butte Trailhead. (FYI: If you want drinks and snacks, you have the option of leaving the paved path here by turning left on Row River Road and stocking up at the River Store.)

12.6 Arrive at the end of the trail marked TRAIL'S END. Turn around and retrace the route back to the trailhead.

25.2 Arrive at the Mosby Creek Trailhead.

Ride Information

Local Information

Cottage Grove Chamber of Commerce, 700 East Gibbs, Suite C, P.O. Box 587, Cottage Grove, OR 97424; (541) 942-2411; www.cgchamber.com.

Local Events and Attractions

Bohemia Mining Days, held in mid-July, Cottage Grove; (541) 942-6125.

Fall Harvest Festival, held in October, Cottage Grove; (541) 942-2411.

Honorable Mentions

Compiled here is an index of great rides located around Eugene and Oakridge. Check them out and let us know what you think. You may decide that one or more of these rides deserves higher status in future editions, or perhaps you have a ride of your own that merits some attention.

R Elijah Bristow State Park

This 847-acre park is located on the south bank of the Middle Fork of the Willamette River. It is host to 12 miles of interconnected multiuse trails that travel through oak woodlands, open meadows, and deciduous forests. This park is open year-round. Some trails, however, may be closed during the winter months because of flooding.

To get there from I–5 in Eugene, take exit 188A for Oregon Highway 58/ Oakridge/Klamath Falls. Head east on Highway 58 for about 10 miles to the junction with Wheeler Road. Turn left and go 0.3 mile to the park entrance. Turn right and travel 1 mile to a day use parking area at the road's end. For more information contact Oregon Parks and Recreation, Suite 1, 1115 Commercial Street NE, Salem, OR 97301; (800) 551–6949; www.oregonstateparks.org/park_83.php. *DeLorme: Oregon Atlas & Gazetteer:* Page 42 A2.

S Goodman Trail

This 8-mile, intermediate, out-and-back, singletrack trail weaves through a corridor of stately red cedar and Douglas fir trees in the Willamette National Forest.

To get there from I–5 in Eugene, take exit 188A for Oregon Highway 58/Oakridge/Klamath Falls. Head east on Highway 58 for about 21 miles to a parking area on the right side of the road.

Start riding uphill on the signed singletrack trail for 4 miles to your turnaround point at the junction with Forest Road 5833 (Goodman Creek Road). Enjoy an inspiring descent on the same route back to the trailhead. The best time to ride this route is May through October.

For more information contact the Willamette National Forest, Middle Fork Ranger District, Lowell Office, 60 South Pioneer Street, Lowell, OR 97452; (541) 937–2129; www.fs.fed.us/r6/willamette. A good reference map for this ride is the Middle Fork Ranger District Map. *DeLorme: Oregon Atlas & Gazetteer:* Page 42 B3.

T Hardesty Trail

The advanced, 12.2-mile Hardesty Trail tests your aerobic fitness and technical prowess with its steep grade and multiple obstacles.

To get there from I–5 in Eugene, take exit 188A for Oregon Highway 58/Oakridge/Klamath Falls. Head east on Highway 58 for about 20 miles to a gravel parking area on the right side of the road.

The trail ascends Hardesty Mountain at a wicked rate as it climbs over 900 feet for 6.1 miles to your turnaround point at the upper trailhead. Descend with care, making sure to watch for hikers on this popular trail. The best time to ride this route is May through October.

This ride requires a $5.00 Northwest Forest Pass. You can purchase it by calling (800) 270–7504 or online at www.naturenw.org.

For more information contact the Willamette National Forest, Middle Fork Ranger District, Lowell Office, 60 South Pioneer Street, Lowell, OR 97452; (541) 937–2129; www.fs.fed.us/r6/willamette. A good reference map for this ride is the Middle Fork Ranger District Map. *DeLorme: Oregon Atlas & Gazetteer:* Page 42 B3.

U Flat Creek-Dead Mountain Trail

This 6.6-mile, out-and-back, intermediate trail combines a short warm-up on paved and gravel forest service roads with a fun ride on Flat Creek Trail 3566.

To get there from I–5 in Eugene, take exit 188A for Oregon Highway 58/Oakridge/Klamath Falls. Head east on Highway 58 for about 36 miles to Oakridge. From the bridge crossing Salmon Creek in Oakridge, continue 1.2 miles east on Highway 58 to Fish Hatchery Road. Turn left, go 1.3 miles, and turn right on Salmon Creek Road. Go about 1.5 miles and turn into the Rigdon/Oakridge Ranger Station on the right side of the road. (You'll reach this turnoff area immediately after you cross a bridge over Salmon Creek.)

Start by riding out to Forest Road 24 (Salmon Creek Road) and turning right. Ride 0.2 mile and turn left onto FR 2404. Continue for 0.6 mile (staying to the left at a road junction after 0.4 mile) to the Flat Creek Trailhead on the left. Ascend the singletrack trail for 2.5 miles to the turnaround point, where the trail intersects with FR 190. Enjoy a thrilling descent on the same route back to your starting point. The best time to ride this route is May through October.

This ride requires a $5.00 Northwest Forest Pass. You can purchase one by calling (800) 270–7504 or online at www.naturenw.org.

For more information contact the Willamette National Forest, Middle Fork Ranger District, Lowell Office, 60 South Pioneer Street, Lowell, OR 97452; (541) 937–2129; www.fs.fed.us/r6/willamette. A good reference map for this ride is the Middle Fork Ranger District Map. *DeLorme: Oregon Atlas & Gazetteer:* Page 43 B5.

V Larison Rock

This 10.2-mile, advanced loop is a classic Oakridge tour with its steep climbing, roots, rocks, exposure, and tough switchbacks. An added bonus is a side trail to the top of Larison Rock.

To get there from I–5 in Eugene, take exit 188A for Oregon Highway 58/ Oakridge/Klamath Falls. Head east on Highway 58 for about 36 miles to Oakridge, then continue east on Highway 58 for about 1.8 miles to Kitson Springs Road. Turn right, continue 0.5 mile, and turn right on Forest Road 21 (Rigdon Road). Go 0.3 mile and turn right on FR 5852 (South Bank Road). Continue about 1 mile to a parking area on the right side of the road.

Start the ride by turning left on FR 5852 and riding 0.9 mile to the junction with FR 21. Turn right and go 0.8 mile to FR 2101 (Larison Rock Road). Turn right and ride for 4.4 miles to the Larison Rock Trailhead on the right. Enjoy a thrilling and tricky descent for 3.4 miles on the Larison Rock Trail to the junction with FR 5852. Turn right and go 0.7 mile to the trailhead on the left side of the road. The best time to ride this route is May through October.

This ride requires a $5.00 Northwest Forest Pass, which can be purchased by calling (800) 270–7504 or online at www.naturenw.org.

For more information contact the Willamette National Forest, Middle Fork Ranger District, Lowell Office, 60 South Pioneer Street, Lowell, OR 97452; (541) 937–2129; www.fs.fed.us/r6/willamette. A good reference map for this ride is the Middle Fork Ranger District Map. *DeLorme: Oregon Atlas & Gazetteer:* Page 43 C5.

W Middle Fork Willamette River

This 19.4-mile, out-and-back, singletrack ride glides along a scenic section of the Middle Fork Willamette River in the Willamette National Forest. The trail challenges you with roots, rocks, sand traps, and drop-offs and inspires you with its soothing river sounds and shady mixed conifer, cottonwood, and bigleaf maple forest.

From I–5 in Eugene, take exit 188A for Oregon Highway 58/Oakridge/Klamath Falls. Head east on Highway 58 for about 36 miles to Oakridge, then continue east on Highway 58 for about 1.8 miles to Kitson Springs Road. Turn right, continue 0.5 mile, turn right on Forest Road 21 (Rigdon Road), and go 11.6 miles to Sand Prairie Campground. Turn right onto the campground entrance road and drive through the campground (staying to the right at road junctions) to a day use parking area.

Pedal upriver on the signed singletrack trail for 5.3 miles to the junction with FR 21. Turn right and go a short distance to the junction with FR 2127. Turn right and cross the river; then take a quick left on the singletrack trail and follow it for another 4.4 miles upriver to the junction with FR 2133 (your turnaround point). Retrace the route back to the trailhead. The best time to ride this route is May through October.

For more information contact the Willamette National Forest, Middle Fork Ranger District, Lowell Office, 60 South Pioneer Street, Lowell, OR 97452; (541) 937–2129; www.fs.fed.us/r6/willamette. A good reference map for this ride is the Middle Fork Ranger District Map. *DeLorme: Oregon Atlas & Gazetteer:* Page 43 D5.

✕ Moon Point-Youngs Rock Loop

This 18.6-mile, advanced route takes you on a wild ride on the Moon Rock Trail and the Youngs Rock Trail in the Willamette National Forest.

From I–5 in Eugene, take exit 188A for Oregon Highway 58/Oakridge/Klamath Falls. Head east on Highway 58 for about 36 miles to Oakridge, then continue east on Highway 58 for about 1.8 miles to Kitson Springs Road. Turn right, continue 0.5 mile, then turn right on Forest Road 21 (Rigdon Road), and go about 17 miles to the Youngs Flat parking area on the right.

Start the ride by turning right (south) on FR 21, pedaling 0.3 mile, and then taking a left on FR 2129 (Youngs Creek Road). Ascend about 8 miles and then turn right on FR 439. Go 1.5 miles and turn right on Moon Point Trail 3688. Following signs, pedal on this fabulous singletrack for 0.8 mile to a trail junction. Go right and continue 0.4 mile to the Moon Rock Viewpoint. Turn around and head back to the trail junction; go right to continue on your downhill odyssey. After 3.6 miles you'll reach a trail junction. Turn left toward Campers Flat Campground and pedal another 1.6 miles to the junction with FR 21. Go right and ride about 2 miles to your starting point.

The best time to ride this route is May through October.

For more information contact the Willamette National Forest, Middle Fork Ranger District, Lowell Office, 60 South Pioneer Street, Lowell, OR 97452; (541) 937–2129; www.fs.fed.us/r6/willamette. A good reference map for this ride is the Middle Fork Ranger District Map. *DeLorme: Oregon Atlas & Gazetteer:* Page 43 D5.

✕ Waldo Lake Loop

This is an advanced, 21-mile, classic singletrack ride around Waldo Lake (located approximately 75 miles southeast of Eugene).

To get there from I–5 in Eugene, take exit 188A for Oregon Highway 58/Oakridge/Klamath Falls. Head southeast on Highway 58 for about 60 miles to the junction with Forest Road 5897. Turn left and travel for 7 miles to the junction with FR 5896. Turn left and continue about 2 miles to the boat ramp parking area at Shadow Bay Campground.

Look for the start of Waldo Lake Trail 3590 south of the parking lot. This ride is usually open late June through October.

This ride requires a $5.00 Northwest Forest Pass. You can purchase it by calling (800) 270–7504 or online at www.naturenw.org.

For more information, contact the Willamette National Forest, Middle Fork Ranger District, Lowell Office, 60 South Pioneer Street, Lowell, OR 97452; (541) 937–2129; www.fs.fed.us/r6/willamette. *DeLorme: Oregon Atlas & Gazetteer:* Page 43 C8.

Z Brice Creek

This 11-mile, intermediate, out-and-back, singletrack tour takes you on a spin along the banks of bouldery Brice Creek through a towering old-growth Douglas fir and red cedar in the Umpqua National Forest.

To get there from Eugene, travel about 18 miles south on I–5 to Cottage Grove, exit 174. At the end of the off-ramp, turn left (east) onto Row River Road and continue 4.3 miles to the junction with Shoreview Drive. Continue straight on Shoreview Drive (Row River Road heads left) for 7 miles to where it merges with Row River Road. Bear right and continue east on Row River Road 8.1 miles and then turn right onto Brice Creek Road (which turns into Forest Road 22). Proceed 3.4 miles on FR 22 and park in the West Brice Creek Trailhead pullout on the left side of the road.

Start pedaling upstream on the signed trail. Follow the singletrack for 5.5 miles to your turnaround point at the East Trailhead. Retrace the same route back to the trailhead. The best time to ride this route is May through October.

For more information contact Umpqua National Forest, Cottage Grove District, 78405 Cedar Park Road, Cottage Grove, OR, 97424; (541) 942–5591; www.fs.fed.us/r6/umpqua. *DeLorme: Oregon Atlas & Gazetteer:* Page 42 C3.

Bend and Central Oregon

A high desert ecosystem of sagebrush, juniper, and ponderosa pine is featured in the dry, central part of this state where volcanic activity and erosion have formed amazing gorges and unique rock formations all throughout the region. Coursing through all of this is central Oregon's mighty Deschutes River, beginning high in the Cascade Mountains and traveling north to south through the heart of Bend, central Oregon's largest city.

Many consider Bend the gateway to the Cascade High Lakes Region and Deschutes National Forest. Located just a few minutes to a few hours from Bend are scores of accessible mountain bike trails that travel through pine forests, circle high glacial lakes, and offer stunning views of the Central Cascade Mountains. One classic singletrack trail that shouldn't be missed is the Newberry Crater Rim Loop Trail—located approximately 38 miles southeast of Bend in the center of the Newberry Crater National Monument. This route circles Paulina and East Lakes, both of which are cradled in a huge caldera.

To the northeast of Bend is the Crooked River National Grassland, with hundreds of forest service roads traveling through a sagebrush-and-juniper steppe surrounded by buttes and canyons. Two great rides in this area are located at Smith Rock State Park and Gray Butte. The Smith Rock State Park route leads you through a canyon carved by the Crooked River and lined with 400-foot cliffs. The Gray Butte Loop winds its way around Gray Butte, the tallest butte in the region, then sends you careening into Sherwood Canyon. Both of these rides offer challenging terrain, magnificent scenery, and spectacular views of the Central Cascade Mountains.

Northwest of Bend is the small, western town of Sisters, hub for an excellent, linked mountain bike trail system managed by the Deschutes National Forest. There are dozens of trails in the Sisters area that take you through open, ponderosa pine forests and through picturesque alpine meadows.

28 Haystack Reservoir

Have you ever wanted to try bicycle camping? If the answer is "Yes," you'll want to try this easy route that takes you through the Crooked River National Grassland and drops you off at Haystack Reservoir Campground. After you set up camp, take a swim and soak in views of the unique central Oregon high desert.

Start: Intersection of Forest Road 5710 and Lone Pine Road, approximately 9 miles northeast of Terrebonne.
Length: 22 miles out and back.
Approximate riding time: 3 to 5 hours.
Difficulty: Moderate, due to the large amount of elevation gain.
Total climbing: 2,000 feet.
Trail surface: Doubletrack and paved road.
Land status: National grassland.
Seasons: April through October.
Nearest town: Terrebonne.
Other trail users: Hikers.

Canine compatibility: Dogs permitted.
Wheels: Fine for hybrids or bikes without dual suspensions.
Trail contacts: Crooked River National Grassland, 813 SW Highway 97, Madras, OR 97741; (541) 475-9272; www.fs.fed.us/r6/centraloregon.
Fees and permits: No fees or permits are required. However, if you camp overnight at Haystack Reservoir, the camping fee is $8.00 per night.
Maps: Maptech maps: Gray Butte; Opal City.

Finding the Trailhead

From Redmond, drive 4.5 miles north on U.S. Highway 97 to the small town of Terrebonne. At the flashing yellow light, turn east on B Avenue, which turns into Smith Rock Way in a short distance. Follow Smith Rock Way for 4.9 miles. Turn left on Lone Pine Road, follow it for 4.4 miles, and turn left on FR 5710. Park on the right side of the road. *DeLorme: Oregon Atlas & Gazetteer:* Page 51 A7.

The Ride

Established in 1962, the 111,352–acre Crooked River National Grassland is filled with rolling plateaus of sagebrush, juniper trees, basalt rimrock, rounded buttes, and steep gorges. The dry, open landscape here is a perfect habitat for a variety of raptors and other wildlife, including pronghorn antelope, mule deer, jackrabbits, and coyotes.

Long before mountain bikes rolled through these grassy hills and plains, homesteaders populated them with grazing livestock. At the turn of the century, ranching and farming were the primary industries in this part of Oregon. Many of these homesteads failed during the Great Depression in the 1930s, however, and the Resettlement Administration purchased much of the land. In 1960 this land became part of the National Forest System. Today the Crooked River National Grassland is

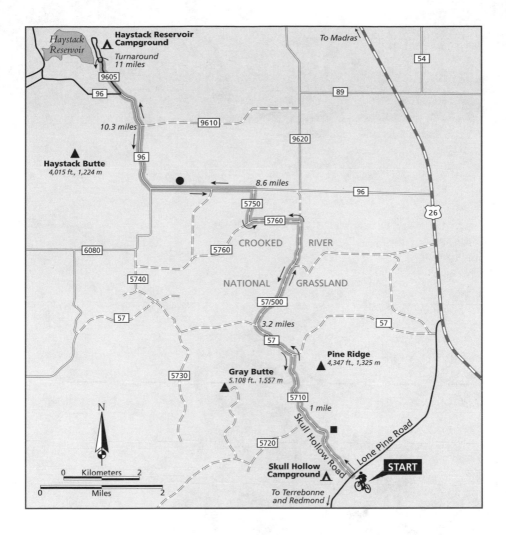

the only grassland in Oregon and Washington managed by the National Forest Service.

This easy doubletrack route starts at the intersection of Lone Pine Road and FR 5710. It winds steeply up Skull Hollow Canyon, filled with scattered junipers and sharp, protruding rock outcroppings. FR 5710 is the main arterial to a multitude of roads and trails that crisscross the plateaus and buttes in this region. As you ride up the canyon, you'll see 5,108-foot Gray Butte on your left—the tallest butte in the region. On your right will be Pine Ridge, a craggy, eroding rimrock with a greenish cast to it. You'll also notice the telltale signs of grazing cattle (cow pies and hoof-worn trails). If you happen to be biking with a canine companion, be sure to keep a close eye on him if there are cows nearby. Livestock in this area are a precious commodity, and ranchers don't appreciate dogs chasing them.

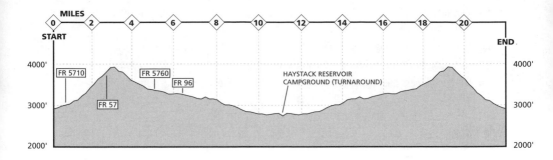

After a few miles you'll reach the top of the canyon and begin riding in an open sagebrush plateau filled with small springs, creeks, marshes, and wild bunch grass. There are several side trips that can be taken off the main route. If you want to try some singletrack riding, consider the Gray Butte Loop (Ride 29). You'll pass this trailhead 3.2 miles from your starting point on the left side of the road. After about 4 miles, you'll see spectacular views to the west of Mount Jefferson, Black Butte, and the Three Sisters. If you're lucky, you'll also catch a glimpse of the many red-tailed hawks and other birds of prey living in this area. If you look to the northwest, you'll see the 4,015-foot Haystack Butte. (This butte is thought to resemble an old-fashioned haystack, hence the name.) When you reach Haystack Reservoir Campground, you'll see a sign and fee station on your right. The overnight fee is $8.00. Pick out a campsite, unpack your gear, and go for a refreshing swim. If you decide to make this a day trip, turn around and head back the way you came.

Haystack Reservoir Trail is an excellent introduction to bicycle camping. The campground has water, rest rooms, and tent sites overlooking Haystack Reservoir. It's a great place to camp if this is your first overnight trip. If this interests you, be sure to check out the In Addition about bicycle camping for suggestions on what to bring.

Miles and Directions

0.0 Start at the intersection of FR 5710 and Lone Pine Road approximately 9 miles northeast of Terrebonne. You'll follow this doubletrack road as it winds up Skull Hollow Canyon. As you ride up the canyon, you'll see 5,108-foot Gray Butte on your left and Pine Ridge on your right.

1.0 Continue straight (right) on FR 5710. (FYI: FR 5720 heads left at this junction.)

2.5 Turn left on FR 57.

3.2 Pass the Gray Butte Trailhead on your left. **Side trip:** If you want to take a side trip, this trail offers some good singletrack riding. See Ride 29. Turn right on FR 57/500.

5.2 Turn left on FR 5760. Look to the west to see spectacular views of Mount Jefferson, Black Butte, and the Three Sisters.

◀ *Checking out the lake scene at Haystack Reservoir.*

6.3 Turn right on FR 5750 and ride until this road ends and intersects with FR 96. (Note: This road can be busy with car traffic, so use extra caution.)

8.6 Turn left on SE Springer Road (FR 96). The gravel road turns to pavement.

10.3 Turn right on FR 9605, which is the entrance to Haystack Reservoir Campground.

11.0 For day-trippers this is your turnaround point. Overnighters can camp here; the fee is $8.00.

Ride Information

Local Information

Redmond Chamber of Commerce, 446 SW Seventh Street, Redmond, OR 97756; (541) 923–5191; www.redmondcofc.com.

LEARN THE LINGO ...

Cowboy Talk

· A cow or calf that is sick: ADR or Ain't do'in right

· A cranky horse or cow: A bugger

· A horse that doesn't want to work and wants to go home: Barn sour

· Animal without a brand: Slick-ear

· Cowboy: Cowpoke, cow-waddie, buckaroo, and vaquero

· Getting a gift that was bought in town: A stay-at-home present

· Herding the cows: Round-up, branding

· Hereford–Angus cross cow: Black baldy

· Ranch: Spread, cow outfit

· Telling the dogs to round up the cows: Get'em up

· Telling the dogs they are done herding the cows for the day: That'll do

· Whiskey: Bug juice, mule, red-eye, forty-rod, chain-lightning, barbwire booze

· Worming and vaccinating the cows: Working the cows

· You'd better get up and get to work: You're burn'in daylight

29 Gray Butte Loop

Central Oregon, where cattle roam and coyotes howl, is a place of wide-open, high sagebrush desert. The singletrack Gray Butte Trail parallels the base of 5,108-foot Gray Butte located in the Crooked River National Grassland. After riding along the singletrack for about 5 miles, you'll careen down a steep jeep track into Sherwood Canyon. And then—you guessed it—there's a grueling 1,000-foot climb back to your starting point.

Start: Gray Butte Trailhead, approximately 18 miles northeast of Redmond off Forest Road 5710.
Length: 11.6-mile loop.
Approximate riding time: 2 to 4 hours.
Difficulty: Difficult, due to technical terrain and elevation gain.
Total climbing: 2,500 feet.
Trail surface: Singletrack trail and doubletrack roads.
Land status: National grassland.
Seasons: April through October.

Nearest town: Terrebonne.
Other trail users: Hikers.
Canine compatibility: Dogs permitted.
Wheels: A bike with dual suspension is recommended.
Trail contacts: Crooked River National Grassland, 813 SW Highway 97, Madras, OR 97741; (541) 475-9272; www.fs.fed.us/r6/centraloregon.
Fees and permits: No fees or permits are required.
Maps: Maptech map: Gray Butte.

Finding the Trailhead

From Redmond travel 4.5 miles north on U.S. Highway 97 to the small town of Terrebonne. At the flashing yellow light in Terrebonne, turn east on B Avenue (after a short distance it turns into Smith Rock Way). Continue 4.9 miles on Smith Rock Way to Lone Pine Road, turn left, and go 4.4 miles to FR 5710. Turn left (you'll pass Skull Hollow Campground on your left) and follow FR 5710 as it winds up Skull Hollow Canyon for 2.6 miles. Turn left on FR 57. Continue 0.6 mile to a gravel pullout on the left side of the road. *DeLorme: Oregon Atlas & Gazetteer:* Page 51 B7.

The Ride

Gray Butte rises 5,108 feet above the central Oregon high desert and is part of a series of rounded buttes that provide a unique texture to this open, juniper and sagebrush landscape. Gray Butte is part of the Crooked River National Grassland established in 1960.

Large portions of the Crooked River National Grassland are open to range cattle from April through October. Although this is public property managed by the National Forest Service, ranchers are allowed to graze their cattle here. Limiting the months they can do this, though, gives the land a chance to replenish itself by allowing early spring grass to grow before cattle can graze again. There are multitudes of

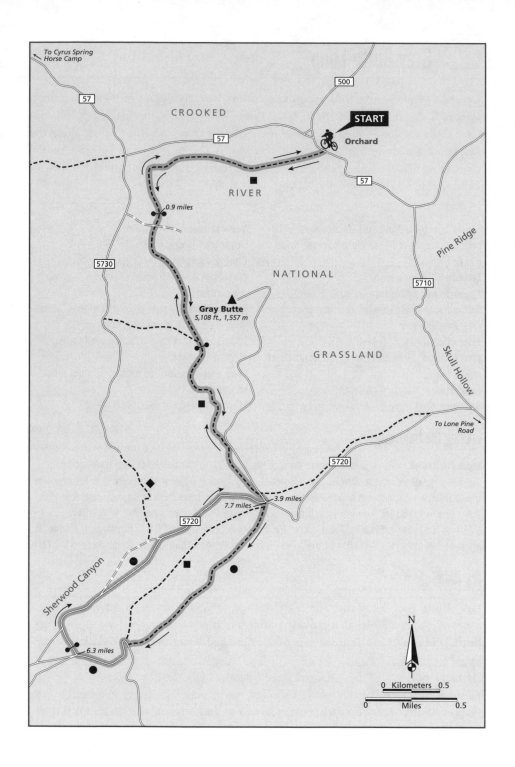

To Cyrus Spring
Horse Camp

500

57

CROOKED

57

START

Orchard

57

RIVER

Pine Ridge

0.9 miles

5730

NATIONAL

5710

Gray Butte
5,108 ft., 1,557 m

GRASSLAND

Skull Hollow

To Lone Pine
Road

5720

3.9 miles

5720

7.7 miles

Sherwood Canyon

6.3 miles

N

0   Kilometers   0.5

0   Miles   0.5

doubletrack dirt roads crisscrossing this vast grassland, used by ranchers to water and check up on their cattle. These roads are also designated as multiuse roads, open for public use.

The snowcapped Cascade Mountains are just west of Gray Butte, dividing Oregon between east and west (read about the Cascades for mountain names). Sixty miles to the east, the Ochoco (OH-chuh-ko) Mountains rise high above the desert plateau. They are the source of the Crooked River, which carves the picturesque gorge running through Smith Rock State Park, approximately 4 miles southwest of Gray Butte.

▶ **QUITE A LINEUP ...**

Oregon's Cascade Mountains from north to south

Mount Hood (11,235 feet)

Mount Jefferson (10,497 feet)

Three Fingered Jack (7,841 feet)

Mount Washington (7,749 feet)

Black Butte (6,436 feet)

North Sister (10,094 feet)

Middle Sister (10,054 feet)

South Sister (10,385 feet)

Broken Top (9,175 feet)

Mount Bachelor (9,065 feet)

The multicolored crags and spires at Smith Rock State Park are part of the Gray Butte Complex, comprising several different types of volcanic rock. Weather and time have produced a variety of formations that vary from smooth, basalt columns to knobby, multipitch walls. Rock climbers from all over the world come here to test their skills on the multifaceted cliff faces. Names of climbs like Heinous Cling, Chain Reaction, Deliverance, and Amphetamine Grip are all part of the colorful climbing culture that has evolved here. Hikers, bird-watchers, and mountain bikers also frequent Smith Rock State Park to enjoy the views of the Cascade Mountain Range and possibly spot wildlife, such as deer, otter, beaver, coyotes, and jackrabbits.

A scenic and somewhat strenuous singletrack trail that catches the highlights of the Cascades and the central Oregon desert is the 11.6-mile Gray Butte Loop Trail. This singletrack trail is located approximately 18 miles northeast of Redmond and skirts Gray Butte, crosses another ridge, then drops more than 1,000 feet into Sherwood Canyon—located to the north of Smith Rock State Park.

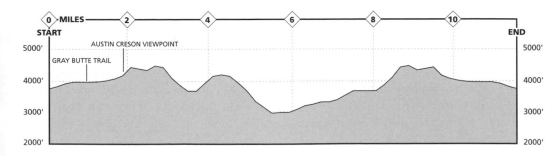

Cranking on the Gray Butte Trail.

The first 5 miles of the ride are along a singletrack trail that can be dusty, rocky, and sometimes full of cowpats. This part of the ride is fairly level with some short, twisty descents and a few short hill climbs. In addition to views of the Cascade Mountains to the west along this section of the trail, you're almost certain to see some of the local range cows that frequent the area from April to October. Most of the time these cows are fairly complacent and their calves tend to be quite curious. It's always a good idea to be cautious, however, especially if you see a large bull wandering into your path!

After 5.4 miles the singletrack trail ends and you'll begin a steep descent for the next 2 miles into Sherwood Canyon along a rocky, rutted, jeep track. You'll have a steep climb back out of the canyon until intersecting with the Gray Butte Trail. Complete the route by riding on the Gray Butte Trail back to your starting point.

This trail is only one of dozens you can explore around Gray Butte (other rides in this area to try are Smith Rock State Park and Haystack Reservoir, both covered in this book). If you want to stay overnight and spend a few days exploring this area, you can set up a base camp at the Skull Hollow Campground at the intersection of FR 5710 and Lone Pine Road. If you like dry, open, sagebrush country with awesome views of snow-covered mountains and high buttes, this ride will satisfy your cravings.

Miles and Directions

0.0 Start on the singletrack trail at the Gray Butte Trailhead located on the left side of the road off FR 57.

0.3 Turn left at the trail fork.

0.4 Cross a doubletrack road and continue straight.

0.9 Go through a green metal gate.

1.9 Arrive at the Austin Creson Viewpoint on your right. (FYI: From this high vantage point you'll have a sweeping view of the Central Cascade peaks.)

2.8 Arrive at a T-intersection. Turn left and go through a green metal gate.

3.9 Cross a doubletrack dirt road (unsigned FR 5720) and continue straight on the single-track trail to begin the loop portion of the route.

4.9 Go through a green metal gate and continue on the singletrack trail.

5.4 Arrive at a four-way intersection. Turn right and continue descending steeply down a very rutted, rocky, eroded four-wheel-drive road.

6.0 The road forks. Turn right.

6.3 Arrive at a T-intersection. Turn right and ride approximately 50 yards, then go through a metal gate. Stay to the right once you go through the gate.

7.0 An intersecting road comes in from the left. Continue riding straight on the main road.

7.7 The loop portion of the ride ends. Turn left on the Gray Butte singletrack trail. Follow it 3.9 miles back to your starting point.

11.6 Arrive back at the Gray Butte Trailhead.

Ride Information

Local Information

Redmond Chamber of Commerce, 446 SW Seventh Street, Redmond, OR 97756; (541) 923-5191; www.redmondcofc.com.

30 Smith Rock State Park

"A diamond in the rough" only begins to describe Smith Rock State Park. An intense singletrack and doubletrack route travels through the heart of this state park, which consists of magnificent multicolored cliffs carved by the Crooked River. The route descends into the canyon, where you'll possibly see rock climbers clinging to the jagged, 400-foot cliffs. After a few miles, you'll begin a thigh-burning mile climb to the top of Staender Ridge, where you will be rewarded with a panoramic view of the Three Sisters Mountains and other Cascade peaks.

Start: Smith Rock State Park main parking lot.
Length: 5.2 miles out and back (with other options).
Approximate riding time: 1.5 to 2 hours.
Difficulty: Difficult. Some sections of this trail are unridable due to steepness and eroded trail conditions. The ride up Burma Ridge is very steep and strenuous along a rocky, rutted road.
Total climbing: 1,120 feet.
Trail surface: Singletrack and doubletrack road.
Land status: State park.
Seasons: Open year-round.

Nearest town: Terrebonne.
Other trail users: Hikers.
Canine compatibility: Leashed dogs permitted.
Wheels: A bike with dual suspension is recommended.
Trail contacts: Crooked River National Grassland, 813 SW Highway 97, Madras, OR 97741; (541) 475-9272; www.fs.fed.us/r6/centraloregon.
Fees and permits: No fees or permits are required.
Maps: Maptech maps: Gray Butte; Opal City; Redmond; O'Neil.

Finding the Trailhead

From Redmond travel 4.5 miles north on U.S. Highway 97 to the small town of Terrebonne. At the flashing yellow light, turn right on B Avenue, which turns into Smith Rock Way after the first stop sign. Continue 3.3 miles northeast, following the signs to Smith Rock State Park. *DeLorme: Oregon Atlas & Gazetteer:* Page 51 B7.

The Ride

A cathedral of multicolored cliffs carved by the Crooked River forms the backdrop to the scenic, 641-acre Smith Rock State Park, located approximately 8 miles northeast of Redmond. The park's jagged, 400-foot cliffs are remnants of ash deposits left from ancient volcanoes. The Gray Butte Complex, of which these volcanoes are a part, is made up of several different volcanic rock types from the Miocene period nearly 17 to 19 million years ago. Millions of years later, a variety of surfaces and textures have formed to create rough-faced cliffs and dihedrals, attracting climbers from all over the world.

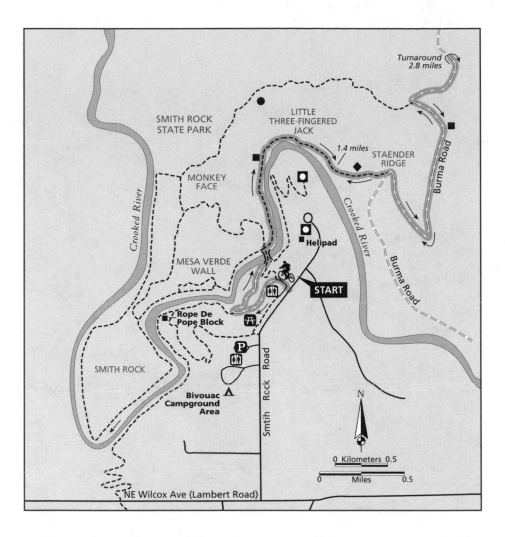

Five explorers who passed through the area in 1867 named the park after its original discoverer, John Smith. A well-known public official, Smith was the Linn County sheriff from 1855 to 1859 and served in the Oregon State Legislature in 1862. He was later appointed as an agent for the Warm Springs Indian Agency, where he served until his death in 1886.

The park rests in the heart of central Oregon on farmland filled with green pastures, beef and dairy cattle, llamas, horses, sheep, and buffalo.

Smith Rock State Park is a main attraction for climbers, but it also attracts hikers, cyclists, and wildlife watchers. With more than 7 miles of hiking and biking trails, the park is a haven for those wanting to view some magnificent scenery and wildlife. River otter, porcupine, muskrats, mule deer, cottontail rabbits, coyotes, red-tailed hawks, and Canada geese are but a few of the residents living full-time at or near the

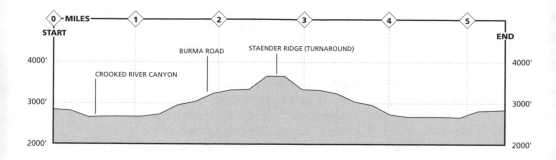

park. Golden eagles and peregrine falcons also nest in the park. During the spring nesting season, park officials close climbing routes near the nesting areas so the chicks will not be disturbed. The park also provides a day use area with rest rooms, picnic tables, drinking water, and barbecue grills, and a small bivouac area for walk-in camping.

For mountain bikers, a steep, scenic, 5.6-mile, out-and-back route descends into the canyon from the main parking lot, parallels the Crooked River, and goes up to the top of Staender Ridge. On the way into the canyon, you'll pass an overlook on your right that provides a spectacular view of the Crooked River Canyon and the rocky cliff faces that shoot skyward from the canyon floor. You'll also see evidence of a devastating fire that roared through this section of the canyon in the summer of 1996. Main areas in the park have been fenced or roped off to encourage new vegetation growth and to help prevent soil erosion. At the bottom of the canyon, you'll cross the meandering Crooked River. Sadly, this river is polluted from agricultural fertilizers and runoff. Fortunately, though, it's still able to support waterfowl, beaver, and river otters. You'll cross a footbridge, then turn right along a singletrack trail that parallels the Crooked River and takes you to the base of Staender Ridge. To get to the top, you'll have to push your bike up some very steep and rocky singletrack that winds up a gully and deposits you on Burma Road. Then you'll burn your thighs for another mile to reach the summit of Staender Ridge. The reward for this feat is a panoramic view of the magnificent Three Sisters and other Central Cascade peaks—a picturesque backdrop to the flat central Oregon farmland.

Miles and Directions

- **0.0** Start from the Smith Rock State Park main parking lot and ride down into the Crooked River Canyon on the main service road.
- **0.4** At the bottom of the canyon, cross a wooden footbridge, then turn right on a singletrack trail. **Option:** If you go left at this intersection, you can ride for 2.1 miles along the Deschutes River.

◀ *Scenic Smith Rock State Park.*

1.4 Turn left on a singletrack trail and begin a very steep climb (you may have to push your bike up some sections of this trail). Stay left at all trail junctions.

1.6 Turn left on the doubletrack Burma Road and begin a steep ascent to the top of Staender Ridge.

2.0 Ride around a green metal gate.

2.6 Arrive at the top of Staender Ridge. Take the time to catch the spectacular views of central Oregon and the Cascade Mountains to the west. This is your turnaround point. Return to the main parking lot by reversing the ride directions. **Option:** If you want a longer ride, you have the option of hooking up with the Gray Butte singletrack trail accessed from the top of the ridge.

Ride Information

Local Information
Redmond Chamber of Commerce, 446 SW Seventh Street, Redmond, OR 97756; (541) 923–5191; www.redmondcofc.com.

SMITH ROCK REGION

The jagged 400-foot cliffs of Smith Rock rise from the gray sagebrush landscape of central Oregon like castle remains. Ashen remnants of an ancient volcano, this orange-tinged complex of pinnacles, columns, and cathedral cliffs stands to the north side of a horseshoe bend of the Crooked River (which couldn't be more aptly named). Of the thousands of visitors a year who descend upon (or should we say ascend?) Smith Rock State Park's 623 acres, maybe twelve aren't there to rock climb. World renowned as a rock-climbing mecca, Smith Rock is host to climbers of every nationality and every skill level. One of the most prominent landmarks in the park is Monkey Face—a striking 400-foot column that rises like an accusatory finger above the Crooked River. But should you forget your rock-climbing gear (which might just be unforgivable), there are miles of hiking and biking trails throughout the park, along the river, and up the mountainous crags.

In Addition

Mountain Biking with Your Dog

Many people love to bring their canine companion along on mountain bike trails. Our furry friends make great trail partners because they're always good company and they never complain. If you take your dog mountain biking with you, or you're considering it, remember there are a number of important items to keep in mind before hitting the trails.

Getting in Shape

Even with four paws, keeping up with a mountain bike is hard work. And if your pet has been a foot-warmer much of his life, you'll need to help him get into reasonable shape before taking him along on those long weekend bike rides.

You can start your dog's training regimen by running or walking him around the neighborhood or, better yet, a local park. Frisbees and balls are also great tools to help get your dog physically fit for those upcoming mountain bike rides. Always remember that on a trail your dog probably runs twice as far as you ride. Build your dog's exercise regimen based on the mileage you plan to ride each time you head out. If you're going on a 5-mile trail, assume your dog needs to be in shape for a 10-mile trail. Gradually build up your dog's stamina over several weeks before committing him to arduous afternoons of trying to keep up with you on the trail.

Training

Teaching your dog simple obedience commands will improve everyone's experience on public trails. The most important lesson is to train your dog to come when called. This will ensure he doesn't stray too far from the trail and possibly get lost. It may also keep him from getting into trouble with other trail users or local wildlife. Teach your dog the "get behind" command. This comes in handy when you're on a singletrack trail and you run into other bikers. Teaching your dog to stay behind your bike and to follow your lead until the trail is clear can be a valuable and important lesson. Remember to always carry a long leash with you in case, despite all your prior training, you have to tie your dog up to a tree at a campsite or succumb to local leash laws on crowded trails. There are a number of good dog training books on the market or look to your local SPCA or kennel club for a qualified dog trainer.

Nutrition

Nutrition is important for all dogs. Never exercise a dog right after a large meal for the same reasons people shouldn't exercise right after eating. Feed your dog a high-quality diet. Higher-quality dog foods may be more expensive than some generic brands, but your dog doesn't need to eat as much of it to get the same nutrition and calories. On long rides your dog needs to refuel just like you do. Zuke's Treats for Dogs (866–ZUKE–DOG; www.zukes.com) carries a wide assortment of high-quality trail treats for your trail partner, including high-energy Power Bones, Trek 'n Treats (a lower-calorie version of Power Bones), Hip Action Snacks (each treat contains glucosamine and chondroitin, which help older dogs with joint soreness), and Jerky Natural Treats.

Paw Protection

If it's hard for you to imagine going barefoot on a rocky trail or hot pavement, imagine what your best friend must be going through. You need to consider protecting your dog's paws from gravel roads, hot asphalt, chemicals, abrasive sand, broken glass, grass stubble, mud, ice, burrs, grass seeds, and dozens of other trail hazards. One of the best ways to combat these outdoor nuisances is to invest in canine footwear. Dog boots protect your pal's paws from getting cut, bruised, and cracked from the elements. Two manufacturers that make high-quality dog boots are Muttluk (888–MUTTLUK; www.muttluks.com) and Ruff Wear (888–783–3932; www.ruffwear.com).

Trail Tips

- Try to pick your riding trails near lakes or streams. The biggest threat to your dog when biking is the heat, and water is essential to keep him cool. If the trail doesn't have water nearby, you need to bring as much liquid for him as you would drink yourself. A small, lightweight plastic bowl can be used, or you can purchase a collapsible water bowl made from waterproof nylon (call Ruff Wear at 888–783–3932; www.ruffwear.com). Also, you can use a water bottle to squirt water into your dog's mouth. An inventive sport bottle made by Cool Pooch (877–CLPOOCH; www.coolpooch.com) allows you and your best friend to drink from the same bottle. You drink water from a plastic straw and your dog drinks out of the lid, which is in the shape of a cup. To fill up the cup for your dog, just bend the straw and squeeze the water bottle.

- Try not to take your dog riding with you on a really hot day—hotter than 80 degrees. To avoid these temperatures, take your dog riding in the early morning or evening when the air is cooler and safer for your pet.

- Watch for signs of heat stroke. Dogs with heat stroke will pant excessively; lie down and refuse to get up; become lethargic and disoriented. If your dog shows any of these signs, immediately hose him down with cool water and let him rest. If you're on the trail and nowhere near a hose, find a cool stream and lay your

Dogs make great trail partners.

dog in the water to help bring his body temperature back to normal. Encourage him to drink and stay put until his symptoms begin to subside. Once he is stabilized take him to a veterinarian for assessment.

- Avoid the common footpad injuries. Don't run your dog on hot pavement or along long stretches of gravel road. Always bring a first-aid kit that includes disinfectant, cotton wrap, and stretchy foot-bandage tape so you can treat and wrap your dog's paw if it becomes injured. As mentioned above, paw protection is important to keep your dog's feet in tip-top running shape.

- Be sure to keep your dog's nails trimmed. Otherwise, they might snag an object along the trail and cause soft tissue or joint injuries.

- Don't take your dog on crowded trails and always carry a leash with you. Remember, just because you love your dog doesn't mean other people will.

31 Peterson Ridge-Eagle Rock Loops

The Peterson Ridge and Eagle Rock loops make up a fun trail system right on the edge of Sisters. It consists of the easy, 5.5-mile Eagle Rock Loop and the moderate, 16-mile Peterson Ridge Loop. The latter is a combination of single and doubletrack that winds through Douglas fir, old-growth juniper, and ponderosa pine. Great Cascade Mountain views and fun singletrack riding make this a favorite local riding hot spot.

Start: The corner of Tyee Drive and Elm Street in Sisters.
Length: 16-mile loop (with shorter options).
Approximate riding time: 2 to 4 hours.
Difficulty: Moderate, due a few trail obstacles combined with a moderate amount of elevation gain.
Total climbing: 640 feet.
Trail surface: Singletrack and doubletrack.
Land status: National forest.
Seasons: April through October.
Nearest town: Sisters.
Other trail users: Hikers.

Canine compatibility: Dogs permitted.
Wheels: A bike with front suspension is nice to have to handle occasional technical obstacles on this route.
Trail contacts: Deschutes National Forest, Sisters Ranger District, P.O. Box 249, Sisters, OR 97759; (541) 549-7700; www.fs.fed.us/r6/centraloregon.
Fees and permits: $5.00 Northwest Forest Pass. You can purchase it by calling (800) 270-7504 or online at www.naturenw.org.
Maps: Maptech maps: Sisters; Three Creek Butte.

Finding the Trailhead

From downtown Sisters go west on U.S. Highway 20. Just at the edge of the city limits, turn left (south) on Elm Street. Continue 0.5 mile, turn left on Tyee Drive, and park on the right side of the road. Immediately on the right are a red fire hydrant and a trail sign that mark the start of this ride as well as the shorter (5.5-mile) Eagle Rock Loop. *DeLorme: Oregon Atlas & Gazetteer:* Page 50 B4.

The Ride

Three snow-peaked mountains, known as the Three Sisters, dominate the central Oregon landscape and together lend their name to a small western-style town near their base called Sisters. These mountains, extinct volcanoes that are now part of the vast Cascade Mountain Range, are a well-known landmark in central Oregon. Early settlers gave these impressive peaks the equally august names of Faith, Hope, and Charity. Together they stand sentinel over this region.

During the late 1800s and early 1900s, after several wagon roads had been established for travelers following dreams of gold in eastern Oregon and Idaho, the population in the region grew dramatically. The town of Sisters became a center for the

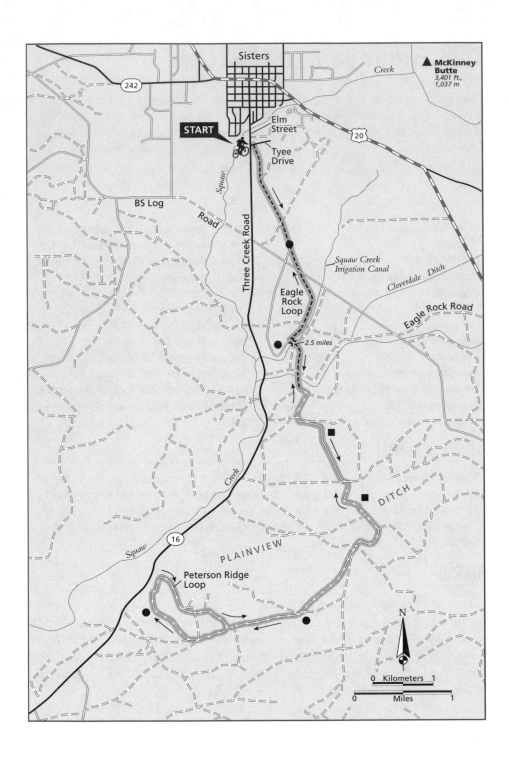

Sisters

▲ **McKinney Butte**
3,401 ft.,
1,037 m

Creek

242

20

START

Elm Street

Tyee Drive

BS Log

Road

Three Creek Road

Squaw

Squaw Creek Irrigation Canal

Cloverdale Ditch

Eagle Rock Loop

Eagle Rock Road

2.5 miles

Creek

DITCH

16

Squaw

PLAINVIEW

Peterson Ridge Loop

N

0   Kilometers   1

0   Miles   1

local ranching and farming community to shop for supplies and goods. It also served as an ideal stopover for travelers heading east or west.

In the 1960s a company called Brooks Resources Corporation envisioned more than just a commercial center in Sisters and began building the Black Butte Ranch and Resort approximately 10 miles west of town. Brooks Resources saw a real opportunity to create a hub for tourism and shopping for visitors in this small, picturesque town. To encourage this structured growth, the corporation offered a $1,500 incentive for businesses to build period-style storefronts resembling 1880s architecture. Eventually the trend took hold, and now these 1880s adornments are part of the city building code. As a result, Sisters has a distinctive, western small-town appeal, making it a great destination and popular stopover for visitors to Central Oregon.

Located right at the edge of city limits is a great two-loop trail system called "The Sisters Mountain Bike Trail." This trail presents cyclists with all types of off-road terrain and fantastic views of the Three Sisters and Cascade Mountain Range.

The Peterson Ridge and Eagle Rock Loops begin at the red fire hydrant located at the corner of Tyee Drive and Elm Street (Forest Road 16). The first couple of miles along the trail are fairly flat, with several curves and whoop-de-doo hills that serve as a good warm-up. This part of the trail also has some soft sections and rocks that you'll need to watch out for. There are trail signs every tenth of a mile to help you navigate turns and intersections.

At the 2.5-mile mark, you'll come to a major trail intersection. Turn right if you want to ride the easy Eagle Rock Loop. Continue straight to stay on the Peterson Ridge Loop. Cross a wooden bridge spanning the Squaw Creek Irrigation Canal, then immediately veer to the right and look for the trail sign marking the continuation of the Peterson Ridge Loop.

You'll climb up Peterson Ridge through old-growth junipers and Douglas firs on a combination of singletrack and doubletrack trails. The trail climbs at a fairly steady grade, with a few short grind-the-pedal sections to get your heart pumping. Upon reaching the top of the ridge, you'll be rewarded for your efforts with a sweeping view to the west of the snowcapped Cascade Mountains.

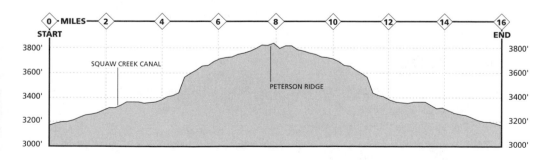

Riding through the sage on the Eagle Rock Loop.

The trail flattens out and for the next 7 miles you'll ride along the ridge, complete a short loop, and return along the same portion of trail. At the 9.7-mile mark, you'll begin a fast, exhilarating descent around trees and rocks and eventually return to the Squaw Creek Irrigation Canal. At the 13.5-mile mark, you'll intersect with the wooden bridge again. After crossing the bridge, you have the option of continuing straight (making the 2.5-mile trip back to your starting point) or, for a change of pace, turning left and pedaling on the Eagle Rock Loop back to your starting point.

This trail is a great introduction to mountain biking in the Sisters area and is a definite "must-ride" for those anxious to push pedals on some great central Oregon singletrack.

Miles and Directions

0.0 Start at the red fire hydrant at the corner of Elm Street and Tyee Drive in Sisters.

0.3 Go straight across a dirt road.

1.7 Cross the bridge and continue straight across a dirt road.

2.5 Go straight (left) and cross the wooden bridge spanning the Squaw Creek Irrigation Canal. Turn right after crossing the bridge and look for the trail sign.

2.7 Turn left at the trail fork.

4.2 Ride straight across a road. Look for the trail sign.

4.4 Turn left at the trail fork and cross a small stream.

5.3 Ride straight across a red-cinder road.

6.1 Turn right at the trail fork.

7.2 Turn right at the trail fork.

7.9 Turn right at the trail fork.

9.7 Turn left and begin to descend Peterson Ridge.

10.4 Ride straight across a red-cinder road and look for the trail sign.

11.6 Ride straight across another red-cinder road.

13.1 Turn right. Ride parallel to the Squaw Creek Irrigation Canal.

13.5 Cross the bridge and continue straight, riding 2.5 miles back to your starting point.
Option: If you turn left you can ride on the Eagle Rock Loop for 3 miles back to the trailhead.

16.0 Arrive back at your starting point.

Ride Information

Local Information
Sisters Chamber of Commerce, 164 North Elm Street, Sisters, OR 97759; (541) 549-0251; www.sisterschamber.com.

32 Suttle Tie–Suttle Lake Loop

Great singletrack and doubletrack riding weaves through a scenic forest of Douglas fir, incense cedar, ponderosa pine, and grand fir, while offering glimpses of Mount Washington. As you cruise around Suttle Lake, you should see abundant vine maple that, in the fall months, displays an amazing show of flaming oranges, burnt reds, and bright yellows, contrasting sharply with the other forest greenery. This ride shows off some great central Oregon scenery and is sure to keep you grinning.

Start: Parking area at the Suttle Tie trailhead off U.S. Highway 20.
Other starting locations: Suttle Lake parking area. If you just want to ride the portion of this route that circles Suttle Lake, you can ride on the loop trail that starts at the main parking area at Suttle Lake, located 13.5 miles northwest of Sisters off U.S. Highway 20.
Length: 13.6-mile loop.
Approximate riding time: 2 to 3 hours.
Difficulty: Easy, due to level singletrack combined with doubletrack trail riding.
Total climbing: 750 feet.
Trail surface: Singletrack and doubletrack.
Land status: National forest.
Seasons: June through October.

Nearest town: Sisters.
Other trail users: Hikers.
Canine compatibility: Leashed dogs permitted.
Wheels: A bike with front suspension is recommended to handle the occasional technical obstacles on this route.
Trail contacts: Deschutes National Forest, Sisters Ranger District, P.O. Box 249, Sisters, OR 97759; (541) 549-7700; www.fs.fed.us/r6/centraloregon.
Fees and permits: $5.00 Northwest Forest Pass. You can purchase it by calling (800) 270-7504 or online at www.naturenw.org.
Maps: Maptech maps: Suttle Lake; Three Fingered Jack.

Finding the Trailhead

From Sisters head west on U.S. Highway 20 for about 10 miles. Turn left on Geo. McAllister Road. Park in the gravel pullout immediately on your right. *DeLorme: Oregon Atlas & Gazetteer: Page 50 B4.*

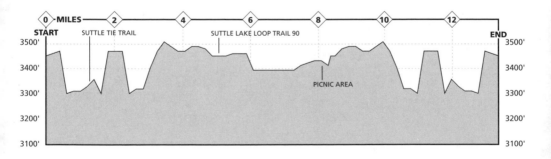

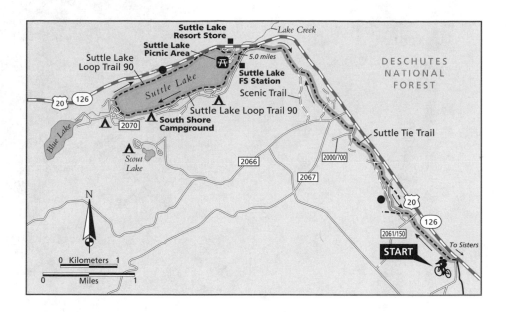

The Ride

The Deschutes National Forest manages an extensive mountain bike trail system around the Sisters area, with several routes linked together, giving mountain bikers many opportunities to ride a variety of trails in different combinations. One trail combination worth exploring is the Suttle Tie/Suttle Lake Loop Trail. The 5-mile Suttle Tie Trail is singletrack and doubletrack riding that weaves through a scenic forest of Douglas fir, incense cedar, ponderosa pine, and grand fir. It then hooks up with the Suttle Lake Loop Trail and follows the shoreline of Suttle Lake.

In the first few miles on the Suttle Tie Trail, you'll have several opportunities to view the snow-covered crest of 7,749-foot Mount Washington in the distance. Classified as a late Pleistocene shield volcano with a prominent cinder cone core, Mount Washington is part of a Central Cascade volcanic platform of overlapping basalt lava flows that runs north to south and is up to 30 miles wide. Mount Washington formed millions of years ago when lava flowed from a central vent in the earth's core and formed a gently sloping, dome-shaped cone. Over millions of years, much of this dome-shaped cone eroded away to form the sharp, angular peak that you see today.

Along this section of the ride, you'll also have a good chance to spot red-tailed hawks soaring in the skies above the trail. These heavy-bodied birds perch high in the treetops where they scan openings in the forest for small game. It's easy to identify red-tailed hawks by their distinctive reddish brown tail and cinnamon brown and white undersides. Continuing along Suttle Tie Trail, you may wonder why the trees

are spaced widely apart and there is very little undergrowth. As you near Suttle Lake, however, tree growth is more concentrated and the undergrowth is much denser. This change in vegetation is due to differences in precipitation—the Suttle Lake region receives 50 to 60 inches of rain a year, compared to the drier area around Sisters, which gets just 14 inches a year.

Just before reaching Suttle Lake, you'll ride next to Lake Creek, the outlet stream for the lake. Obsidian flakes have been found near Lake Creek dated between 4,500 and 2,000 years old. Obsidian is black or banded, hard volcanic glass formed by the rapid cooling of lava. It displays shiny, curved surfaces when fractured. It's thought that Native Americans once met here after gathering obsidian in a quarry near the Three Sisters Mountains.

A glacier that extended to Mount Washington about 25,000 years ago formed Suttle Lake; you may notice its elongated shape and steep banks typical of glacial

DESCHUTES NATIONAL FOREST FACTS

The Deschutes National Forest:

- Contains 182,740 acres of designated wilderness, distributed among five wilderness areas.
- Is twice as large as the state of Rhode Island.
- Is within 150 miles of 80 percent of Oregon's total population.
- Has been inhabited and used by people for over 9,000 years.
- Has 1,388 miles of trails, including nearly 60 miles of the Pacific Crest National Scenic Trail.
- Includes the headwaters of the Deschutes and Metolius Rivers, which support ten species of game fish.
- Has 157 lakes and reservoirs providing sport-fishing opportunities. Hosmer Lake is famous for its Atlantic salmon.
- Has the largest variety of volcanic formations in the lower forty-eight states and is known internationally for such.
- Has one of the finest examples of an obsidian flow in the world.
- Is the largest supplier of pumice in the Northwest.
- Was the training grounds for the Apollo astronaut program in the 1960s.
- Is located on the shores of the ancient Fort Rock Lake.
- Has one of the highest geothermal potentials in the United States.
- Has the largest collection of "bugs" (especially in our trees) in the Pacific Northwest.

◀ *Suttle Lake Trail.*

lakes. Originally, Suttle Lake was called Butte Lake by two early explorers named Andrew Wiley and John Gray, who sought a wagon route over the Cascades in 1859. This name didn't last long, however. In 1866 a pioneer named John Settle stumbled upon the lake while on a hunting trip. Unaware of its existing name, he pridefully called it Settles. Suttle has since become the geographic name for the lake, most likely due to a spelling error.

As you ride around the lake, it's easy to see why this lake has been a gathering place for people throughout history. The lake's gently sloping, sandy shores make great camping spots, and the abundant fish make this a favorite hole for anglers. Suttle Lake Lodge was built in 1925 to accommodate the growing number of visitors frequenting the lake in the summer. The potential for winter recreation at Suttle Lake didn't go unnoticed either, and a ski hill was built southwest of the lake back in the 1930s. In 1939 cross-country ski trails were cut in the Blue Lake/Suttle Lake area. Blue Lake, a close neighbor of Suttle Lake, is sometimes called the "Crater Lake of Central Oregon" due to its striking blue color, which comes from its depth of over 300 feet—a sharp contrast to Suttle Lake's paltry 75-foot depth. Unlike Suttle Lake's glacial history, a violent volcanic explosion about 1,500 years ago formed Blue Lake.

In several places around Suttle Lake, you'll ride through camping, picnic, and swimming areas, and you will cross several boat ramps. The numerous access points along the shoreline are a sure sign of this lake's popularity during the summertime. It's recommended that you ride the Suttle Lake Loop Trail in the fall months when the summer crowds have gone and you can enjoy the scenery.

Miles and Directions

0.0 Start from the parking area and begin riding on the doubletrack road at the trailhead sign. (FYI: Be on the lookout for bike trail signs that appear about every half mile along Suttle Tie Trail.)

0.9 Cross Forest Road 2061/150 and continue straight.

1.0 Turn right at the trail fork.

1.2 Turn right at the trail fork. Turn left at the next intersection marked by a bike trail sign.

2.3 Turn right on FR 2000/700. FR 2000/720 veers left.

2.4 Turn left at the bike trail sign.

2.7 Cross FR 2067 and continue straight on the Suttle Tie Trail.

2.9 Turn left at the trail fork and continue riding on the Suttle Tie Trail.

3.4 Cross two wooden bridges over two small creeks.

4.4 Cross a scenic trail and continue straight.

4.6 Cross a paved road and continue straight.

4.7 Turn left at the trail fork.

4.9 The Suttle Tie Trail ends. Continue straight on the Suttle Lake Loop Trail 90 that parallels Lake Creek.

5.0 Turn left and continue riding on Suttle Lake Loop Trail 90.

5.4 Cross a boat ramp and continue straight.

6.7 Cross another paved boat ramp and picnic area and continue riding straight.

6.8 Ride over a wooden footbridge, cross another boat ramp, and continue straight.

8.3 Arrive at a picnic area. Ride through the picnic area (the trail is hard to distinguish here) and look for a wooden building in front of you. The Suttle Lake Loop Trail 90 starts up again about 50 feet to the left of the building.

8.5 The trail intersects a paved road. Continue straight on the road and pass Suttle Lake Resort and store on your right.

8.6 Look for the Suttle Lake Loop Trail sign and veer left. Ride parallel to Lake Creek. The trail is hard to distinguish here.

8.7 Arrive at an old concrete foundation next to Lake Creek and a SUTTLE LAKE TRAIL 90 sign. Turn right and cross a wooden bridge over Lake Creek. Immediately after you cross the bridge, take a very sharp left turn back on the Suttle Tie Trail. This trail is easy to miss! Ride 4.9 miles back to your starting point, reversing the route for the first 4.9 miles.

13.6 Arrive back at the trailhead.

Ride Information

Local Information

Sisters Chamber of Commerce, 164 North Elm Street, Sisters, OR 97759; (541) 549-0251; www.sisterschamber.com.

33 Upper Black Butte Loop

This great intermediate trail circles the million-year-old Black Butte, a well-known landmark in the Sisters area. The route travels through a majestic ponderosa pine and Douglas fir forest on a mainly doubletrack road. Fantastic views of the Three Sisters and other Cascade peaks can be seen to the west. If you want to go exploring, this trail hooks up with other mountain bike trails around Sisters that have their own secrets worth discovering.

Start: The trailhead is located off Forest Road 1110.
Length: 14.3-mile loop.
Approximate riding time: 3 to 4 hours.
Difficulty: Moderate, due to some steep ascents on a loose trail surface.
Total climbing: 800 feet.
Trail surface: Doubletrack and singletrack.
Land status: National forest.
Seasons: May through October.
Nearest town: Sisters.
Other trail users: Hikers.
Canine compatibility: Dogs permitted.

Wheels: A bike with front suspension is nice to have to handle the occasional technical sections on this route.
Trail contacts: Deschutes National Forest, Sisters Ranger District, P.O. Box 249, Sisters, OR 97759; (541) 549-7700; www.fs.fed.us/r6/centraloregon.
Fees and permits: $5.00 Northwest Forest Pass. You can purchase one by calling (800) 270-7504 or online at www.naturenw.org.
Maps: Maptech maps: Black Butte; Little Squaw Back.

Finding the Trailhead

From Sisters travel approximately 5.5 miles west on U.S. Highway 20. Turn right on FR 11 (Green Ridge Road). Continue 3.8 miles and turn left on FR 1110. Go 1 mile and look for a dirt road on the left side of the road and the trailhead. *DeLorme: Oregon Atlas & Gazetteer:* Page 50 A4.

The Ride

Black Butte is a well-known landmark in the Sisters area, resting on the southern border of the Metolius Basin. This prominent butte is classified as a stratovolcano and

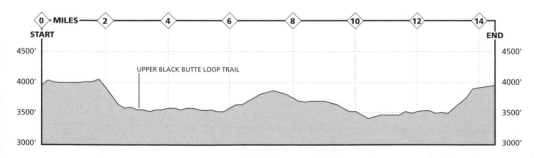

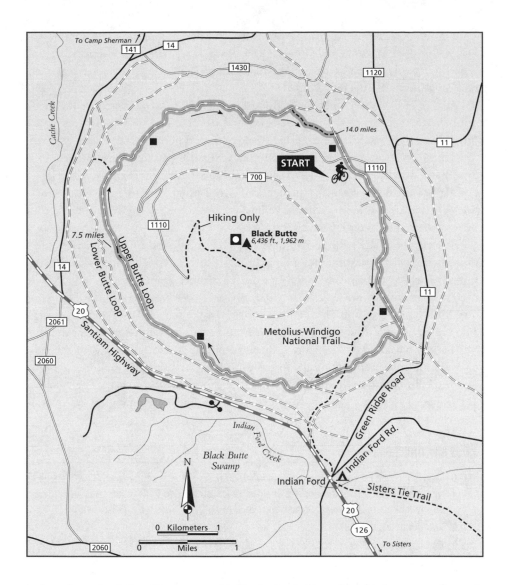

is thought to be 1.5 million years old. Geologists believe that this butte was formed by hundreds of layers of basalt lava flows that built up over hundreds of years. Near the base of Black Butte is a swampy area created by water filtering through the porous volcanic rock beneath the butte. Apparently, an old streambed on this spot was buried when Black Butte first erupted. Today much of the water filters through an underground aquifer surfacing just north of Black Butte at Metolius Springs— the origin of the pure, crystal-clear, Metolius River. The Metolius River is also known by the Warm Springs Indians as the Metolius, a word that translates to "whitefish," for the light-colored salmon that spawn here.

Those interested in exploring Black Butte and the surrounding area should start by cycling along the 14.3-mile Upper Black Butte Loop. This fun, intermediate trail is part of a two-loop trail system in the Black Butte vicinity, offering a variety of terrain on a mostly doubletrack trail.

At the start of the Upper Black Butte Loop, you'll make a short ascent along a doubletrack trail carpeted with pine cones and needles. The trail levels, then winds through a parklike setting of towering Douglas fir and ponderosa pine, the predominant tree species in this area. Ponderosa pine are usually characterized by their "yellow" bark, which is usually 3 to 4 inches thick. You'll notice that many of the larger ponderosas do not have many branches. When natural, low-intensity fires spread through this area, some branches were burned, but the trees survived because they were protected by their especially thick bark.

After about 4 miles the terrain becomes very rough and rocky. This is where a bike with shocks is a wonderful luxury. It may also help to let a little bit of the air out of your tires to help absorb some of the extra shock from the trail. When you're tired of grinding through rocks, stop and cast your eyes west toward the Three Sisters, Mount Jefferson, and Three Fingered Jack. For the remainder of the route, you'll ride mostly along a doubletrack trail with a short section of singletrack near the end.

If you have some extra energy to burn off when you're finished with the ride, take the 3.8-mile round-trip hike to the top of Black Butte. To reach the trailhead for this hike, continue driving on FR 1110 to the end of the road. The hike has 1,600 feet of elevation gain and the broad, flat summit has far-ranging views of all the major Cascade peaks.

Miles and Directions

0.0 Start 1 mile off FR 1110 on a dirt road located on the left side of the road. There's a sign with a map that shows the Upper and Lower Black Butte Loop Trails. (Note: As you ride, be on the lookout for trail signs posted every mile or so that prove to be indispensable.)

0.9 Turn left at the trail fork.

2.1 Turn left at the trail fork.

2.2 Turn right at the signed trail intersection.

4.3 There is a three-way intersection. You'll continue straight. **Option:** If you want to explore the Lower Butte Loop, you can turn left here.

7.3 Look for the trail sign that indicates that you will need to take a sharp left turn. Continue riding for 0.2 mile on a singletrack trail that winds quietly through a thick stand of Douglas fir trees.

7.5 The trail turns back into a doubletrack road.

8.4 Continue straight. **Option:** If you want to explore the Lower Butte Loop, you have the option of turning left here. You'll have a fun descent for the next few miles. Occasionally along this section, you'll have to try a few stump jumps, or just carry your bike over small logs that have fallen across the trail.

11.8 Look for the trail marker and turn sharply to the right. Continue riding on a singletrack trail.

Leading the way on the Black Butte Trail.

14.0 Turn right at the trail fork.

14.3 Intersect with FR 1110 and arrive back at your starting point.

Ride Information

Local Information

Sisters Chamber of Commerce, 164 North Elm Street, Sisters, OR 97759; (541) 549-0251; www.sisterschamber.com.

34 Shevlin Park

Only minutes from downtown Bend, this fun ride winds through a ponderosa and Douglas fir forest along the banks of picturesque Tumalo Creek in Shevlin Park.

Start: The trailhead is at the entrance to Shevlin Park, located about 4 miles west of Bend on Shevlin Park Road.
Length: 4.9-mile loop.
Approximate riding time: 1 to 1.5 hours.
Difficulty: Moderate, due to a few technical obstacles in the trail.
Total climbing: 250 feet.
Trail surface: Singletrack and doubletrack.
Land status: City park.
Seasons: Late April to October.
Nearest town: Bend.
Other trail users: Hikers and runners.

Canine compatibility: Leashed dogs permitted.
Wheels: A bike with front suspension is not essential on this route but is nice to have on a few isolated technical sections.
Trail contacts: Bend Metro Park & Recreation District, 200 NW Pacific Park Lane, Bend, OR 97701; (541) 389-7275; www.bendparks andrec.org.
Fees and permits: No permits or fees required.
Maps: Maptech map: Bend.

Finding the Trailhead

From the intersection of U.S. Highway 97 in Bend, head west onto Greenwood Avenue and follow it through downtown as it turns into NW Newport Avenue. At the junction with NW Fifth Street, zero out your odometer and continue 3.7 miles west on Newport Avenue (this turns into Shevlin Park Road after 1.9 miles) to the entrance to Shevlin Park Road. Turn left at the park entrance and park in the paved parking area by the wood trail sign. *DeLorme: Oregon Atlas & Gazetteer:* Page 51 D5.

The Ride

The city of Bend is host to thirty-seven developed parks that cover more than 1,800 acres. This route explores 603-acre Shevlin Park, which was donated by the Shevlin-Hixon Company to the city of Bend in 1920. The park is named after the company's

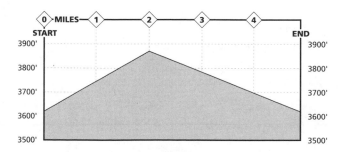

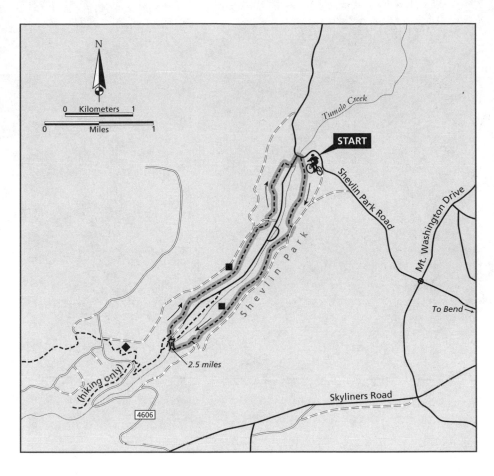

president, Thomas H. Shevlin. At one time Shevlin-Hixon operated one of the largest lumber mills in the country. Its first mill in Bend was opened in 1916 and began processing what seemed at that time to be an endless supply of trees. By 1950 the tree supply began to dwindle and Shevlin-Hixon sold out to its rival, Brooks-Scanlon.

This route is very convenient to downtown Bend and is very popular with local riders. You'll begin by riding through a stand of shimmering aspen trees and then crossing rambling Tumalo Creek. You'll then power up a short hill on some switchbacks to the top of the ridge. The route sails along the ridgeline above the creek through an old-growth ponderosa pine forest blanketed with leafy green manzanita. The stately ponderosa pine tree forms parklike stands and can be recognized by its yellowish bark and large cylindrical cones. The trees can grow to heights of more than 120 feet and live to be 400 to 500 years old. Periodically the park is subjected to prescribed burns to keep the forest healthy by eliminating dead brush and promoting new growth.

Shevlin Park is a great place to ride close to Bend.

From the ridgeline you'll enjoy a fast descent back to the creek. You'll cross a picturesque wood bridge and finish the loop on a combination of singletrack and doubletrack back to your starting point. In order to keep this route open to mountain biking, avoid riding here when the trails are soggy. Watch your speed and be on the lookout for hikers and runners.

Miles and Directions

0.0 From the paved parking area, go around a metal gate. Start riding on the singletrack trail that starts on the left side of a large, wood, trail sign. (FYI: This section of the trail is virtually flat and takes you through a thick grove of aspens.)

0.1 Turn left and follow the singletrack trail for about 100 yards until you reach a wood bridge over Tumalo Creek. Cross the bridge, turn right, and follow the singletrack trail about 25 yards upstream. The trail then curves sharply to the left and switchbacks steeply uphill.

0.2 Turn right at a T-intersection.

0.3 Turn right at the trail fork and continue cruising through a clear-cut area on a high ridge above the creek.

0.8 Turn left. (Note: Ignore the spur trail that heads downhill to the creek.)

0.9 Turn right on a doubletrack road.

1.2 Turn right on a singletrack trail.

1.5 (Note: Watch for a large boulder in the trail.)

1.9 Turn left and continue cruising on the singletrack trail along the ridge. (Note: Ignore the singletrack trail that heads downhill to the right.)

2.0 Turn right on a doubletrack road. The route takes you downhill toward the creek. Then you'll cross over a drainage pipe and head uphill.

2.1 Turn right on a doubletrack road. Go about 25 yards and arrive at a T-intersection. Turn left on a singletrack trail.

2.5 Cross a narrow wood bridge over Tumalo Creek. After crossing the bridge continue on the singletrack trail as it heads downstream.

2.7 Arrive at a somewhat confusing five-way intersection. Go left on an unsigned singletrack trail that heads slightly uphill.

4.0 Turn right on a singletrack trail.

4.1 Cross a doubletrack road and continue pedaling on the singletrack trail.

4.7 Turn left on the paved park-entrance road.

4.9 Arrive back at the trailhead.

Ride Information

Local Information

Bend Chamber Visitor & Convention Bureau, 63085 North U.S. Highway 97, Bend, OR 97701; (800) 905-2363; www.visitbend.com.

Local Events and Attractions

High Desert Museum, 59800 South U.S. Highway 97, Bend; (541) 382-4754; www.high desert.org.

Accommodations

Lara House B&B, 640 NW Congress, Bend; (541) 388-4064; www.larahouse.com.

Restaurants

Deschutes Brewery, 1044 NW Bond Street, Bend; (541) 382-9242; www.deschutes brewery.com.

35 Deschutes River Trail–First Street Rapids Park

This easy route takes you along a scenic section of the rambling Deschutes River. The trail begins at First Street Rapids Park and heads north along the river's edge. After about a mile you'll parallel a golf course as the trail winds through a mix of juniper, sage, and yellow-barked ponderosa pine trees. The last half of the trail winds high on the canyon rim and affords stunning views of Mount Washington and Black Butte to the northwest and the Deschutes River far below.

Start: The trailhead is at First Street Rapids Park in downtown Bend.
Length: 6 miles out and back.
Approximate riding time: 1 to 1.5 hours.
Difficulty: Easy, due to smooth trail surface and minimal elevation gain.
Total climbing: 120 feet.
Trail surface: Wood-chip trail and paved road.
Land status: City park.
Seasons: Year-round.
Nearest town: Bend.
Other trail users: Hikers and runners.

Canine compatibility: Leashed dogs permitted.
Wheels: A bike without front suspension will work fine due to the smooth surface and easy grade.
Trail contacts: Bend Metro Park & Recreation District, 200 NW Pacific Park Lane, Bend, OR 97701; (541) 389-7275; www.bendparksandrec.org.
Fees and permits: No fees or permits required.
Maps: Maptech maps: Bend.

Finding the Trailhead

From U.S. Highway 97 in Bend, turn right on Division Street. Go 0.8 mile and turn right on Revere Avenue. Continue 0.2 mile and turn left on Hill Avenue. Proceed 0.2 mile and turn right on Portland Avenue. Go 0.2 mile and turn right on First Street. Continue 0.3 mile to where the street dead-ends at First Street Rapids Park. *DeLorme: Oregon Atlas & Gazetteer:* Page 51 D6.

The Ride

First Street Rapids Park is one of ten parks in Bend that line the banks of the Deschutes River. The majority of the route is on a wide, wood-chip trail that parallels the river through downtown Bend. It is part of the Deschutes River Trail Action Plan that was developed with the input of many citizens and community groups. Construction of the trail began in the late 1980s. When it is completed it will link Shevlin Park (located 4 miles west of Bend) to Tumalo State Park (5 miles northwest of Bend).

First Street Rapids Park is a popular put-in spot for kayakers and most likely you'll see paddlers playing in the rapids. Watch for small groups of ducks, blue herons, and Canada geese feeding along the riverbank. At 0.8 mile you'll cross Mount Washington Drive and continue on the smooth grade of the wood-chip trail

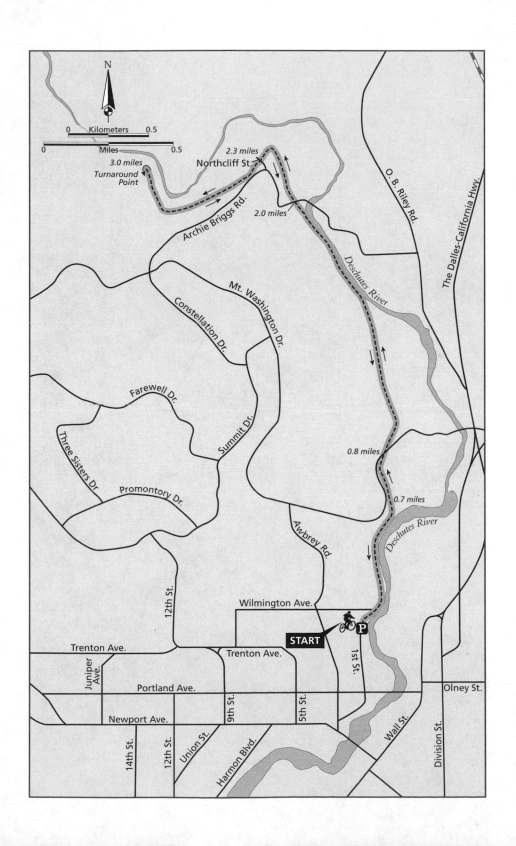

N

0 Kilometers 0.5
0 Miles 0.5

3.0 miles
Turnaround
Point

2.3 miles
Northcliff St.

Archie Briggs Rd.

2.0 miles

Mt. Washington Dr.

Constellation Dr.

Deschutes River

O. B. Riley Rd.

The Dalles-California Hwy.

Farewell Dr.

Summit Dr.

Three Sisters Dr.

Promontory Dr.

0.8 miles

0.7 miles

Deschutes River

Awbrey Rd.

12th St.

Wilmington Ave.

START

P

1st St.

Trenton Ave.

Trenton Ave.

Juniper Ave.

Portland Ave.

Olney St.

9th St.

5th St.

Newport Ave.

14th St.

12th St.

Union St.

Harmon Blvd.

Wall St.

Division St.

as it continues north. At this point the trail parallels the greens of the River's Edge Golf Course before it enters a forest corridor that passes through several residential areas. This is one of twenty-four golf courses in central Oregon. Not surprisingly, central Oregon is not only a mountain biking mecca but was also named in the April 2000 issue of *Golf Digest* as the twenty-third top-golfing destination in the world out of fifty destinations selected.

Over the next 2 miles, you'll cross two more paved roads as the path winds through an area of expensive homes high above the river. From this vantage point the snowcapped peaks of Mount Washington, Black Butte, and other Central Cascade Mountains dominate the skyline to the west. Near the trail's turnaround point is a fun downhill section followed by one last uphill crank to the trail's end.

Miles and Directions

0.0 From First Street Rapids Park, begin riding north on the wood-chip trail that parallels the scenic Deschutes River.

0.7 Turn left on the wood-chip trail (don't go right toward the golf course). The trail intersects with the paved Mount Washington Drive. Turn right and follow the wood-chip trail downhill as it parallels Mount Washington Drive. (Note: Look for the small Deschutes River Trail signs marking the trail.)

0.8 Turn left and cross Mount Washington Drive. Pick up the wood-chip trail on the other side. The trail parallels a paved path for a short distance but then turns back to wood chip only.

2.0 Cross Archie Briggs Road and continue on the wood-chip trail on the other side.

2.3 The trail crosses unmarked Northcliff Street in a residential area and then hugs the ridgeline high above the Deschutes River. (FYI: From this section of the trail, you'll have grand views of Mount Washington, Black Butte, and other Central Cascade peaks.)

3.0 Arrive at the route's turnaround point at the trail's end. Retrace the route back to your starting point.

6.0 Arrive at the trailhead at First Street Rapids Park.

Ride Information

Local Information
Bend Chamber Visitor & Convention Bureau,
63085 North U.S. Highway 97, Bend, OR 97701; (800) 905-2363; www.visitbend.com

◀ *The Deschutes River.*

36 Phil's Trail-Kent's Trail Loop

This fun loop route sails through a lodgepole and ponderosa pine forest right on the edge of Bend's city limits. This route is only one of many possibilities that you can explore on this extensive trail system, which has routes ranging from easy cruises to tough and technical singletrack.

Start: Phil's Trailhead, located approximately 3.5 miles west of Bend off Skyliners Road.
Length: 8.5-mile loop.
Approximate riding time: 1.5 to 2 hours.
Difficulty: Moderate, due to some short, steep ascents and occasional technical obstacles.
Total climbing: 500 feet.
Trail surface: Singletrack and doubletrack.
Land status: National forest.
Seasons: Late April through October.
Nearest town: Bend.
Other trail users: Hikers and runners.

Canine compatibility: Dogs permitted.
Wheels: A bike with front suspension will smooth your journey through the intermittent rocky sections.
Trail contacts: Deschutes National Forest, 1645 Highway 20 East, Bend, OR 97701; (541) 383-5300; www.fs.fed.us/r6/centraloregon.
Fees and permits: $5.00 Northwest Forest Pass. You can purchase it by calling (800) 270-7504 or online at www.naturenw.org.
Maps: Maptech map: Shevlin Park.

Finding the Trailhead

From U.S. Highway 97 in Bend, head west on Franklin Avenue (this turns into Riverside Boulevard) and travel 1.2 miles to the junction with Tumalo Avenue. Turn right on Tumalo Avenue (this turns into Galveston Avenue and then into Skyliners Road) and go 3.3 miles west. Turn left on Forest Road 220, go 0.5 mile, and turn right into the trailhead parking area. *DeLorme: Oregon Atlas & Gazetteer:* Page 51 D5.

The Ride

Located at an elevation of 3,600 feet at the foot of the Central Cascade Mountains, Bend is an outdoor lover's paradise with tons of mountain biking opportunities. Eight major peaks—Mount Bachelor; Broken Top; North, Middle, and South Sister;

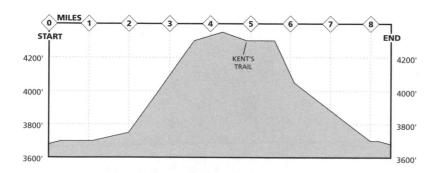

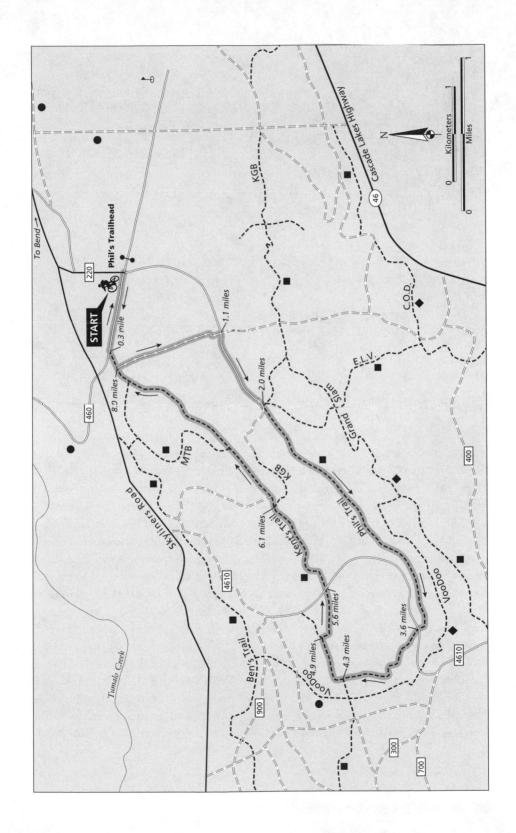

Early spring snow on Phil's Trail.

Mount Washington; Three Fingered Jack; and Mount Jefferson—between 7,749 and 10,497 feet dominate its western horizon. The Deschutes National Forest is located right out Bend's back door and has hundreds of miles of trails open to mountain bikes.

This loop route is part of the network of trails developed by the founding members of the Central Oregon Trails Alliance—a Bend-based mountain biking advocacy group that started in the late 1980s. This group, in cooperation with the USDA Forest Service and Bureau of Land Management, helps to keep trails open to mountain biking by maintaining existing trails, and helping to plan and build new ones. Trails here appeal to all levels of riders. With names like KGB, CIA, Storm King, VooDoo, Laura's Lane, and Woody's Way to choose from, you can find the perfect route to fit your mood and energy level.

This intermediate loop combines Phil's Trail with Kent's Trail. The route starts off through a thick lodgepole pine forest, follows Phil's Connect Trail for 2 miles, and then hooks up with Phil's Trail. This buff trail twists and turns uphill through open forest for 1.3 miles and then joins Kent's Trail at the 4.3-mile mark. From this junction stay on Kent's Trail for the remainder of the ride, which combines a short uphill crank with a downhill surf back to the trailhead. Try this loop for starters and then get creative and invent your own ride.

Miles and Directions

0.0 Start the ride on the singletrack trail that heads off into the woods from the parking area.

0.3 Turn left at the trail junction.

0.4 Turn left on the signed Phil's Connect Trail/H Trail. Continue cruising through a thick lodge-pole pine and ponderosa pine forest.

1.1 Turn right on a doubletrack road where a sign reads PHIL'S CONNECT/PHIL'S TRAIL/H TRAIL.

1.7 Continue straight on the signed Phil's Connect/H Trail.

2.0 Continue straight at the four-way junction on the signed Phil's Trail/H Trail.

3.6 Cross a doubletrack road and continue on the signed Phil's Trail.

4.3 Turn right on the signed Kent's Trail. Phil's Trail/H Trail heads left at this junction.

4.9 Take a sharp right on the signed Kent's Trail and crank up a steep hill. As you ascend, ignore a spur trail that heads left.

5.6 Cross a doubletrack road and continue riding on the singletrack trail.

6.1 Continue straight on the signed Kent's Trail. The KGB Trail heads right.

6.3 Continue straight on the signed Kent's Trail.

6.7 Continue straight on the signed Kent's Trail. The Sandista Trail goes left.

7.9 Turn right where a sign indicates KENT'S TRAIL—TO TRAILHEAD.

8.0 The loop portion of the route ends. Continue straight (left) where a sign indicates TRAILHEAD.

8.2 Stay right at the trail junction.

8.5 Arrive back at the trailhead.

Ride Information

Local Information

Bend Chamber Visitor & Convention Bureau,
63085 North U.S. Highway 97, Bend, OR
97701; (800) 905-2363; www.visitbend.com.

37 Deschutes River Trail

A local Oregon favorite, this trail swerves in and out of a Douglas fir forest paralleling the mesmerizing waters of the Deschutes River. A river with many faces, the Deschutes has sections that are slow and meandering and others where it crashes and tumbles through deep lava shoots and over rocky falls.

Start: The trailhead is located at the Meadow Picnic Area about 7.5 miles west of downtown Bend off the Cascade Lakes Highway.
Length: 16.6 miles out and back.
Approximate riding time: 4 to 5 hours.
Difficulty: Moderate, due to some technical sections on the trail.
Total climbing: 360 feet.
Trail surface: Singletrack and doubletrack.
Land status: National forest.
Seasons: Year-round (snow can be present during the winter months).
Nearest town: Bend.
Other trail users: Hikers.
Canine compatibility: Leashed dogs permitted.

Wheels: A bike with front suspension is nice to have to handle some of the technical sections on this trail.
Trail contacts: Deschutes National Forest, 1645 Highway 20 East, Bend, OR 97701; (541) 383-5300; www.fs.fed.us/r6/centraloregon.
Fees and permits: No permits required if you start from the Meadow Picnic Area. All other Deschutes River trailheads require a $5.00 Northwest Forest Pass. You can purchase one by calling (800) 270-7504 or online at www.naturenw.org.
Maps: Maptech maps: Benham Falls. The USFS Deschutes River Trail Map is available online at www.fs.fed.us/r6/centraloregon.

Finding the Trailhead

Head 6.2 miles west of Bend on the Cascade Lakes Highway (Oregon Highway 46) and turn left on the gravel Forest Road 100 at the MEADOW PICNIC AREA sign. Continue 1.4 miles to the parking area and trailhead. *DeLorme: Oregon Atlas & Gazetteer:* Page 45 A5.

The Ride

With a population of over 30,000, Bend is one of the fastest growing cities in Oregon. Located at the base of the Oregon Cascades, it is only 22 miles from Mount Bachelor, which offers some of the best powder skiing in Oregon. The Deschutes River also flows through the city and is a popular spot for fishing, whitewater rafting, and other outdoor adventures.

U.S. Highway 97 travels right through the heart of this outdoor-oriented city. Although this serves to bolster the local economy, many feel that it threatens the quaint appeal this town thrives on. Several miles of fast-food restaurants, shopping malls, car lots, and real estate offices line this stretch of highway. But not far past this main arterial, a city of delightful parks, cafes, coffee houses, and the Deschutes

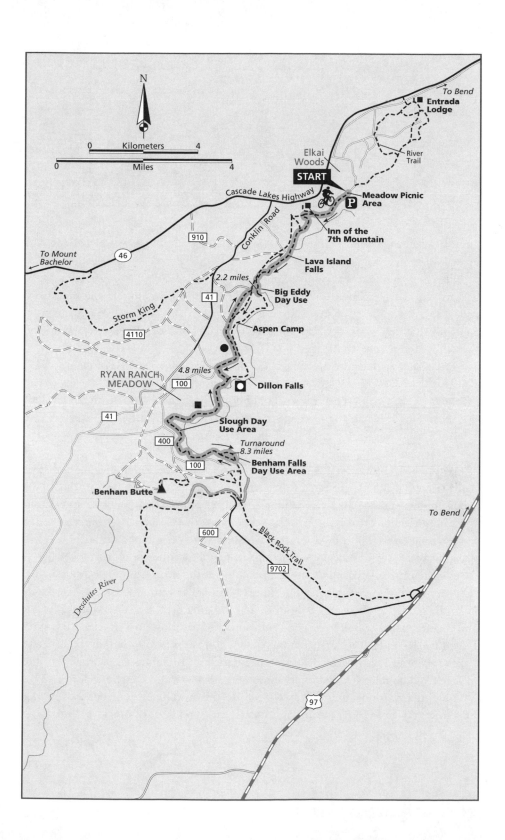

N

Kilometers
0   4
0   Miles   4

→ To Bend

■ **Entrada Lodge**

River Trail

Elkai Woods →

START

Cascade Lakes Highway

🚲

P   **Meadow Picnic Area**

Inn of the 7th Mountain

Conklin Road

910

46

To Mount Bachelor

Lava Island Falls

2.2 miles

41

Big Eddy Day Use

Storm King

4110

Aspen Camp

●

4.8 miles

RYAN RANCH MEADOW

100

■

◙   **Dillon Falls**

41

Slough Day Use Area

400

Turnaround 8.3 miles

100

Benham Falls Day Use Area

Benham Butte ▲

600

Black Rock Trail

9702

To Bend →

Deshutes River

97

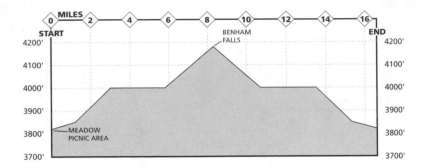

Brewery—arguably one of the best microbreweries in the state—give Bend the appeal for which it is so popular.

This burgeoning town was first known as Farewell Bend when several roads met at a fork in the Deschutes River. Originating at Little Lava Lake in the high Cascade Mountains, the river snakes its way down from the hills and travels north to south for 252 miles through a gauntlet of reservoirs and dams before reaching the Columbia River near The Dalles.

The Klamath Indians originally called the Deschutes River "Kolamkeni Koke." Kolam was a wild root used as a common source of food. "Keni" means place. "Koke" was the general term for stream. This name changed in the early 1800s during the fur trade when the river was called "Rivière des Chutes" or "Rivière aux Chutes," translating to River of the Falls. The name eventually was shortened simply to Deschutes.

Bend's early economy was built on ranching. Soon thereafter, logging and steel had their reign for many years as the region's main industries. Then, in the 1940s when the Deschutes River was dammed, ranching and farming once again became most important to the economy, as the new dams provided a reliable source of water for growing crops. This new source of irrigated water, combined with the region's warm, dry climate, was ideal for growing alfalfa, wheat, mint, and other crops.

For the off-road cycling enthusiast, Bend lies at the heart of numerous mountain bike opportunities through the Deschutes National Forest and the Cascade High Lakes Region. Trails here are easily accessible and offer cyclists a variety of challenges and breathtaking scenery. A good introduction to this area is the 16.6-mile Deschutes River Trail, located approximately 7.5 miles west of Bend off the Cascade Lakes Highway. This intermediate, out-and-back ride is composed primarily of singletrack and doubletrack and offers some great views of the Deschutes River.

As you ride along the trail, you'll see the many different personalities of the Deschutes River. In some sections it is meandering and slow. In others it rages down

The Deschutes River.

lava canyons, tumbling over steep, rocky falls. Examples of this can be seen at Dillon Falls and Benham Falls. As you ride, you'll most likely see some of the local blue herons feeding in the marshy stretches of the river. Look high enough into the tree-tops of the Douglas firs and you'll see osprey atop their lofty perches, spying for their next meal.

The only drawback to this ride may be its popularity. Weekends can be very crowded, and severe overuse and inattention to the fragile ecosystem here have heavily damaged stretches of the riverbank. Also, bring your bug spray. Mosquitoes here can be fierce.

Miles and Directions

0.0 Start riding south on a singletrack trail where a sign reads DESCHUTES RIVER TRAILS/LAVA ISLAND ROCK SHELTER 1/LAVA ISLAND FALLS 1.2/DILLON FALLS 4.5/BENHAM FALLS 8.5. Follow the trail as it heads up a short hill and then winds around lava outcrops above the river through a gorgeous ponderosa pine forest.

0.5 Turn left as the trail passes a pond on the left. Ignore side trails that head right.

1.2 Arrive at Lava Island Shelter. Go about 100 yards and keep following the main trail as it follows the riverbank.

2.0 The singletrack joins a doubletrack road. Ride on the doubletrack road and then veer left back onto the singletrack trail.

2.2 Go right at the signed trail junction.

2.4 Go straight at a four-way junction.

3.4 Pedal through a boat launch area and veer left.

3.9 Turn right at a trail junction.

4.1 Turn left at a trail junction.

4.4 Continue straight (right).

4.8 Veer left onto a doubletrack at Dillon Falls Campground.

4.9 Ride through an opening in the fence.

6.3 Turn right at the trail junction.

7.4 Continue straight (left).

7.9 Turn left at the trail junction.

8.3 Arrive at the Benham Falls parking area. Walk down a hiking path to view the falls and retrace the route back to the trailhead.

16.6 Arrive at the trailhead.

Ride Information

Local Information

Bend Chamber Visitor & Convention Bureau,
63085 North U.S. Highway 97, Bend, OR
97701; (800) 905-2363; www.visitbend.com.

38 Swampy Lakes–Swede Ridge Loop

This local ride is a great afternoon or weekend getaway in the Deschutes National Forest. The route follows a popular cross-country skiing route and twists and turns through a lodgepole pine and cedar forest to the Swampy Lakes Shelter. It continues by traversing a ridge to the Swede Ridge Shelter, where you'll have grand views of Broken Top. You'll complete the loop by a series of ups and downs and then get one last cardio rush on an intense hill climb back to the Swampy Lakes Sno-Park.

Start: The trailhead is located at the Swampy Lakes Sno-Park 16.5 miles west of Bend off the Cascade Lakes Highway (Oregon Highway 46).
Length: 8.2-mile loop.
Approximate riding time: 1.5 to 2 hours.
Difficulty: Moderate, due to technical obstacles on the trail.
Total climbing: 400 feet.
Trail surface: 6.5 miles of singletrack and 1.6 miles of doubletrack.
Land status: National forest.
Seasons: June through October.
Nearest town: Bend.

Other trail users: Hikers.
Canine compatibility: Dogs permitted.
Wheels: A bike with front suspension is handy for occasional root bundles, rock outcroppings, and a creek crossing.
Trail contacts: Deschutes National Forest, 1645 Highway 20 East, Bend, OR 97701; (541) 383-5300; www.fs.fed.us/r6/centraloregon.
Fees and permits: $5.00 Northwest Forest Pass. You can purchase it by calling (800) 270-7504 or online at www.naturenw.org.
Maps: Maptech maps: Wanoga Butte; Tumalo Falls.

Finding the Trailhead

From Bend travel 16.5 miles west on the Cascade Lakes Highway to the Swampy Lakes Sno-Park, located on the right side of the road. Turn right and go 0.2 mile to the parking area and trailhead. *DeLorme: Oregon Atlas & Gazetteer:* Page 44 A4.

The Ride

This intermediate ride follows a popular cross-country ski route in the Deschutes National Forest within a twenty-minute drive of Bend off the Cascade Lakes Highway. The trail starts at the Swampy Sno-Park and heads uphill at a gentle pace through an open, lodgepole pine and cedar forest. This trail is characteristically soft and dusty due to the soft volcanic soil prevalent in this area. Periodically, you'll have to crank hard through soft spots in the trail and dodge some roots and rocks. After 1.5 miles you'll zip downhill to a creek crossing over a wobbly wood footbridge. This small creek meanders through an open meadow dotted with wildflowers. At 2.1 miles you'll arrive at Swampy Lakes Shelter. This cozy wood shelter has a wood stove and is used as a warming hut in the winter months by cross-country skiers.

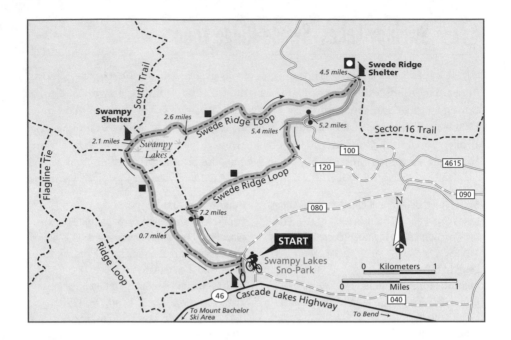

Over the next 2.4 miles, you'll pedal on many fun ups and downs as you head east. At 4 miles the trail traverses through an old burn area, the location of the Bridge Creek fire that was started by an abandoned campfire on July 24, 1979. By the time the fire was put out, it had burned 2,500 acres of national forest land and 1,800 acres of privately owned land and destroyed $6.5 million of timber. The area was replanted and the small trees are thriving in the sunny central Oregon climate. As you traverse the ridge, look west to view the jagged pinnacles of 9,175-foot Broken Top, which were carved by glacial erosion and are a reminder of this area's intense volcanic past. After 4.5 miles you'll arrive at a trail junction where you have the option of turning left and riding 50 yards down a short hill to check out the Swede Ridge Shelter. This is a good spot to take a break and fuel up for the remainder of the loop. Over the next 2.8 miles, the route ascends at a moderate pace through a thick lodgepole pine forest. At 7.3 miles you'll ride around a yellow gate and then begin a fun descent on an eroded doubletrack road for 0.7 mile until you turn onto a singletrack trail at the 8-mile mark. From here it's a quick spin back to your starting point at the Swampy Sno-Park.

Miles and Directions

0.0 Begin riding on the signed Swampy Lakes Trail No. 23, located on the right side of the rest rooms. Pedal a short distance to a trail fork. Turn right toward Swampy Lakes and Swede Ridge.

0.1 Turn left toward the Swampy Lakes Shelter and begin a gradual ascent.

0.7 Continue straight where a sign indicates SWAMPY SHELTER 1.5/RIDGE AND SWAMPY LOOPS.

0.9 Continue straight on the signed Swampy Loop toward Swampy Lakes Shelter. The Swampy Tie Trail heads left.

1.5 Continue straight and ignore the trail that heads right. Begin a fun downhill toward the Swampy Lakes Shelter.

1.9 Cross a wobbly wood bridge over a small bubbling creek lined with bright wildflowers. Go 10 yards and turn right at the trail junction toward the signed Swampy Lakes Shelter. The Flagline Trail heads left.

2.1 Arrive at Swampy Lakes Shelter. Turn right (east) at the trail fork toward the Swampy Sno-Park. (FYI: The trail that heads left will reach Tumalo Falls in 3.5 miles.) From here begin a fast descent on tight, curvy switchbacks.

2.3 Arrive at a bouldery creek crossing. Bold riders may attempt to ride across, but others may just want to walk their bikes across.

2.6 Turn left toward the signed Swede Ridge Shelter. Begin a fun roller-coaster ride on many fun ups and downs.

4.0 The route traverses a ridge with good views looking west of the Bridge Creek Burn and Broken Top.

4.5 Turn right on FR 100 toward the signed Swampy Sno-Park. (FYI: The Swede Ridge Shelter is located 50 yards from this intersection on the left.)

5.2 Ride around a yellow metal gate and turn right (west) on FR 140 where a sign indicates SWAMPY SNO-PARK 2¾.

5.4 Turn left on an unsigned singletrack trail. From here you'll begin climbing.

7.2 Turn left at the four-way intersection toward the Swampy Sno-Park.

7.3 Ride around a metal gate and continue straight on a doubletrack road. Begin a fun descent.

8.0 Turn right on the singletrack trail at the four-way intersection toward the Swampy Sno-Park.

8.1 Continue straight.

8.2 Arrive at the trailhead at Swampy Sno-Park.

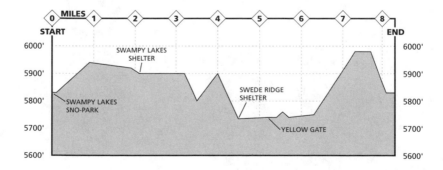

Ride Information

Local Information

Bend Chamber Visitor & Convention Bureau, 63085 North U.S. Highway 97, Bend, OR 97701; (800) 905-2363; www.visitbend.com.

Local Events and Attractions

High Desert Museum, 59800 South U.S. Highway 97, Bend; (541) 382-4754; www.highdesert.org.

Accommodations

Lava Lake Campground at Lava Lake, Deschutes National Forest, Bend; (541) 383-5300; www.fs.fed.us/r6/centraloregon.

Lara House B&B, 640 NW Congress, Bend; (541) 388-4064; www.larahouse.com.

Restaurants

Deschutes Brewery, 1044 NW Bond Street, Bend; (541) 382-9242; www.deschutesbrewery.com.

◀ *View of Broken Top from the Swede Ridge Shelter.*

39 Lava Lake Loop

Get ready to crank on this awesome central Oregon singletrack filled with many challenges that will test your technical prowess. The gorgeous mountain and lake scenery and nonstop action on this trail make it one of the best rides in the region.

Start: The Lava Lake Day Use Parking Area, located 39.5 miles southwest of Bend off the Cascade Lakes Highway (Oregon Highway 46).
Length: 24.2-mile loop.
Approximate riding time: 4 to 6 hours.
Difficulty: Strenuous, due to length of the route and advanced technical obstacles on the trail.
Total climbing: 685 feet.
Trail surface: 10.5 miles of singletrack; 0.2 miles of gravel road; 13.5 miles of pavement.
Land status: National forest.
Seasons: June through October.
Nearest town: Bend.

Other trail users: Hikers and equestrians.
Canine compatibility: Dogs permitted.
Wheels: A bike with front suspension is nice for the nonstop technical action on this trail.
Trail contacts: Deschutes National Forest, 1645 Highway 20 East, Bend, OR 97701; (541) 383–5300; www.fs.fed.us/r6/centraloregon.
Fees and permits: $5.00 Northwest Forest Pass. You can purchase it by calling (800) 270–7504 or online at www.naturenw.org.
Maps: Maptech maps: Elk Lake; Bachelor Butte; Broken Top.

Finding the Trailhead

From Bend head west on the Cascade Lakes Highway for about 39.5 miles to the Lava Lake Resort turnoff. Turn left on Lava Lake Road and travel 1 mile on a paved road to the day use parking area at Lava Lake. *DeLorme: Oregon Atlas & Gazetteer:* Page 44 A2 and Page 50 D3.

The Ride

The Cascade High Lakes Region of central Oregon has stunning scenery and some of the best singletrack riding in the state. The region is host to more than a hundred lakes that have been formed by volcanic activity and the gouging action of glaciers.

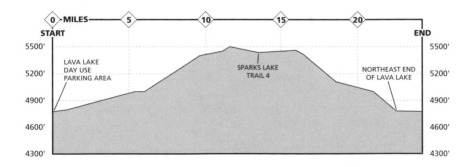

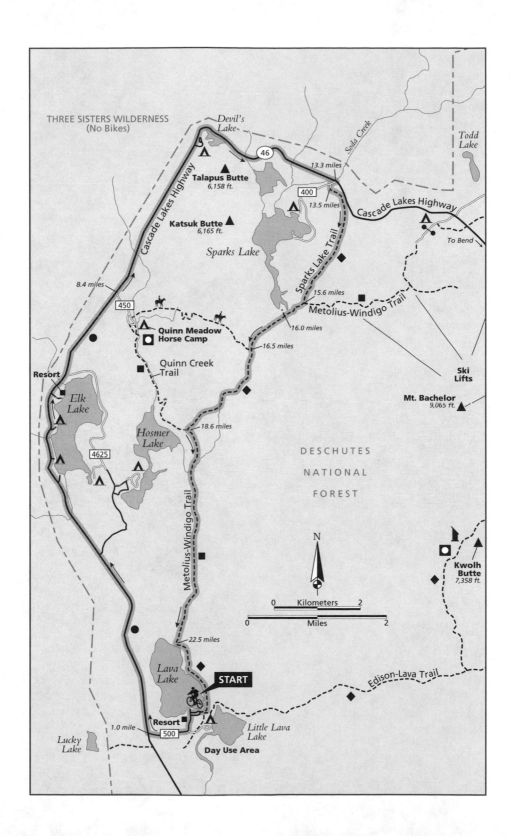

THREE SISTERS WILDERNESS
(No Bikes)

Devil's Lake

46

13.3 miles

Talapus Butte
6,158 ft.

400

13.5 miles

Cascade Lakes Highway

To Bend

Soda Creek

Todd Lake

Katsuk Butte
6,165 ft.

Sparks Lake

Cascade Lakes Highway

8.4 miles

450

15.6 miles

Sparks Lake Trail

Metolius-Windigo Trail

Ski Lifts

**Quinn Meadow
Horse Camp**

16.0 miles

16.5 miles

Mt. Bachelor
9,065 ft.

Quinn Creek
Trail

Resort

Elk Lake

18.6 miles

Hosner Lake

DESCHUTES

NATIONAL

4625

FOREST

N

**Kwolh
Butte**
7,358 ft.

Metolius-Windigo Trail

0   Kilometers   2

0   Miles   2

22.5 miles

Lava Lake

START

Edison-Lava Trail

Lucky Lake

1.0 mile

Resort

500

Little Lava Lake

Day Use Area

Located 39.5 miles southwest of Bend, 350-acre Lava Lake is one of the main attractions along this scenic stretch of the Cascade Lakes Highway. Fishing enthusiasts congregate here in the summertime to try their luck at catching rainbow and brook trout in the cool waters of the spring-fed lake. Others come here to mountain bike, hike, and camp.

This technically challenging and entertaining ride begins at the south end of Lava Lake and heads north on the Cascade Lakes Highway for 13.3 miles. Along this section of the route you'll climb more than 625 feet, but you won't notice the elevation gain because you'll be too busy admiring the high mountain scenery. To the north, 10,358-foot South Sister dominates the horizon with its red-cinder peak contrasting brightly against the blue sky. Many hike to the summit of this peak on the South Sister Trail, and if you look closely you can see a faint trail up to the top.

To the northeast 9,065-foot Mount Bachelor, home to the well-known Mount Bachelor Ski Resort, rises prominently above the forested landscape. This young volcano was formed about 14,000 years ago and is covered with thick stands of western and Engelmann spruce, ponderosa pine, Douglas fir, and sugar pine.

After 13.5 miles of paved road riding, you'll turn off the highway and begin pedaling on a brilliant singletrack for the next 10.5 miles. The trail, which tends to be dusty because of the soft volcanic soil, heads south and throws everything at you all at once. It races through jagged lava flows on a series of intense ups and downs through a maze of roots, drop-offs, lava shelves, water bars, and sand traps. At 16.5 miles you'll continue south toward Hosmer Lake; the trail mellows out a bit with some longer downhill sections of smoother terrain mixed in with just enough rocks, roots, and water bars to keep things interesting. After 18.6 miles you'll continue your journey south through a maze of gorgeous lava flows and descend a little over 300 feet until you reach the north end of Lava Lake at the 22.5-mile mark. Be sure to watch your speed on blind corners, because you're sharing the trail with equestrians, which is very obvious by the periodic horse droppings on the trail.

Once you reach the northeast end of the lake, get psyched to navigate this technically tough 1.5-mile section of the trail that winds around the east side of the lake. If you desire, this is also your chance to wash off trail dust by taking a well-earned dip into the delightfully cool lake waters. After 24.2 miles you'll arrive back at the day use area. A large campground adjacent to it is a great place to set up base camp. The lake also has a store where you can stock up on supplies and buy tokens to take a hot shower (in case you didn't opt for the cold lake version) after your ride.

◄ *The Lava Lake Loop has some of the best technical singletrack riding in the Cascade Lakes region.*

Miles and Directions

0.0 From the day use parking area, pedal on paved Lava Lake Road to the junction with the Cascade Lakes Highway.

1.0 Turn right (north) on the Cascade Lakes Highway. (Note: Be careful on this stretch due to the narrow shoulder and fast traffic.)

13.3 Turn right on FR 400 at the Sparks Lake Recreation sign. At the road fork turn left toward the Sparks Lake boat ramp and trailheads.

13.5 Turn left into the gravel trailhead parking area. From here begin pedaling south on the singletrack trail where a sign indicates SPARKS LAKE TRAIL NO. 4/METOLIUS-WINDIGO TRAIL 2/LAVA LAKE 9.

15.6 Turn right where a sign indicates QUINN MEADOW 5. (FYI: The trail that heads left continues to Todd Creek and Highway 46.)

16.0 Continue straight (left) toward Hosmer Lake.

16.5 Continue straight on the Metolius-Windigo Trail where a sign indicates LAVA LAKE 5.

18.6 Turn left where a sign indicates LAVA LAKE 3.5/LUCKY LAKE 7.5.

21.2 (FYI: Stop to admire the deep blue waters of Lava Lake to the south.)

22.5 Arrive at the northeast tip of Lava Lake. As you continue around the east side of the lake, get ready to tackle some technical singletrack.

24.0 Turn right toward the boat ramp. Ride across the gravel boat ramp parking area and continue west on a paved road.

24.1 Turn right on paved Lava Lake Road.

24.2 Turn right into the day use area.

Ride Information

Local Information

Bend Chamber Visitor & Convention Bureau, 63085 North U.S. Highway 97, Bend, OR 97701; (800) 905-2363; www.visitbend.com.

Local Events and Attractions

High Desert Museum, 59800 South U.S. Highway 97, Bend; (541) 382-4754; www.highdesert.org.

Accommodations

Lava Lake Campground at Lava Lake, Deschutes National Forest, Bend; (541) 383-5300; www.fs.fed.us/r6/centraloregon.

Lara House B&B, 640 NW Congress, Bend; (541) 388-4064; www.larahouse.com.

Restaurants

Deschutes Brewery, 1044 NW Bond Street, Bend; (541) 382-9242; www.deschutes brewery.com.

40 Cultus Lake Loop

Fabulous singletrack riding is featured next to the glimmering, high mountain Cultus Lake. You'll also glide by Deer Lake and Little Cultus Lake along the way. These pristine pools harbor lake trout, a favorite meal for the local osprey that are often seen soaring high above in the blue Oregon skies. These lakes also offer plenty of opportunities to cool off on a hot summer day.

Start: Day use area at Cultus Lake off Forest Road 4635/100.
Length: 12.4-mile loop.
Approximate riding time: 3 to 4 hours.
Difficulty: Moderate, due to moderate climbing and distance.
Total climbing: 400 feet.
Trail surface: Singletrack, doubletrack, gravel roads, and pavement.
Land status: National forest.
Seasons: July through October.
Nearest town: Bend.
Other trail users: Hikers.

Canine compatibility: Dogs permitted.
Wheels: A bike with front suspension is recommended for the occasional technical sections on this route.
Trail contacts: Deschutes National Forest, 1645 Highway 20 East, Bend, OR 97701; (541) 383-5300; www.fs.fed.us/r6/centraloregon.
Fees and permits: $5.00 Northwest Forest Pass. You can purchase one by calling (800) 270-7504 or online at www.naturenw.org.
Maps: Maptech maps: Irish Mountain; Crane Prairie Reservoir.

Finding the Trailhead

From U.S. Highway 97 in Bend, turn west on Franklin Avenue toward Mount Bachelor and the Cascade Lakes. Continue 1.2 miles until you reach a stop sign. Turn right on Tumalo Avenue (which soon turns into NW Galveston). Continue 0.5 mile and turn left on NW Fourteenth (there is a Dairy Queen on the corner). This street soon turns into Cascade Lakes Highway (Oregon Highway 46). Drive 46 miles on the Cascade Lakes Highway to FR 4635 at the Cultus Lake Resort sign. Turn right on FR 4635 and travel 2 miles to a fork. Turn right on FR 4635/100 (if you go left here, you'll go to Cultus Lake Resort). Continue 0.3 mile and park in a gravel parking lot on the left side of the road in the day use area. *DeLorme: Oregon Atlas & Gazetteer:* Page 44 B1.

The Ride

With more than 500 named and unnamed lakes, central Oregon is well known for its scenic bodies of water. The Cascade High Lakes form a great part of this watery treasure. Many of these high mountain lakes were formed when lava flows blocked off mountain streams, when water collected in inactive craters, or simply when springs welled up through the porous layers of lava and collected in oval-shaped cavities left by receded glaciers.

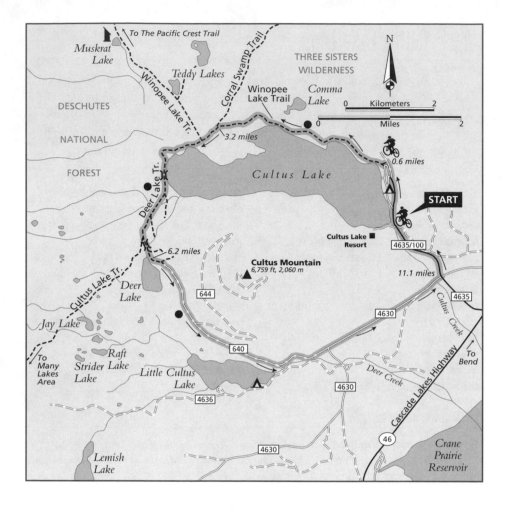

The Cascade Lakes Highway (Oregon Highway 46) travels right through the heart of the Cascade High Lakes Region. This scenic highway starts in Bend and travels 20 miles west to Mount Bachelor, then turns south for approximately 80 miles. Cultus Lake, located about 46 miles southwest of Bend, was carved by an advancing glacier nearly 25,000 years ago.

Cultus Lake covers approximately 791 square acres with an average depth of 80 feet. Its smaller neighbor, Little Cultus Lake, covers 156 square acres with an average depth of 17 feet. The outflow stream for Cultus Lake is Cultus Creek, and Deer Creek is the outflow stream for Little Cultus Lake. Both of these streams eventually flow into Crane Prairie Reservoir located to the south.

These lakes are stocked with brook, rainbow, and cutthroat trout. These fish are not only sought by anglers, but are also the main course for the osprey. Related to both the hawk and eagle, ospreys are classified in their own family called Pandion-idae. These magnificent birds weigh up to 4.5 pounds and have a 6-foot wingspan.

They have striking yellow-orange eyes and a predominantly white underside, with black markings on the top of their wings. Their heads are white with a distinctive black band across the eyes and cheeks.

Also known as the "fish hawk," the osprey's diet is made up almost entirely of fish. The osprey has the ability to reverse its outer claw, having talons facing both forward and backward so that it can more easily hold onto its catch. As you cycle along, you may notice these hard-working birds soaring tirelessly above many of the lakes. They can also see fish from as high as 90 feet. Once they spot a good catch, they'll make a fast, arrowlike dive, plunging as far as 4 feet into the water

▶ **MORE TRIVIA...**

Deschutes County Facts:

Established: 1816

Square area: 3,055 miles

Elevation at Bend: 3,623 feet

Average temperature: January 30.5 degrees; July 62.5 degrees

Annual precipitation: 12.04 inches

Snowfall: 33.88 inches

Thirty years ago, though, these tough, dynamic birds were a rare sight. Their environment was plagued by the chemical DDT, which found its way into the food chain, contaminating the fish these birds caught and ate. This harmful chemical caused the shells of the ospreys' eggs to become very thin, causing them to break. On average, ospreys have just one to two chicks each year, but because of DDT, many pairs were unable to successfully hatch their young and the osprey population went into a steep decline. DDT was eventually banned for most uses in 1972 and the osprey has been able to make a successful comeback. They are once again a common sight in the area and are wonderful to watch as they fish Oregon's high mountain lakes for their next meal.

The 12.4-mile Cultus Loop Trail gives cyclists an excellent opportunity to spot these elegant birds soaring high above Cultus Lake, Little Cultus Lake, and Deer Lake. This loop begins at the day use area at Cultus Lake. It then hooks up with the Winopee Lake singletrack trail and skirts the edge of Cultus Lake, winding through a cool, thick, pine forest. The singletrack here is fast and easy, with some great rocky outcroppings along the shore, providing fantastic views of Cultus Lake.

From the lake you'll turn on Deer Lake Trail (singletrack) that takes you around the backside of the 6,759-foot Cultus Mountain, paralleling Deer Lake. This small,

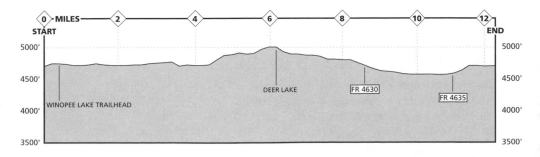

shallow, isolated lake is one of the best places to spot osprey. The many snags and shallow depth of the lake provides an excellent hunting habitat for the osprey. Look for the birds soaring above the lake and then listen for their distinctive "Kree, Kree, Kree."

Continue along Deer Lake Trail until intersecting with FR 640 at Little Cultus Lake. If it's a hot summer day, feel welcome to take a refreshing swim in Deer Lake or Little Cultus Lake. Complete the remaining 3 miles of the trail on a washboard gravel and pavement road that can be somewhat annoying, thanks to the cars that frequent this stretch.

There are so many other off-road cycling opportunities in this area that you should consider the option of sticking around for some overnight camping. Consider staying at Little Cultus Lake, where the camping fee is only $5.00 per vehicle, and it's quieter than the more popular Cultus Lake Campground.

Miles and Directions

0.0 Start at the parking lot at the day use area at Cultus Lake. From the gravel parking area, turn left on FR 4635/100.

0.4 Turn right at the road fork.

0.6 Turn left on the singletrack Winopee Lake Trail.

3.2 Arrive at the junction with the Corral Swamp Trail (it heads to the right). Continue straight.

3.4 Turn left toward Deer Lake. (FYI: A sign indicates that if you turn right you'll head toward the Pacific Crest Trail. This is the Winopee Trail.)

4.0 Cross a wooden bridge and arrive at a trail fork. Turn right.

4.8 Turn right toward Deer Lake.

5.9 Reach the junction with the Cultus Lake Trail. Turn left and continue on the Deer Lake Trail. (FYI: If you turn right, a sign indicates that you'll head toward the Many Lakes Area and Taylor Burn Road.)

6.2 Turn right. You are now at Deer Lake. (FYI: If it's a hot day, this is a good place to go swimming. Also, be on the lookout for osprey. They are frequently seen here soaring above the lake trying to catch their next meal.)

6.5 Turn right at the trail fork.

8.3 Turn right on FR 640.

8.6 Turn left and continue riding on FR 4630.

11.1 Turn left on paved FR 4635 and continue riding toward Cultus Lake.

12.1 Turn right on FR 4635/100. (FYI: If you go left you'll go toward Cultus Lake Resort.)

12.4 Arrive back at the trailhead.

Ride Information

Local Information

Bend Chamber Visitor & Convention Bureau,
63085 North U.S. Highway 97, Bend, OR
97701; (800) 905-2363; www.visitbend.com.

41 Charlton Lake Trail

This route takes you on a grand tour through the Cascade High Lakes Region. The route begins just past Little Cultus Lake and climbs steeply up technical singletrack through an alpine forest before reaching the picturesque Charlton Lake. On the way back, the trail will send you on a wind-whipping descent packed full of logs, roots, stream crossings, and stump jumps, guaranteed to send you smiling all the way to the trailhead.

Start: From a dirt pullout off Forest Road 4636, 3.4 miles past Little Cultus Lake.
Length: 15.2 miles out and back.
Approximate riding time: 4 to 5 hours.
Difficulty: Difficult, due to technical terrain and steep ascents.
Total climbing: 1,000 feet.
Trail surface: Singletrack and doubletrack.
Land status: National forest.
Seasons: July through October.
Nearest town: Bend.
Other trail users: Hikers.

Canine compatibility: Dogs permitted.
Wheels: A bike with front suspension is recommended for the technical sections on this route.
Trail contacts: Deschutes National Forest, 1645 Highway 20 East, Bend, OR 97701; (541) 383-5300; www.fs.fed.us/r6/centraloregon.
Fees and permits: No permits or fees required.
Maps: Maptech map: The Twins; Irish Mountain.

Finding the Trailhead

From U.S. Highway 97 in Bend, turn west on Franklin Avenue toward Mount Bachelor and the Cascade Lakes. Continue 1.2 miles until you reach a stop sign. Turn right on Tumalo Avenue (which soon turns into NW Galveston). Continue 0.5 mile and turn left on NW Fourteenth (there is a Dairy Queen on the corner). The street soon turns into Cascade Lakes Highway (Oregon Highway 46). Drive 46 miles on the Cascade Lakes Highway to FR 4635 at the Cultus Lake Resort sign. Turn right and proceed 0.8 mile. At the road junction, turn left on FR 4630 toward Little Cultus Lake/Taylor Lakes. When you reach the next junction, stay to the right (the road turns into FR 4636). Once you reach Little Cultus Lake, continue another 3.4 miles on FR 4636 to a dirt pullout on the right side of the road. *DeLorme: Oregon Atlas & Gazetteer:* Page 44 B1.

The Ride

The 15.2-mile, advanced Charlton Lake Trail, located approximately 50 miles southwest of Bend, takes you on a grand tour through the Cascade High Lakes Region. You can access this ride by treating yourself to a drive on the scenic Cascade Lakes Highway, which starts in Bend and winds through the Central Cascade Mountains. Sagebrush and bitterbrush intermingle in a predominantly Douglas fir and ponderosa pine forest, creating a lush and distracting roadside landscape as you make your way west on the picturesque highway. About 7 miles outside of Bend, you'll skim through the

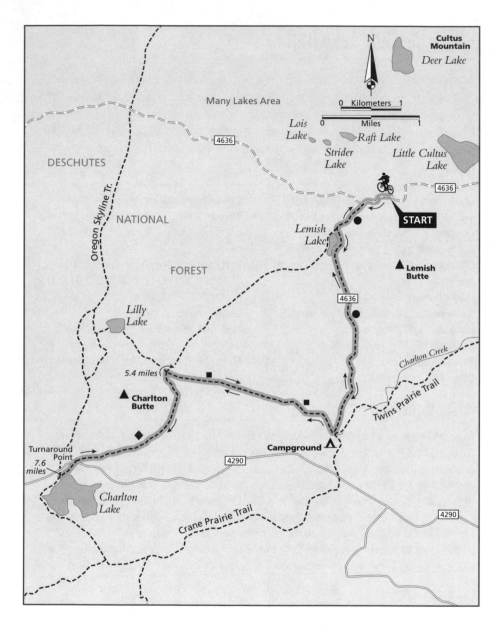

Deschutes National Recreation Area, where you'll discover several hiking, mountain biking, and equestrian trails that parallel the Deschutes River.

Eventually, the Cascade Lakes Highway becomes a National Forest Scenic Byway with a noticeably steeper pitch. After about 20 miles, 9,065-foot Mount Bachelor dominates the scene. This 14,000-year-old volcanic peak is home to the Mount Bachelor Ski Resort, one of Oregon's premier ski areas. Beyond Mount Bachelor, encounter more than your fair share of spectacular views in Dutchman Flat, a pumice-filled valley that offers grand tableaus of Broken Top, Three Fingered Jack, and South Sister in the distance. Driving through this area, you also pass Todd and Sparks Lakes.

After a few more miles, the road turns south, and you glimpse Devils Lake before entering the Elk Lake Recreation Area. Sailors and sailboarders enjoy Elk Lake's 390 acres, while fishermen troll for the brook, brown, and rainbow trout that thrive in this high alpine lake. Your course also skirts Lava Lake, the headwaters for the Deschutes River, on the east side of the highway.

No matter how plush your car upholstery, this 46-mile tour of idyllic mountain scenery will leave you anxious to get outside to enjoy the landscape. To reach your ride's starting point, turn right at the Cultus Lake Resort turnoff, and, in about 5 more miles, you'll arrive at the trailhead, located not far past Little Cultus Lake. You begin this course on a doubletrack forest road, but before you know it, you're on a fun singletrack trail that goes by Lemish Lake and then on a steep ascent toward Charlton Lake. The trail is rocky and narrow as it winds through a high alpine forest. After almost 7 miles of climbing, you enjoy a short, steep descent to Charlton Lake. This is your turnaround point, but before heading back, reward yourself for all that hard climbing with a refreshing swim in the small alpine lake.

Keep in mind that several different trails in this area are open to mountain biking. You can create shorter or longer routes depending on how much time you have. If you plan on camping, the Little Cultus Lake Campground is highly recommended. The camping fee is only $5.00 per night, and it's less crowded than the more popular Cultus Lake Campground.

Another highlight worth investigating is Osprey Point, located south of the Cultus Lake Resort turnoff (on Oregon Highway 46) on the west bank of the 3,850-acre Crane Prairie Reservoir. At the point, a shoreline trail offers prime osprey viewing. Half of Oregon's migrating osprey population nests here and can be seen April through October. You may also encounter other avian wildlife, including Canada geese, great blue herons, bald eagles, and sandhill cranes.

Miles and Directions

0.0 From the dirt pullout turn right and begin riding down FR 4636.

0.2 Turn left toward Lemish Lake.

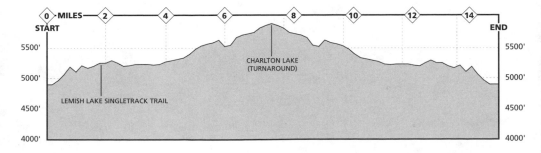

Charlton Lake.

1.9 Turn left and ride on the Lemish Lake singletrack trail.

2.5 Turn right toward Charlton Lake.

5.4 Reach a four-way intersection. Turn left and continue riding toward Charlton Lake.

7.3 Cross FR 4290 and continue riding straight.

7.6 Reach Charlton Lake, which is your turnaround point. This lake is a great place to take a swim. Return the same way back to the starting point.

15.2 Arrive at your starting point.

Ride Information

Local Information
Bend Chamber Visitor & Convention Bureau, 63085 North U.S. Highway 97, Bend, OR 97701; (800) 905-2363; www.visitbend.com.

Local Events and Attractions
High Desert Museum, 59800 South U.S. Highway 97, Bend; (541) 382-4754; www.highdesert.org.

Accommodations
Lara House B&B, 640 NW Congress, Bend; (541) 388-4064; www.larahouse.com.

Restaurants
Deschutes Brewery, 1044 NW Bond Street, Bend; (541) 382-9242; www. deschutesbrewery.com.

◀ *On the Charlton Lake Trail.*

42 Fall River Trail

This beautiful river trail follows the course of the crystal-clear, spring-fed Fall River. This uncrowded route takes you through immense groves of ponderosa pine trees and has many scenic viewpoints of the river, where you may see Canada geese, ospreys, and mallards.

Start: The trailhead is 0.7 mile west of Fall River Campground.
Length: 6.4 miles out and back.
Approximate riding time: 1 to 1.5 hours.
Difficulty: Easy.
Total climbing: 100 feet. Elevation profiles are not provided for rides with little or no elevation gain.
Trail surface: Singletrack trail and doubletrack road.
Land status: National forest.
Seasons: April through November.

Nearest town: Bend.
Other trail users: Hikers.
Canine compatibility: Dogs permitted.
Wheels: A hybrid bike will do fine on this easy, nontechnical trail.
Trail contacts: Deschutes National Forest, 1645 Highway 20 East, Bend, OR 97701; (541) 383-5300; www.fs.fed.us/r6/centraloregon.
Fees and permits: No fees or permits are required.
Maps: Maptech map: Pistol Butte.

Finding the Trailhead

From the intersection of Greenwood Avenue and U.S. Highway 97 in Bend, travel 16.7 miles south on U.S. Highway 97. Turn right (west) on Vandevert Road at the VANDEVERT ROAD/FALL RIVER sign. Continue for 1 mile to the junction with South Century Drive. Turn left and go 1 mile to the junction with Cascade Lakes Highway (Oregon Highway 46). Go right and continue 10.4 miles (you'll pass Fall River Campground on the left after 9.7 miles) to an unsigned, gravel, circular parking area on the left side of the road. A green forest service building is located adjacent to the parking area. *DeLorme: Oregon Atlas & Gazetteer:* Page 44 B4.

The Ride

Located in the Deschutes National Forest southwest of Bend, Fall River is a beautiful spring-fed river that is stocked with brown, brook, and rainbow trout. The source of the river is about 2 miles northwest of Pringle Falls on the Deschutes River. From there Fall River meanders northeast for 8 miles until it joins the Deschutes River about 6 miles below Pringle Falls.

This route parallels the course of the river for 3.2 miles. With a combination of singletrack and doubletrack riding with few obstacles, the tour takes you through a forest corridor of stately ponderosa pine trees. These yellow-barked giants are prized for their clear, even grain, which is used for door and window frames. This hardy tree is fire resistant and survives drought better than any other Northwest tree; its

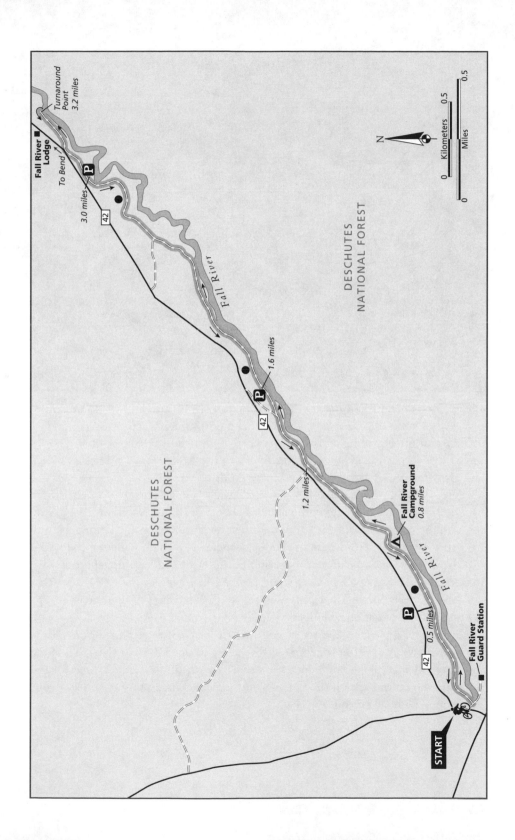

Canada geese feeding in Fall River.

root system is deep and extensively branched, and it can survive on only 8 to 12 inches of rain per year. These amazing trees can live to be 400 to 500 years of age and grow to be over 120 feet tall and 5 feet in diameter.

After 0.7 mile you'll arrive at quiet Fall River Campground. This forest service campground has ten tent sites with picnic tables, fire grills, and rest rooms. You'll ride through the campground for 0.1 mile and then begin riding on the singletrack trail next to Campsite 8. From here the forest deepens with thick stands of lodgepole pine trees. These trees are also drought and fire resistant and have the ability to live in poor soils. They grow very slowly, and it may take a century for a tree to reach a height of 60 feet. Native Americans used the long, thin trunks of these trees as supporting poles for their tepee lodges.

As the trail approaches the river's edge, watch for Canada geese and ducks feeding in the river. Also be on the lookout for osprey perched in dead tree snags along the edge. After 1.2 miles you'll ride on a short stretch of doubletrack road for 0.4 mile and then turn back on the fast and fun singletrack trail until its end and your turnaround point at 3.2 miles.

Miles and Directions

0.0 Look to your left and begin riding on the doubletrack road that begins adjacent to a wood pole fence. Go 75 yards and then veer left on a smaller doubletrack road. This road soon turns into a wide singletrack trail that takes you through a corridor of large ponderosa pine trees.

0.5 Arrive at a sign (facing the other way) that reads END OF TRAIL/PARKING ON ROAD 42. Ignore the sign and continue heading east as the trail parallels Fall River.

0.6 Veer to the right at the brown hiker sign. (FYI: Just past this junction you'll pass a picturesque wood bridge that spans Fall Creek.)

0.7 Arrive at Fall River Campground Day Use Area. (FYI: Rest rooms are available on your left.) Turn onto the gravel campground loop road and continue through the campground.

0.8 Veer right on the unsigned singletrack Fall River Trail that begins just to the left of Campsite 8 and takes you through a thick lodgepole pine forest right near the river's edge.

1.2 The trail intersects a red-cinder road. Turn right on the cinder road.

1.5 Turn right on the unsigned doubletrack road.

1.6 Turn right on an unsigned singletrack trail just before the doubletrack road meets a red-cinder road.

3.0 Continue straight across a parking area and continue riding on the signed Fall River Trail.

3.2 Arrive at a rock dam across the river and arrive at an END OF TRAIL sign. This is your turnaround point. Retrace the route back to your starting point.

6.4 Arrive back at the trailhead.

Ride Information

Local Information
Bend Chamber Visitor & Convention Bureau, 63085 North U.S. Highway 97, Bend, OR 97701; (800) 905-2363; www.visitbend.com.

Local Events and Attractions
High Desert Museum, 59800 South U.S. Highway 97, Bend; (541) 382-4754; www.highdesert.org.

Accommodations
Lara House B&B, 640 NW Congress, Bend; (541) 388-4064; www.larahouse.com.

Fall River Campground, Deschutes National Forest; (541) 383-5300; www.fs.fed.us/r6/centraloregon.

Restaurants
Deschutes Brewery, 1044 NW Bond Street, Bend; (541) 382-9242; www.deschutesbrewery.com.

43 Peter Skene Ogden Trail

The Peter Skene Odgen Trail consists of singletrack, doubletrack, and paved roads. The 9-mile singletrack portion of the ride is uphill only and parallels the picturesque Paulina Creek, which is full of swirling pools and tumbling falls. The trail takes you to Paulina Lake, which is a good place to take a refreshing plunge. You'll have an exhilarating descent on paved Paulina Lake Road back to your starting point.

Start: The trailhead is located about 27 miles southeast of Bend off Paulina Lake Road (Forest Road 21) at the Ogden Group Camp.
Length: 19.2-mile loop.
Approximate riding time: 3 to 5 hours.
Difficulty: Difficult, due to a steep ascent and a variety of obstacles, including roots, rocks, pummy (sandy, soft) topsoil, and tree fall.
Total climbing: 2,050 feet.
Trail surface: Paved road, gravel road, doubletrack, singletrack.
Land status: National monument.
Seasons: Mid-July through October.
Nearest towns: La Pine and Bend.
Other trail users: Hikers and equestrians.

Canine compatibility: Leashed dogs permitted.
Wheels: A bike with front suspension is recommended to handle the numerous technical obstacles on this trail.
Trail contacts: Deschutes National Forest, 1645 Highway 20 East, Bend, OR 97701; (541) 383–5300; www.fs.fed.us/r6/centraloregon.
Fees and permits: $5.00 Northwest Forest Pass. You can purchase it by calling (800) 270–7504 or online at www.naturenw.org.
Maps: Maptech map: Paulina Creek; Finley Butte.

Finding the Trailhead

From the intersection of Franklin Avenue and Highway 97 in Bend, head south on Highway 97 for 24 miles to the Newberry Caldera/Paulina–East Lake sign. Turn left on FR 21 (Paulina Lake Road). Continue 2.8 miles on Paulina Lake Road to the Ogden Group Camp. Turn left on a gravel road and continue 0.2 mile and park in the gravel parking lot at the trailhead sign.
From La Pine (to the south), head north approximately 6 miles to FR 21 (Paulina Lake Road) and turn right. Follow the directions above. *DeLorme: Oregon Atlas & Gazetteer:* Page 45 C5.

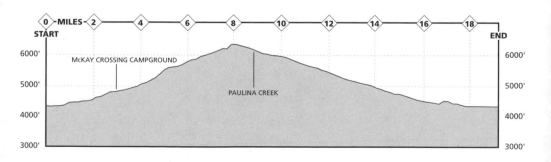

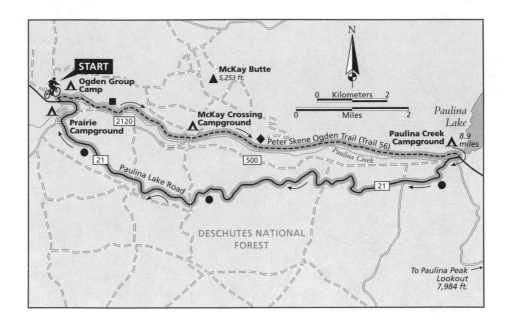

The Ride

A virtual jack-of-all-trades—trapper, trader, explorer, diplomat—Peter Skene Ogden was famous throughout central and eastern Oregon. During his lifetime, this colorful character led dozens of trapping parties across the West for the Hudson's Bay Company. On one of these expeditions, he led what is thought to be the first recorded journey through central and eastern Oregon. Ogden kept a detailed log of his business dealings, giving us a glimpse into his thoughts, as well as some of the perils he faced along the way.

One such expedition began in September of 1826, with its main objective to explore the Sylvailles River (now known as Sylvies River) in Klamath County. It was a river reported to be rich with beaver. Ogden's expedition started in the first part of October at The Dalles in the Columbia Gorge and followed the Deschutes River until reaching the Crooked River.

Over the next few weeks, the expedition followed a route that took the trappers to the head of the John Day and Crooked Rivers. At last they reached the Sylvailles River and had great success capturing many beaver in the days that followed their arrival. By mid-October they had trapped 134 beaver and one otter. From here, Ogden's party headed to the Harney Lakes Basin in eastern Oregon. During this part of the expedition, however, cold temperatures, snowfall, and lack of food began to take their toll on the trappers. Ogden noted in his journal: "It is incredible the number of Indians in this quarter. We cannot go 10 yards without finding them. Huts generally of grass of a size to hold six or eight persons. No nation so numerous as

these in all North America. I include both Upper and Lower Snakes, the latter wild as deer . . . An old woman camped with us the other night; and her information I have found most correct. From the severe weather last year, her people were reduced from want of food to subsist on the bodies of relations and children. She herself had not killed any but had fed on two of her own children who died thro' weakness . . . what an example to us at present reduced to one meal a day, how loudly and grievously we complain; when I consider the Snake sufferings compared to our own. Many a day they pass without food and without murmur."

As Odgen and his party traveled through the Harney Lakes Basin, his journal reflects an ongoing feeling of desperation after being unsuccessful at obtaining food: "This adds to the general gloom prevailing in camp with all in a starving condition, so that plots are forming among the Freemen to separate. Should we not find animals our horses will fall to the kettle. I am at a loss how to act." As they continued to travel, their situation became worse with the weather: "Bad as our prospects were yesterday they are worse today. It snowed all night and day. If this snow does not disappear our express men will never reach us . . . I intend to take the nearest route I can discover to the Clammitte [Klamath] Country. My provisions are fast decreasing. The hunters are discouraged."

By the first part of November, they were traveling southwest, back through the central Oregon desert. They were so desperate for water, they had to melt snow in animal skins in an attempt to get their horses to drink. Finally, by mid-November, the party reached Paulina and East Lakes in what is today Newberry Crater National Monument. Ogden writes: "These lakes are a godsend. It was a consolation to see our poor horses quench their thirst. Pines and hemlocks are the only trees. Numbers of bear tracks seen. This is the season bears seek winter lodgings and are fat. Our hunters came in without success."

Today the Peter Skene Ogden Trail (named in tribute to Ogden's travels throughout this area) parallels the bubbling waters of Paulina Creek, which flows from the lake of the same name. Paulina Lake, located in the Newberry Crater National Monument is 250 feet deep and covers 1,531 acres. The 19.2-mile trail consists of singletrack, doubletrack, and paved road. The 9-mile singletrack portion

▶ **OREGON TRIVIA . . .**

Symbols of Oregon
State animal: American beaver
State bird: Western meadowlark
State dance: Square dance
State fish: Chinook salmon
State flower: Oregon grape
State gemstone: Oregon sunstone
State insect: Oregon swallowtail
State rock: Thunderegg
State tree: Douglas fir

◀ *An early spring hike-a-bike expedition on the Peter Skene Odgen Trail.*

of the route travels in an uphill direction only, paralleling the picturesque Paulina Creek, full of swirling pools and tumbling falls. At one time this trail was open to cyclists traveling downhill as well, but later it was limited to uphill use after a few too many cyclists went faster than they could handle and began endangering hikers and equestrians coming in the other direction.

The trail begins at Ogden Group Camp. As you make the steep ascent toward Paulina Lake, you'll experience an assortment of twists, turns, and short ups and downs. After a few miles the gorge along the creek becomes steeper and you'll climb a series of switchbacks that are sure to test your stamina. There are several points along the trail that offer great views of some of the creek's spectacular falls. When you reach Paulina Lake, be sure to check out the view of Paulina Peak. You can also take advantage of Paulina Lake Resort to get a cold drink. If it's a hot summer day, take a refreshing plunge into the lake.

You'll have a fun, fast, 10-mile descent on Paulina Lake Road (FR 21), which takes you back to your starting point. Should you be interested in staying overnight, there are many places to camp along Paulina Lake and Paulina Creek. While you're in the area, you should also try out the Newberry Crater Rim Loop (see the next ride), which will take you on a steep, scenic ride around Paulina and East Lakes. After a hot and dusty uphill climb along the Peter Skene Ogden Trail or a grueling ride on the Newberry Crater Rim Loop, you too will think, like Ogden, that these lakes and their refreshingly cool water are a godsend.

Miles and Directions

0.0 Start from the parking lot and look for the trailhead sign, indicating Paulina Lake is 8.5 miles away. Cross a wooden bridge.

0.3 Turn right and ride up a short, steep hill.

0.8 Turn right on a doubletrack dirt road. Ride approximately 20 feet. At the three-way intersection, turn left.

1.0 Cross a wooden bridge.

2.6 (FYI: There is a good viewpoint of a waterfall.)

2.9 Cross a gravel road and continue straight. You'll ride through McKay Crossing Campground.

5.6 Turn left at the trail fork.

6.4 Turn right at the trail fork.

8.9 Turn right on a paved road and cross a concrete bridge over the start of Paulina Creek.

9.0 Turn right on FR 21 and cruise for 10 miles on a fun, paved downhill to Ogden Group Camp.

19.0 Turn right on a gravel road (at Ogden Group Camp) and ride 0.2 mile back to the gravel parking lot and your vehicle.

19.2 Arrive back at the trailhead.

Ride Information

Local Information

Bend Chamber Visitor & Convention Bureau, 63085 North U.S. Highway 97, Bend, OR 97701; (800) 905-2363; www.visitbend.com.

Local Events and Attractions

High Desert Museum, 59800 South U.S. Highway 97, Bend; (541) 382-4754; www.highdesert.org.

Accommodations

Lara House B&B, 640 NW Congress, Bend; (541) 388-4064; www.larahouse.com.

Restaurants

Deschutes Brewery, 1044 NW Bond Street, Bend; (541) 382-9242; www.deschutes brewery.com.

44 Newberry Crater Rim Loop

Here's a classic singletrack trail, which circles Paulina and East Lakes, two glacial melts cradled within a huge caldera and surrounded by giant obsidian flows. The route climbs steeply for several miles along the crater rim, offering plenty of opportunities to view the lakes and Paulina Peak. Designated as a wildlife refuge, these lakes support a number of unusual birds and animals. Just when you thought things couldn't get much better, there is a thrilling singletrack descent back to your starting point.

Start: Paulina Lake Campground in the Newberry National Volcanic Monument.
Length: 18.9-mile loop.
Approximate riding time: 3 to 5 hours.
Difficulty: Difficult, due to a large amount of elevation gain, moderate technical obstacles, and the length of the route.
Total climbing: 1,200 feet.
Trail surface: Singletrack, doubletrack, gravel road, and pavement.
Land status: National monument.
Seasons: Mid-July through October.
Nearest Towns: La Pine and Bend.
Other trail users: Hikers and equestrians.

Canine compatibility: Leashed dogs permitted.
Wheels: A bike with front suspension is recommended to handle the technical obstacles on this trail.
Trail contacts: Deschutes National Forest, 1645 Highway 20 East, Bend, OR 97701; (541) 383-5300; www.fs.fed.us/r6/centraloregon.
Fees and permits: $5.00 Northwest Forest Pass. You can purchase it by calling (800) 270-7504 or online at www.naturenw.org.
Maps: Maptech map: Paulina Creek; Finley Butte

Finding the Trailhead

From the intersection of Franklin Avenue and Highway 97 in Bend, head south on U. S. Highway 97 for 24 miles to the Newberry Caldera/Paulina/East Lake sign. Turn left on Forest Road 21 (Paulina Lake Road). Continue 13.4 miles to the Paulina Lake Campground on your left and park in the boat ramp area next to some rest rooms. You'll have to pay a $5.00 parking fee at the entrance booth to the Newberry National Volcanic Monument. *DeLorme: Oregon Atlas & Gazetteer:* Page 45 C7.

The Ride

At first glance, central Oregon may seem to be characterized by its wide-open spaces, sagebrush- and juniper-scattered plateaus, rounded buttes, forested ridges, and snowcapped mountains. But not far off the main highways are some of the most unique and dramatic features in the world—the dramatic remains of volcanic activity that, geologically speaking, occurred fairly recently.

One of the most stunning of these geological features is at the 50,000-acre Newberry National Volcanic Monument, located 38 miles southeast of Bend off U.S.

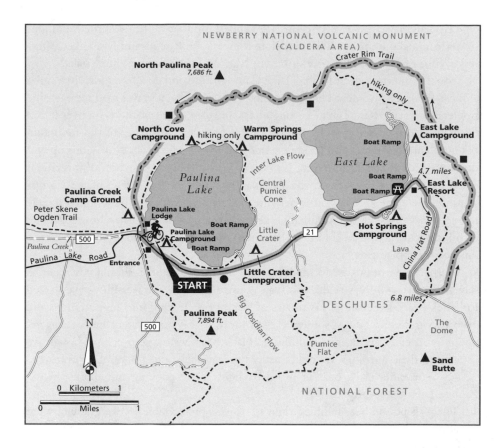

Highway 97. This national preserve was established in 1990 as the volcanic center-piece of the central Oregon region. At the heart of this preserve is the 500-square-mile Newberry Caldera crater, which cradles two pristine alpine lakes named Paulina and East.

Paulina Lake (250 feet deep) and East Lake (180 feet deep) were a single, very large lake until approximately 6,200 years ago when lava flows split them apart. Today these two separate lakes are designated as a wildlife refuge, supporting bald eagles, ducks, geese, osprey, and tundra swans. Mammals—including badgers, black bears, deer, elk, and pine marten—roam the shores and surrounding peaks and valleys as well. Both lakes are popular fishing spots for trout and other varieties.

The Newberry Volcano, located along a group of faults called the Northwest Rift Zone, is one of the largest shield volcanoes in the United States. Shield volcanoes are formed mainly by fluid lava flows pouring from a central vent to form a broad, gently sloping, dome-shaped cone. The volcano's most recent activity occurred 1,300 years ago when it deposited over 170 million cubic yards of obsidian and pumice into what is now called the Big Obsidian Flow, located just east of Paulina Lake Lodge.

Crater Rim Trail is a very scenic, 18.9-mile loop that captures all the highlights of this national monument. This moderate route circles Paulina and East Lakes, offering cyclists great vistas that overlook both lakes and their surrounding peaks.

You'll begin the ride at Paulina Lake Campground and go approximately 5 miles along fairly level pavement before climbing 2 miles of steep gravel road to reach the singletrack Crater Rim Trail. The singletrack portion of this route is often soft and dusty from the ashlike pummy topsoil that is prevalent on many of the mountain bike trails around Bend. You'll ride on this trail for 12-plus miles as it winds up and down forested ridges surrounding Newberry Crater. The end portion of this ride is a screaming downhill back to the Paulina Lake Resort and Paulina Lake Campground. There are so many other activities in the area, you may be tempted to stay for a few days. Besides the mountain bike trails, there are more than a hundred miles of hiking trails, abundant fishing in the lakes, and cool dips in an alpine lake after a long off-road bike ride.

Many campgrounds are located throughout the monument, should you want to stay a few days. And if you do, you may want to keep an extra-cautious eye peeled for black bears. Everyone hears stories of black bears tearing into tents, trailers, and even cars to have a bite of someone else's meal. It was no different here, as several people warned us about the possibility of black bears visiting our camp. Though we listened to their warnings, we didn't really think much about it—until we were visited by a juvenile black bear in broad daylight while cooking our dinner in the Paulina Lake Campground.

The 275-pound bear rambled right up to our picnic table (as we grabbed what we could and headed for the safety of our vehicles), then preceded to knock the top off our cooler and eat a quarter pound of hot-pepper-jack cheese and a whole package of whole wheat tortillas—all in about 30 seconds flat. So much for the burritos we were planning for dinner! Our bear encounter certainly made us more wary. But if anything, it added to the experience we had while visiting this very unique section of central Oregon.

Miles and Directions

0.0 Start from the boat ramp at the Paulina Lake Campground. Ride out to FR 21 (Paulina Lake Road).

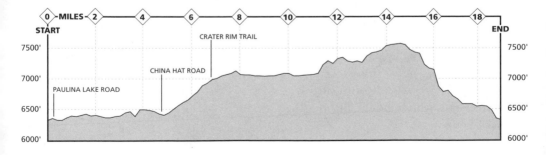

0.2 Turn left on FR 21 (Paulina Lake Road).

4.7 Turn right on paved China Hat Road.

4.9 (Note: The pavement turns to gravel.)

6.8 Turn left on the singletrack Crater Rim Trail. Immediately after turning on this trail, the trail forks. At the fork, turn right.

14.2 Turn left at the trail fork.

18.6 Ride around a green metal gate. The trail comes to a T-intersection at a paved road. Turn right and cross a concrete bridge.

18.7 Take an immediate left on a singletrack trail and follow it as it winds back through the Paulina Lake Campground

18.9 Arrive back at your starting point at the boat ramp.

Ride Information

Local Information

Bend Chamber Visitor & Convention Bureau, 63085 North U.S. Highway 97, Bend, OR 97701; (800) 905-2363; www.visitbend.com.

Local Events and Attractions

High Desert Museum, 59800 South U.S. Highway 97, Bend; (541) 382-4754; www.highdesert.org.

Accommodations

Lara House B&B, 640 NW Congress, Bend; (541) 388-4064; www.larahouse.com.

Restaurants

Deschutes Brewery, 1044 NW Bond Street, Bend; (541) 382-9242; www.deschutes brewery.com.

Honorable Mentions

Compiled here is an index of great rides in Bend and central Oregon. Check them out and let us know what you think. You may decide that one or more of these rides deserves higher status in future editions or perhaps you have a ride of your own that merits some attention.

AA Mzarek

This 18-mile, out-and-back, intermediate ride close to Bend races through an open lodgepole and ponderosa pine forest and keeps you grinning for its entire length.

From the intersection of U.S. Highway 97 in Bend, head west onto Greenwood Avenue and follow it through downtown as it turns into NW Newport Avenue. At the junction with NW Fifth Street, zero out your odometer and continue 3.7 miles west on Newport Avenue (this turns into Shevlin Park Road after 1.9 miles) to the entrance to Shevlin Park Road. Turn left at the park entrance and continue to a gravel parking area on the right.

Start pedaling on the trail that begins on the right side of the parking area. Ride the trail as it weaves in and out of an open pine forest for about 9 miles to a turn-around point at Forest Road 4602-400. The best time to ride this route is May through October.

For more information contact the Deschutes National Forest, 1645 Highway 20 East, Bend, OR 97701; (541) 383–5300; www.fs.fed.us/r6/centraloregon. A good reference map for this ride is the *Mountain Biking & Cross-Country Skiing Map Central Oregon,* available from Adventure Maps; (800) 849–6589; www.adventuremaps.com. *DeLorme: Oregon Atlas & Gazetteer:* Page 51 D5.

BB Tumalo Creek–Tumalo Falls

This 7.6-mile, out-and-back tour takes you through a sunny ponderosa pine forest along Tumalo Creek to impressive Tumalo Falls.

To get there from the intersection of NW Franklin and U.S. Highway 97 in Bend, turn west on Franklin Avenue (this turns into Riverside Boulevard). Go 1.2 miles and then turn right on Tumalo Avenue. Continue on Tumalo Avenue (this road turns into Galveston Avenue and then Skyliners Road) for about 12 miles to the Skyliners Snow Play Parking Area on the left.

Start riding on the singletrack trail that begins next to the rest room. At 0.1 mile cross a doubletrack road and continue straight. At 0.8 mile turn right at the trail fork where a sign reads TUMALO FALLS. At 1.1 miles continue straight (left) on the Tumalo Creek Trail. At 3.1 miles cross a footbridge over Tumalo Creek. At 3.2 miles continue straight toward Tumalo Falls. At 3.5 miles cross a footbridge over Tumalo

Creek. At 3.6 miles arrive at a paved parking lot at the Tumalo Falls Picnic Area. Continue on the North Fork Trail, which is adjacent to the large interpretive signs. At 3.8 miles arrive at a gorgeous viewpoint of Tumalo Falls. From here, retrace the route back to your starting point. The best time to ride this route is May through October.

This ride requires a $5.00 Northwest Forest Pass, which can be purchased by calling (800) 270–7504 or online at www.naturenw.org.

For more information contact the Deschutes National Forest, 1645 Highway 20 East, Bend, OR 97701; (541) 383–5300; www.fs.fed.us/r6/centraloregon. A good reference map for this ride is the *Mountain Biking & Cross-Country Skiing Map Central Oregon,* available from Adventure Maps; (800) 849–6589; www.adventuremaps.com. *DeLorme: Oregon Atlas & Gazetteer:* Page 50 D4.

CC North Fork-South Fork-Flagline Loop

Hill climbers will love this 20.5-mile, advanced loop, which starts at Tumalo Falls and climbs almost 3,000 feet in the Deschutes National Forest on the North Fork, South Fork, and Flagline Trails.

From U.S. Highway 97 in Bend, head west on Franklin Avenue (this turns into Riverside Boulevard) and travel 1.2 miles to the junction with Tumalo Avenue. Turn right on Tumalo Avenue (this turns into Galveston Avenue and then into Skyliners Road), go about 13 miles west (the road turns into Forest Road 4603), and park at the Tumalo Falls Picnic Area at the road's end.

Start by climbing steeply toward a viewpoint of Tumalo Falls. Veer right on the North Fork Trail. At 3.4 miles go right at the trail junction. At 3.7 miles turn right, cross a bridge, and continue riding on FR 382. At 4.2 miles turn left on FR 370. At 7.5 miles continue straight (left) on FR 370. After 9.9 miles turn left on the Flagline Trail (this trail is hard to see!). Continue on the Flagline Trail for about 6.9 miles to a trail junction. Turn left on the South Fork Trail. Continue on the South Fork Trail to the 18.7-mile mark. Turn right on the Bridge Creek Trail. At 20.1 miles turn left on the Skyliners Trail and follow it for 0.5 mile back to your starting point. **Important:** The Flagline Trail section of this route stays closed each year until August 15 to help protect elk that are calving in this area.

This route requires a $5.00 Northwest Forest Pass, which is available by calling (800) 270–7504 or online at www.naturenw.org.

For more information contact the Deschutes National Forest, 1645 Highway 20 East, Bend, OR 97701; (541) 383–5300; www.fs.fed.us/r6/centraloregon. A good reference map for this ride is the *Mountain Biking & Cross-Country Skiing Map Central Oregon,* available from Adventure Maps; (800) 849–6589; www.adventuremaps.com. *DeLorme: Oregon Atlas & Gazetteer:* Page 50 D4.

DD Edison-Lava-Kwolh Butte

This 24-mile, out-and-back, advanced trail starts at Edison Sno-Park and takes you on a demanding ride through a ponderosa and lodgepole pine forest past dramatic lava flows to the summit of Kwolh Butte and then to Little Lava Lake and Lava Lake.

To get there head 16 miles west of Bend on the Cascade Lakes Highway (Oregon Highway 46) to the junction with Forest Road 45. Turn left and continue about 6 miles south to Edison Sno-Park.

Start riding on the Edison-Lava Trail and follow it for 5.6 miles to a right turn on a singletrack trail toward Kwolh Butte. Ride 1.6 miles to the summit of Kwolh Butte. Enjoy the views and then turn around for a fast descent back to the Edison-Lava Trail at the 8.8-mile mark. Turn right and continue 4.8 miles to your turn-around point at Lava Lake and Little Lava Lake. Take a swim in either lake before you head 10.2 miles on the Edison-Lava Trail back to your starting point. This ride is open from June through October.

This ride requires a $5.00 Northwest Forest Pass. It can be purchased by calling (800) 270-7504 or online at www.naturenw.org.

For more information contact the Deschutes National Forest, 1645 Highway 20 East, Bend, OR 97701; (541) 383-5300; www.fs.fed.us/r6/centraloregon. A good reference map for this ride is the *Mountain Biking & Cross-Country Skiing Map Central Oregon,* available from Adventure Maps, (800) 849-6589; www.adventuremaps.com. *DeLorme: Oregon Atlas & Gazetteer:* Page 44 A4.

EE Quinn Creek

This intermediate, 7-mile, out-and-back tour parallels cheery Quinn Creek past the north end of Hosmer Lake.

To get there from Bend, travel 31.2 miles west and south on Cascade Lakes Highway (Oregon Highway 46) to Quinn Meadow Horse Camp.

Follow the singletrack trail for 3.5 miles to your turnaround point at the junction with the Metolius-Windigo Trail. If you are looking for a longer ride, you can turn right on the Metolius-Windigo Trail and pedal 5.3 miles one-way on an advanced-intermediate singletrack trail to Lava Lake. This route is open June through October.

For more information contact the Deschutes National Forest, 1645 Highway 20 East, Bend, OR 97701; (541) 383-5300; www.fs.fed.us/r6/centraloregon. A good reference map for this ride is the *Mountain Biking & Cross-Country Skiing Map Central Oregon,* available from Adventure Maps; (800) 849-6589; www.adventuremaps.com. *DeLorme: Oregon Atlas & Gazetteer:* Page 44 A2.

FF Twin Lakes

This easy, 2.4-mile, out-and-back trail starts at North Twin Lake and takes you to South Twin Lake. The route travels through a scenic ponderosa and lodgepole pine forest. This is a great family ride if you are camping at North Twin Lake.

To get to the trailhead from Bend, travel 26.8 miles south on U.S. Highway 97 to Wickiup Junction. Turn right (west) on Forest Road 43 and go 11 miles to the junction with FR 42. Turn west and go 4.6 miles to the junction with FR 4260. Turn left (south) and go 0.2 mile to North Twin Lake Campground.

Start riding on the trail, accessible from North Twin Lake Campground. Follow the trail until it intersects with the South Twin Lake Trail. It is recommended that you stash your bike and take a short, 1.4-mile hike around South Twin Lake Trail (no bikes allowed); then pedal back on the same route back to North Twin Lake Campground. This route is open June through October.

For more information contact the Deschutes National Forest, 1645 Highway 20 East, Bend, OR 97701; (541) 383–5300; www.fs.fed.us/r6/centraloregon. *DeLorme: Oregon Atlas & Gazetteer:* Page 44 C2.

GG La Pine State Park

Located in a forested setting along the banks of the Deschutes and Fall Rivers, this 2,333-acre state park has some prime mountain biking trails that travel next to these two scenic rivers. The park also has a large campground if you want to stay the night.

To get there from Bend, head 23 miles south on U.S. Highway 97 and turn right onto State Park Road at the La Pine State Park sign. Proceed 4.2 miles to a Y junction. Turn right and follow signs for the camping and day use areas. Go 0.2 mile and turn left where the sign reads PICNIC/DAY USE AREA. Arrive at a large parking area in 0.4 mile.

For more information contact Oregon Parks and Recreation, Suite 1, 1115 Commercial Street NE, Salem, OR 97301; (800) 551–6949; www.oregonstateparks. org/park_41.php. *DeLorme: Oregon Atlas & Gazetteer:* Page 44 B4.

HH Sisters Tie Trail

This intermediate, 6.6-mile trail starts about 0.5 mile past the Sisters Ranger Station and travels northwest on dirt roads and singletrack to Indian Ford Campground. This trail links with the Black Butte Loops Trail System.

To get to the trailhead from U.S. Highway 20 in Sisters, turn north on Pine Street and go past the Ranger Station, approximately a half mile. Look for the parking area on the left side of the road after the pavement ends. The best time to ride this route is April through October.

For more information contact Deschutes National Forest, Sisters Ranger District, P.O. Box 249, Sisters, OR 97759; (541) 549–7700; www.fs.fed.us/r6/centraloregon. *DeLorme: Oregon Atlas & Gazetteer:* Page 50 B4.

II Coyote Creek

This 18.4-mile, out-and-back, intermediate route follows a historic pack trail and provides a good workout (with 1,500 feet of elevation gain) and great views of the Ochoco Mountains.

To get there from Prineville, travel east for 25 miles on U.S. Highway 26. Turn left on Forest Road 27 and continue 1 mile. Turn right on FR 2730 and continue 6.5 miles. Turn right turn on FR 2735 and proceed 1.5 miles to the trailhead. For more information contact the Ochoco National Forest, 3160 NE Third Street, Prineville, OR 97754; (541) 416–6500; www.fs.fed.us/r6/centraloregon. *DeLorme: Oregon Atlas & Gazetteer:* Page 80 B3.

JJ Round Mountain

This advanced, 12.5-mile loop climbs to the top of Round Mountain in the Ochoco National Forest (located approximately 30 miles east of Prineville). To get there from Prineville, drive east on U.S. Highway 26 for 15 miles to the intersection of County Road 23. Turn right and drive 9 miles before turning left on Forest Road 22 (toward Walton Lake). Go 7 miles to the Walton Lake Campground, pass the campground, and turn right on FR 148. Continue 0.4 mile to a pullout on the right side of the road, which is the parking area for Trail 805.

The tour starts by riding back down the hill on FR 148 to its intersection with FR 22. Turn right on FR 22 and go to its junction with FR 135, where you'll turn right. Follow the trail markers for approximately 4.5 miles. Turn right on FR 200 (unsigned) and ride to the summit of Round Mountain—your turnaround point. Descend on FR 200 and look for the intersection with Round Mountain Trail 805 on your left. Turn left on this trail and ride back to your starting point.

For more information contact the Ochoco National Forest, 3160 NE Third Street, Prineville, OR 97754; (541) 416–6500; www.fs.fed.us/r6/centraloregon. *DeLorme: Oregon Atlas & Gazetteer:* Page 80 C3.

Oregon Coast

With a diverse landscape made up of mountains, forest, beaches, rivers, lakes, dunes, bays, and estuaries, the Oregon coast is filled with unique mountain biking adventures. The north to south Coast Mountain Range separates the northwest Oregon coastline from the green Willamette Valley to the east. Molded and shaped by a series of geologic events, this mountain range is relatively young in relation to the Cascade Mountain Range located in the central part of the state.

The Coast Mountain Range began as seafloor sediments and basalt seamounts. When the North American continent collided with these seamounts more than forty-five million years ago, a shallow seafloor was created that filled with sediment over the next twenty million years. About twenty-five million years ago, the Coast Range was pushed upward from the sea, and over the next seven million years the Oregon coast landscape evolved into what you see today.

Other volcanic episodes also shaped the basalt headlands along the coast. Over fifteen million years ago, as many as twelve huge basalt lava flows, originating in eastern Oregon and Washington, traveled west to the Pacific Ocean through the ancient Columbia River channel and formed Tillamook Head, Cape Falcon, Cape Meares, Cape Lookout, Cape Kiwanda, Yaquina Head, Depoe Bay, Otter Rocks, and Seal Rocks. You can see some of these prominent headlands on the Neahkahnie Mountain Ride.

If you want to explore the beach scene and view an old shipwreck, be sure to ride the Fort Stevens State Park Route. To ride through more scenic coastal ecosystems, check out the bike paths at Nehalem Bay State Park and South Beach State Park. The Cannon Beach Ride also promises gorgeous ocean scenery and great beach riding. If you're longing for some singletrack, try the Cummins Creek and the Siltcoos Lake Rides.

Keep in mind that riding on the northwest Oregon coast can often be rainy and cool and the trails are often muddy. The best time to ride here is July through October, when the trails are drier.

45 Fort Stevens State Park

Shipwrecks and sandy beaches await those who wander on the paved bicycle paths at Fort Stevens State Park. Cruise through a coastal forest; view the skeletal remains of the *Peter Iredale* shipwreck; and learn about the area's history at the Fort Stevens Military Museum located inside the park.

Start: In the Battery Russell parking lot accessed from the day use area entrance.
Length: 6.5-mile loop.
Approximate riding time: 1 to 2 hours depending on how much exploring you want to do.
Difficulty: Easy, due to flat terrain and smooth riding surface.
Total climbing: 10 feet. Elevation profiles are not provided for rides with little or no elevation gain.
Trail surface: Paved bicycle path and sandy beach.
Land status: State park.
Seasons: Year-round.

Nearest town: Astoria.
Other trail users: Hikers.
Canine compatibility: Leashed dogs permitted.
Wheels: Fine for hybrids or bikes without dual suspensions due to the smooth riding surface.
Trail contacts: Oregon Parks and Recreation, Suite 1, 1115 Commercial Street NE, Salem, OR 97301; (800) 551-6949; www. oregonstateparks.org/park_179.php.
Fees and permits: Day use fee of $3.00 or you can purchase a $25.00 annual permit for access to all Oregon state parks; (800) 551-6949 or www.oregonstateparks.org.
Maps: Maptech Map: Warrenton.

Finding the Trailhead

From Astoria travel south on U. S. Highway 101 and follow signs to Fort Stevens State Park. Once you reach the park, turn west at the signed day use area entrance. Continue 1 mile to the Battery Russell parking area on the left.

From Seaside travel 10 miles north on U. S. Highway 101 and follow the signs to Fort Stevens State Park. Once you reach the park, turn west at the signed day use area entrance. Continue 1 mile to the Battery Russell parking area on the left. *DeLorme: Oregon Atlas & Gazetteer:* Page 70 C2.

The Ride

The whalelike metal skeleton of the *Peter Iredale* invites the curious traveler to Fort Stevens State Park for further inspection. Fort Stevens State Park is situated on Clatsop Spit, a skinny stretch of sand that forms the gateway to the Columbia River. Also known as "Graveyard of the Ships" because of storms, rough seas, and fog, this area has caused more than 2,000 wrecks of ships trying to cross the Columbia bar.

Fort Stevens has an interesting history that dates back to 1863 when it was first established by President Lincoln during the Civil War in an effort to calm western

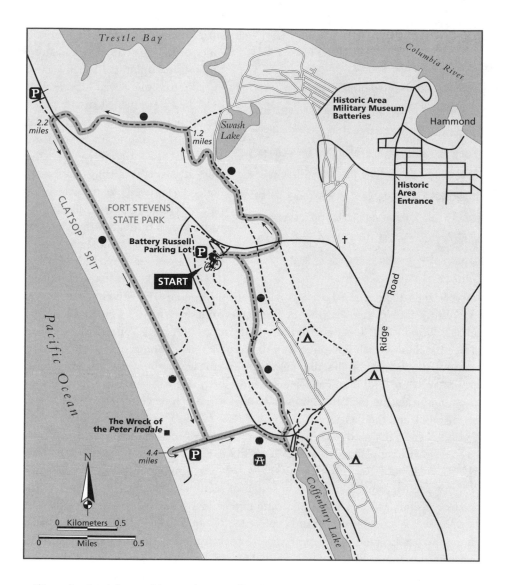

military leaders' fears of increasing conflict in Unionist states and territories. Luckily, the fort never saw any military action. In the early 1900s Fort Stevens served as a strategic garrison to protect trade and transportation routes. And later, during World War II, 2,500 soldiers were stationed here and served in constant fear of attack from the Japanese navy. These fears were realized when a Japanese submarine approached the mouth of the Columbia River on the night of June 21, 1942, and fired on the fort. Luckily, the seventeen shells that were fired did no damage. No firepower was returned either, because the submarine was out of range. The fort was demilitarized after World War II and was then used by the Army reserves and the Coast Guard until 1975, when it was turned into a state park. Today, this park offers more

▶ A PIECE OF HISTORY ...

The Wreck of the *Peter Iredale*

In 1906 the four-masted British freighter *Peter Iredale* was on its way from Australia to Astoria, Oregon, to pick up its next cargo. It was a very foggy, windy day, and as the ship approached the Columbia bar, it became lost. Imagine the crew's frustration and fright when a strong gust of wind blew up and steered the ship aground on Clatsop Spit. Luckily, all of the crew survived, but the ship was so damaged that it had to be abandoned and left to fate.

than 7 miles of paved biking trails, 5 miles of hiking trails, a large campground, and unlimited beach access.

The 6.5-mile paved bicycle path described here hits all of the park's major points of interest. The ride starts at the parking lot next to the Battery Russell. Before you start the ride, it's worth touring the stark, concrete remnants of this old military garrison. The first mile of the route winds through a thick coastal forest of western hemlock, red cedar, bigleaf maple, and red alder. At the 1.2-mile mark, you have the option to veer right to tour the Fort Stevens Military Museum. The museum has several interesting displays that describe the fort's colorful history, focusing especially on the impact World War II had on it and the nearby town of Astoria. You can also pick up a free brochure, which will direct you to the park's many points of historic interest.

Over the next 3.2 miles, the trail opens up and winds through a cascading river of silvery-white sand dunes and short, wind-blown trees that look like twisted sentinels enduring the brutal coastal winds. At 4.4 miles you will reach a wide open, sandy beach and the skeletal remains of the *Peter Iredale*. The rusty frame of this ship, buried deep in the sand, serves as a stark reminder of the brutal storms and merciless seas that have plagued sailors of both the past and present along this stretch of the Pacific Coast. After checking out the *Peter Iredale,* you might be interested to take a short side trip down the beach in search of sea lions frolicking in the surf. Look farther offshore and you may sight some migrating whales.

At the 5.2-mile mark, stop and explore the tranquil Coffenbury Lake, then pedal along the last 1.3 miles of this scenic route back through a green canopy of trees to your starting point. The beauty, accessibility, and large camping facility at this park can draw large crowds during the summer. Dogs, kids, campers, and all the associated paraphernalia can dampen the spirits of any visiting cyclist. It's recommended that you visit the park in the early spring or late fall to really appreciate the park's unique history and scenic beauty.

Miles and Directions

0.0 From the Battery Russell parking lot, look for the bicycle sign. Ride on the paved path toward Coffenbury Lake.

The wreck of the Peter Iredale.

0.1 Turn left toward the "Historic Area/South Jetty."

0.2 Cross a bridge and continue straight.

1.1 Stay to the right.

1.2 Turn left toward the "Beach/Iredale/South Jetty." **Side trip:** You can turn right and ride 0.6 mile to the museum and historic area.

2.2 Cross a paved road and turn left.

3.5 Continue straight.

4.2 Cross the road and turn right.

4.3 Continue straight and ride through the beach parking lot, down a small sandy slope to the beach. Continue riding straight toward the *Peter Iredale* shipwreck.

4.4 Explore the shipwreck, then turn and ride back up the sandy slope, through the beach parking lot, to the paved bicycle path.

4.5 Continue straight on the paved bicycle path.

4.6 Continue straight toward Coffenbury Lake and the camping area.

5.1 Turn right and ride 0.1 mile to view Coffenbury Lake.

5.2 Stop and explore Coffenbury Lake. Ride 0.1 mile back to the paved bicycle path.

5.3 Turn right and ride toward the Battery Russell parking lot.

5.4 Turn left.

6.4 Turn left and follow the signs to the parking lot.

6.5 Arrive back at the Battery Russell parking lot.

Ride Information

Local Information

Astoria/Warrenton Area Chamber of Commerce, 111 West Manor Drive, Astoria, OR 97103; (503) 325-6311; www.oldoregon.com.

Local Events and Attractions

Columbia River Maritime Museum, 1792 Marine Drive, Astoria; (503) 325-2323; www.crmm.org.

Fort Clatsop National Memorial, 92343 Fort Clatsop Road, Astoria; (503) 861-2471 ext. 214; www.nps.gov/focl.

Accommodations

Fort Stevens State Park Campground; (800) 551-6949 (information); (800) 452-5687 (reservations); www.oregonstateparks. org/park_179.php.

Grandview B&B, 1574 Grand Avenue, Astoria; (800) 488-3250; www.moriah.com/ grandview.

Officers' Inn B&B, 540 Russell Place, Hammond; (800) 377-2524; www.moriah.com/officersinn.

46 Cannon Beach

Beach riding at its best. Grab lunch to go at Osburn's Grocery Store and Delicatessen located on Hemlock Street just north of Second Street. Ride south on an endless sandy beach, passing 235-foot Haystack Rock. This distinct rock promontory is designated as part of the Oregon Islands Wildlife Refuge and is an important nesting spot for puffins, pelagic cormorants, pigeon guillemots, and western gulls.

Start: Public parking area in downtown Cannon Beach at Second and Spruce Streets.
Length: 5 miles out and back.
Approximate riding time: 1 to 2 hours.
Difficulty: Easy, due to flat terrain.
Total climbing: None. Elevation profiles are not provided for rides with little or no elevation gain.
Trail surface: Sandy beach and paved road.
Land status: Public beach.
Seasons: Open year-round.

Nearest town: Cannon Beach.
Other trail users: Hikers.
Canine compatibility: Leashed dogs permitted.
Wheels: A hybrid bike will work fine on this ride.
Trail contacts: Cannon Beach Chamber of Commerce, 207 North Spruce Street, P.O. Box 64, Cannon Beach, OR 97110; (503) 436-2623; www.cannonbeach.org.
Fees and permits: No fees or permits required.
Maps: Maptech maps: Tillamook Head; Arch Cape.

Finding the Trailhead

Head about 75 miles west of Portland on U.S. Highway 26 to the intersection with U.S. Highway 101. Turn south on U.S. Highway 101 and take the Cannon Beach exit. Continue driving south through downtown Cannon Beach to a public parking area located at the intersection of Second Street and Spruce Street. *DeLorme: Oregon Atlas & Gazetteer:* Page 64 A1.

The Ride

The small coastal town of Cannon Beach, located approximately 75 miles northwest of Portland, is a popular tourist destination and home of the famous Haystack Rock. Tourists who come here can stroll through the town's art galleries and boutiques; relax at its quaint cafes; and walk along the broad, sandy beach to see the prominent, 235-foot Haystack Rock.

The first white explorers to visit the area were Lewis and Clark during their expedition in 1806. They spent the winter at Fort Clatsop and often sent different groups of men on hunting expeditions for elk, which was a large part of their diet. The party also ate roots, berries, dogs (yes, dogs!), and fresh whale blubber obtained from the local Native Americans. The journal of Meriwether Lewis describes the day of Sunday, January 5, 1806, when two of his party members returned with some fresh whale blubber to eat:

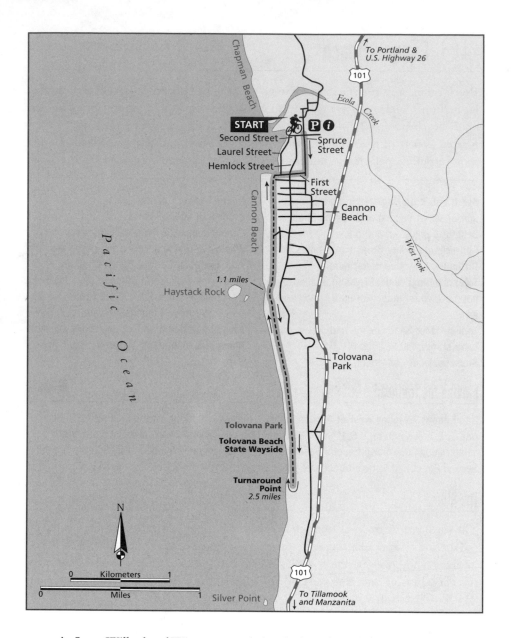

At 5 P.M. Willard and Wiser returned, they had not been lost as we apprehended. They informed us that it was not until the fifth day after leaving the Fort that they could find a convenient place for making salt; that they had at length established themselves on the coast about 15 Miles S.W. from this, near the lodge of some Killamuck families; that the Indians were very friendly and had given them a considerable quantity of the blubber of a whale which perished on the coast some distance S.E. of

Seagulls at Cannon Beach are a common sight.

them; part of this blubber they brought with them, it was white & not unlike the fat of Poork, tho' the texture was more spongey and somewhat coarser. I had a part of it cooked and found it very pallitable and tender, it resembled the beaver or the dog in flavour. it may appear somewhat extraordinary tho' it is a fact that the flesh of the beaver and dog possess a great affinity in point of flavour. (Source: *The Journals of Lewis and Clark,* by Bernard DeVoto, pages 299 and 300)

While you're in the area, it's worth the short drive to visit Ecola (this is the Native American word for "whale") State Park, located just a few miles north of downtown Cannon Beach. It is situated on top of a prominent headland, offering great views of Cannon Beach, Haystack Rock, Tillamook Rock Lighthouse, and the Pacific Ocean. There are picnic tables, rest room facilities, and many hiking trails. One of the hiking trails worth exploring is a 2-mile section of the Oregon Coast Trail, connecting Ecola State Park to Indian Beach (look for the trailhead just to the north of the main parking area). Indian Beach, a popular place for kayaking and surfing, is a small, rocky beach tucked away between local basalt cliffs.

Cannon Beach earned its name after a series of events in the mid-1800s. In 1846 a U.S. survey schooner named *Shark* sank near the mouth of the Columbia River. Within a month three cannons from this wreckage washed up on the beach near Arch Cape, south of what is now Cannon Beach. The cannons later vanished and legends developed regarding their disappearance. When Arch Cape built a post office in 1891, the residents named it Cannon Beach. As the area's population grew, four more post offices were built, three of which were designated with the name Ecola.

In 1922 residents voted to change the name of the post offices from Ecola to Cannon Beach and the name has stayed ever since.

There is a fun, 5–mile, out–and–back beach route worth taking that starts at the parking lot next to the Chamber of Commerce Information Center in downtown Cannon Beach. This route leads you along the sandy shoreline behind the town, and as you ride along you'll see people flying kites, running their dogs, playing with their kids, or just strolling to the sound of the waves.

Once you reach the beach and ride south for about a mile, you'll see Haystack Rock on your right. Haystack Rock began some seventeen million years ago with a series of eruptions that poured molten rock over the Columbia Plateau. The eruptions continued for over ten million years, spreading lava over 78,000 square miles of earth. Some of these lava flows reached all the way to the ocean (it was 25 miles inland from its present location). When the lava invaded the soft marine sediments of the coast, different knobs, sheets, and fingers of rock began to form. As the rock cooled, it turned into basalt. Over millions of years, these basalt formations have eroded away to form the rocky cliffs and headlands that are present today along the Oregon coast. Haystack Rock is one such result of this erosion process.

This easy route along the beach provides one of the best opportunities for seeing the Oregon coast's unique beauty. Remember, though, that salt water can wreck your mountain bike. If possible, rinse your bike off with fresh water after completing this ride (you can obtain fresh water in the public rest rooms located in the parking lot at the start of the ride).

Miles and Directions

0.0 Turn left out of the parking area on Spruce Street.

0.1 Turn right on First Street.

0.2 First Street intersects with Hemlock. Continue straight across Hemlock. You will then intersect with Laurel Street. Continue straight, crossing Laurel Street, and continue riding on a sandy path to the beach. Turn left at the beach and ride south.

1.1 (FYI: Pass Haystack Rock on your right. If it's low tide, take the time to explore the tidal pools located at the base of Haystack Rock. This intertidal ecosystem is home to starfish, barnacles, mussels, crabs, limpets, nudibranches, chitons, and green sea anemones.)

2.5 Reach your turnaround point at Tolovanna Wayside. Return to your starting point on the same route.

5.0 Arrive at your starting point.

Ride Information

Local Information
Cannon Beach Chamber of Commerce,
207 North Spruce Street, P.O. Box 64, Cannon
Beach, OR 97110; (503) 436-2623;
www.cannonbeach.org.

47 Neahkahnie Mountain

If buried treasure and spectacular views sound at all tempting, this is the ride for you. It takes you south along bustling Highway 101, then wanders steeply up the side of 1,631-foot Neahkahnie Mountain, where local legend says buried treasure still exists. Near the summit, stash your bike and hike through an old-growth coastal forest. Eventually the trail deposits you atop the mountain, where (on a clear day) you can see 50 miles in every direction.

Start: Oswald West State Park located 10 miles south of Cannon Beach.
Length: 9.4 miles out and back.
Approximate riding time: 1.5 to 3 hours.
Difficulty: Moderate, due to a steep ascent on a rough, gravel road.
Total climbing: 1,300 feet.
Trail surface: Paved road and gravel road.
Land status: State forest.
Seasons: Open year-round (the route can be muddy during the winter months).
Nearest town: Cannon Beach.

Other trail users: Hikers.
Canine compatibility: Leashed dogs permitted.
Wheels: A bike with suspension is recommended due to the rough gravel road surface.
Trail contacts: Oregon State Parks and Recreation, Suite 1, 1115 Commercial Street NE, Salem, OR 97301; (800) 551-6949; www.oregonstateparks.org/park_195.php.
Fees and permits: No fees or permits required.
Maps: Maptech maps: Arch Cape; Nehalem.

Finding the Trailhead

From Cannon Beach head about 10 miles south (or about 30 miles north of Tillamook) on U.S. Highway 101 to the Oswald West State Park parking area, located on the right (west) side of the road. If this parking area is full, continue south to another parking area on the east side of the highway. *DeLorme: Oregon Atlas & Gazetteer:* Page 64 B1.

The Ride

Some of the most breathtaking views of the northern Oregon coast can be seen from the top of 1,631-foot Neahkahnie Mountain, which is reached by a scenic and strenuous 9.4-mile ride. Starting at Oswald West State Park, about 10 miles south of Cannon Beach off U.S. Highway 101, this ride combines 5.4 miles of paved riding, 3.2 miles of steep doubletrack, and 0.8 mile of hiking. The first leg takes you south from the Oswald West State Park, where you'll begin to climb the side of the headland. As you ride along Highway 101, be sure to stop at the scenic pullouts and catch the magnificent views of Manzanita Beach to the south.

Back in the seventeenth century, it was fairly common to see Spanish sailing vessels along this stretch of coast. Many of them carried cargoes of beeswax (used in candle making), a common item for trade at the time. Ten tons of beeswax have since

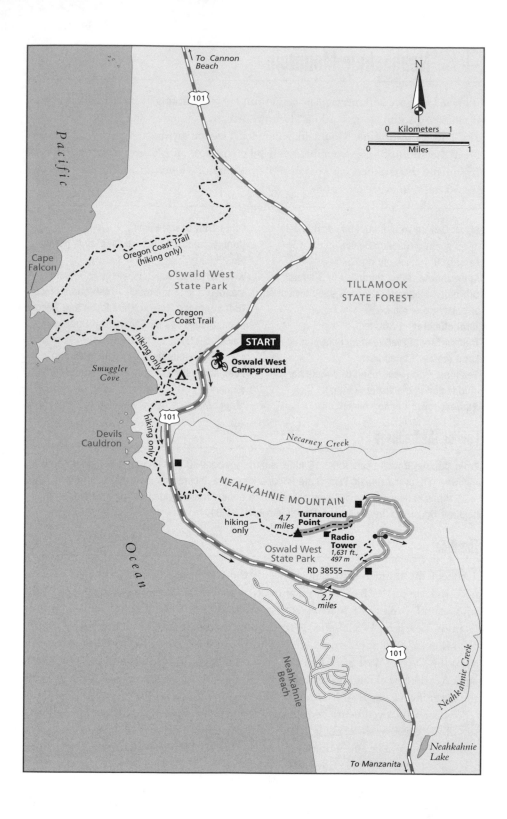

To Cannon Beach

101

N

0 Kilometers 1

0 Miles 1

Pacific

Cape Falcon

Oregon Coast Trail (hiking only)

Oswald West State Park

TILLAMOOK STATE FOREST

Oregon Coast Trail

hiking only

Smuggler Cove

START
Oswald West Campground

101

Devils Cauldron

hiking only

Necarney Creek

NEAHKAHNIE MOUNTAIN

hiking only

4.7 miles

Turnaround Point

Radio Tower
1,631 ft.,
497 m

Oswald West State Park

RD 38555

2.7 miles

Ocean

Neahkahnie Beach

101

Neahkahnie Creek

To Manzanita

Neahkahnie Lake

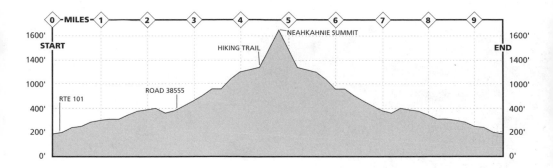

been found along the northern Oregon coast; some of the pieces have elaborate carvings of crucifixes and other designs. Some of them are kept at the Tillamook Pioneer Museum.

The museum is also home to a unique set of rocks found by a farmer at the southern base of Neahkahnie Mountain back in the 1890s. These rocks have carvings thought to reveal the hiding place of a buried treasure near the mountain. For the past hundred years, fortune seekers have hunted for this legendary treasure, but with no luck.

The story begins in the mid–1700s when a Spanish galleon sailing off the Oregon coast was caught in a storm and blown ashore at Cape Foulweather near the base of Neahkahnie Mountain. The ship's crew came ashore and, in desperation, buried a large chest filled with valuables. Some accounts of the story say that a crew member was shot to death, then buried on top of the chest. Native Americans who witnessed the murder abandoned the site out of fear that the spirit of the murdered man would haunt them forever.

After pedaling 2.7 miles along the highway shoulder, you'll turn left on a doubletrack road that winds steeply up the side of the mountain and travels through a dense forest of Sitka spruce, red cedar, and western hemlock. After nearly 1 mile on this doubletrack, the grade becomes so steep you may have to push your bike. After 1.6 miles the road intersects with a hiking trail that is closed to bikes. You'll need to stash your bike and hike the remaining 0.4 mile to the summit. As you climb there are several breaks in the trees that offer great views of the coastline to the north. The last few hundred yards of the trail will snake over a rocky spine to the summit, where your efforts are repaid many times over with the magnificent view of the Oregon coastline and Pacific Ocean.

Miles and Directions

0.0 Start by turning right (south) out of the parking lot on U.S. Highway 101. (FYI: Be sure to stop at the viewpoints along this section of the highway to catch the stunning views.)

2.7 Turn left on Road 38555. Begin a steep ascent up Neahkahnie Mountain.

3.1 Pass a trailhead on your left. Continue straight.

View looking south from the summit of Neahkahnie Mountain.

3.5 Ride through a gate. Continue riding up the hill. (Note: The road becomes very steep here and you may have to push your bike up this section.)

3.9 There is a short descent, after which the road continues climbing very steeply.

4.3 Arrive at a junction of the road with a hiking trail. (FYI: This trail begins at Oswald West State Park Campground and winds about 3.6 miles to the top of the mountain.) Turn right on the hiking trail. You'll have to stash your bike and hike the remaining 0.4 mile to reach the summit. (Bikes are not allowed on this trail.)

4.7 Reach the 1,631-foot summit of Neahkahnie Mountain. On a clear day you can see up to 50 miles in every direction. Retrace the route back to your starting point.

9.4 Arrive back at your starting point.

Ride Information

Local Information
Cannon Beach Chamber of Commerce, 207 North Spruce Street, P.O. Box 64, Cannon Beach, OR 97110; (503) 436–2623; www.cannonbeach.org.

Local Events and Attractions
Tillamook County Pioneer Museum, 2106 Second Street, Tillamook; (503) 842–4553; www.tcpm.org.

48 Siltcoos Lake

You'll have a blast on this short-but-sweet, 4.4-mile, singletrack loop around Siltcoos Lake. This quick it's-over-before-you-can-blink trail winds through a thick coastal forest, taking you to the edge of 3,500-acre Siltcoos Lake—the largest freshwater lake on the Oregon coast. Here you'll have a good chance of seeing blue herons and a variety of other waterfowl. Short intense climbs, fast twisting downhills, and smooth-sailing straightaways make this trail so much fun that you'll want to do it again and again.

Start: Siltcoos Lake Trailhead located 7 miles south of Florence (or 13 miles north of Reedsport) on the east side of U.S. Highway 101.
Length: 4.4-mile loop.
Approximate riding time: 1 hour.
Difficulty: Easy, due to smooth trail surface and minimal elevation gain.
Total climbing: 300 feet.
Trail surface: Singletrack.
Land status: National recreation area.
Seasons: Year-round (the trail can be muddy during the winter months).
Nearest town: Florence.
Other trail users: Hikers.
Canine compatibility: Leashed dogs permitted.

Wheels: A bike with front suspension is recommended to prevent arm jarring on the many fast rolling hills and turns on this route.
Trail contacts: Oregon Dunes National Visitor Center, 855 Highway Avenue, Reedsport, OR 97467; (541) 271-3611; www.fs.fed.us/r6/siuslaw/oregondunes.
Fees and permits: Requires a Northwest Forest $5.00 day pass or you can purchase a $30.00 annual pass. You can purchase it online at www.fs.fed.us/r6/feedemo or by calling (800) 270-7504.
Maps: Maptech maps: Florence; Goose Pasture; Fivemile Creek; Tahkenitch Creek.

Finding the Trailhead

From Florence travel 7 miles south on U.S. Highway 101. Turn left (east) at the Siltcoos Lake Trail sign.
From Reedsport travel about 13 miles north on U.S. Highway 101. Turn right (east) into the Siltcoos Lake Trail parking lot. *DeLorme: Oregon Atlas & Gazetteer:* Page 32, Inset 3, A4.

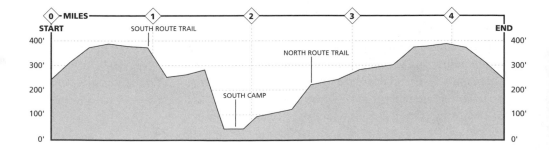

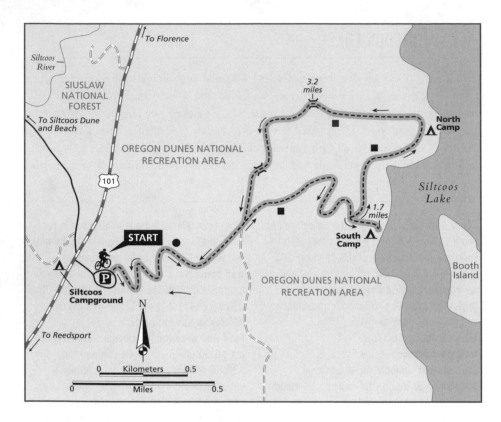

The Ride

The Oregon Dunes National Recreation Area, established in 1972, is a 50-square-mile area of sand dunes along a narrow band of coastline between Florence and North Bend on the southern Oregon coast. These minimountains of sand are constantly being sculpted and resculpted by the Pacific winds and, at times, can reach heights of more than 300 feet.

Millions of years ago this part of Oregon was completely under water. Comprised mostly of sand, the sea floor was eventually raised out of the ocean during the continental uplift to form the sedimentary rock that makes up Oregon's present-day coastal range. As time went on, wind and rain eroded the sandstone of the coastal mountains. The resulting sand was carried by rivers back to the ocean where it was deposited, once again, on the ocean floor. Strong ocean currents moving northward in the winter and southward in the summer keep this sand just offshore. Tides, currents, and waves then deposit it on the gently sloping Oregon shores. Once the sand dries, strong prevailing coastal winds blow the smaller, lighter grains of sand inland to eventually form the giant dunes you see today.

Siltcoos Lake.

These dunes can stretch inland for up to 3 miles and intermingle with coastal forests and freshwater lakes, creating an interesting patchwork of coastal ecosystems. One unique ecosystem worth visiting is the Darlingtonia Botanical Wayside located 5 miles north of Florence off U.S. Highway 101. A short hike into a small wetland takes you to the park's main attraction—the insect-eating cobra lily *(Darlingtonia Californica).* These unique plants have resorted to their meat-eating ways because of the lack of nutrients in the coastal soil. They lure insects into their slow-but-sure traps and digest them for their much-needed nutrients.

A variety of freshwater lakes also exist along this length of coastland as a result of sand dunes blocking small streams that once extended to the ocean. Woahink, Siltcoos, Tahkenitch, and Threemile Lakes, located between Florence and Reedsport, all have something unique to offer. Tahkenitch Dunes Trail, located 5 miles north of Reedsport (or 13 miles south of Florence) off U.S. Highway 101 at the Tahkenitch Campground Trailhead, is a great 6.5-mile-loop hiking trail that winds through marsh, forest, and dunes. This trail heads toward the beach, where visitors can turn south and hook up with the Threemile Lake Trail. If you want to see and climb some really big dunes, go check out the 2.5-mile Umpqua Dunes Trail that starts at the Eel Creek Campground Trailhead 11 miles south of Reedsport (or 16 miles north of Coos Bay) off U.S. Highway 101.

Luckily, mountain bikers can also experience some of this thick coastal forest by riding the short-but-sweet 4.4-mile singletrack loop around Siltcoos Lake, named after a local Indian chief and his family. Located approximately 7 miles south of Florence off U.S. Highway 101, the lake is a popular boating, fishing, and bird-watching spot. It supports a number of islands and freshwater marshes and brims with a variety of fish, such as steelhead, cutthroat trout, bass, perch, bluegill, and catfish.

Miles and Directions

0.0 Start riding at the signed trailhead.

0.8 Turn right and take the south route trail.

1.5 Turn right and ride a steep descent toward South Camp.

1.7 At South Camp, check out the lake, then turn around and ride back up the hill.

2.0 Turn right at the trail fork.

2.3 Turn right at the trail fork.

2.5 Turn left at the trail fork. You'll ride a short distance and reach a campsite. Stay to the left.

2.6 Turn right and follow the north route back to your starting point.

3.6 Turn right at the trail fork.

4.4 Arrive at the trailhead.

Ride Information

Local Information

Florence Chamber of Commerce, 270 Highway 101, Florence, OR 97439; (800) 524-4864; www.florencechamber.com.

MIXED UP . . .

An interesting controversy has developed on the decided "mixed-use" policy of the National Dunes Recreation Area. Nature lovers aren't the only ones attracted to these dunes; so are folks in dune buggies, dirt bikes, and all sorts of off-road contraptions. The United States Forest Service is starting to cut back on off-road vehicle use in an attempt to attract more wildlife and a quieter approach to the dune "experience." The northern half of the recreation area (north of Reedsport) has fewer off-road vehicles and more hiking trails, whereas the lower half is geared more toward off-road vehicle use.

Honorable Mentions

Compiled here is an index of great rides on the Oregon coast. Check them out and let us know what you think. You may decide that one or more of these rides deserves higher status in future editions or perhaps you have a ride of your own that merits some attention.

KK Nehalem Bay State Park

This easy, 2-mile, paved bike path takes you on a tour of a coastal dune ecosystem in Nehalem Bay State Park, an 890-acre park located on a sand spit between Nehalem Bay and the Pacific Ocean.

To get there from Manzanita, travel 3 miles south on U.S. Highway 101 to Carey Street. Turn right (west) on Carey Street and go 1.5 miles to the park entrance. Continue on the park entrance road to a road fork and go on to a parking area.

Start riding on the paved bike path and follow it as it loops 2 miles through the park. This ride is open year-round.

A $3.00 day use parking pass is required.

For more information contact Oregon Parks and Recreation, Suite 1, 1115 Commercial Street NE, Salem, OR 97301-1002; (800) 551–6949; www.oregonstateparks.org/park_201.php. *DeLorme: Oregon Atlas & Gazetteer:* Page 64 C2.

LL South Beach State Park

This 434-acre scenic state park has an easy, 3-mile, out-and-back, paved path that travels from the day use area through a grassy, beach dune environment to the South Jetty.

To get there travel 2 miles south of Newport on U.S. Highway 101 to the park entrance on the right (west) side of the road. Proceed to the day use parking area.

On this ride you'll have great views of the Yaquina Bay Bridge and Yaquina Bay Lighthouse. The park also has a great campground if you want to stay overnight. This ride is open year-round.

For more information contact Oregon Parks and Recreation, Suite 1, 1115 Commercial Street NE, Salem, OR 97301-1002; (800) 551–6949; www.oregonstateparks.org/park_209.php. *DeLorme: Oregon Atlas & Gazetteer:* Page 32, Inset 1, D1.

MM Cummins Creek Loop

This advanced, 10.4-mile loop combines paved roads and singletrack trails that wind through old-growth timber, offering great views of the Pacific Ocean. As an added benefit, it also borders the Cummins Creek Wilderness.

To get there, drive 28 miles south of Newport on U.S. Highway 101. Just past Cape Perpetua, turn left and drive to the Cape Perpetua Visitors Center.

Start the ride by pedaling back out to U.S. Highway 101 from the visitor center. Turn right (north) on U.S. Highway 101 and ride 0.5 mile to Forest Road 55. Turn right on FR 55, then ride up a steep ascent for 4 miles to a gravel parking lot on the right at Cooks Ridge Trailhead. Take this trail for 0.2 miles to a trail junction. Turn left at this junction onto Cummins Creek Trail. Ride about a half mile, then veer left at the next trail intersection. At the next intersection, turn right, continuing to follow the Cummins Creek Trail. After approximately 8.5 miles, the trail intersects with a paved road. Follow this road back to U.S. Highway 101. When you reach it, turn right (north) and ride back to the visitor center. The best time to ride this route is May through October.

A $3.00 day use parking pass is required and can be purchased in the visitor center or from self-pay stations located in the parking lot.

For more information contact Cape Perpetua Interpretive Center, Yachats, OR 97498; (541) 547–3289; www.newportnet.com/capeperpetua. *DeLorme: Oregon Atlas & Gazetteer:* Page 32, Inset 2, B2.

The Art of Mountain Biking

Within the following pages, you will find everything you need to know about off-road bicycling in northwest Oregon. This section begins by exploring the fascinating history of the mountain bike itself, then goes on to discuss everything from the health benefits of off-road cycling to tips and techniques for bicycling over logs and up hills. Also included are the types of clothing to keep you comfortable and in style, essential equipment ideas to keep your rides smooth and trouble-free, and descriptions of off-road terrain to prepare you for the kinds of bumps and bounces you can expect to encounter.

The mountain bike, with its knobby tread and reinforced frame, takes cyclists to places once unheard of—down rugged mountain trails, through streams of rushing water, across the frozen Alaskan tundra, and even to work in the city. There seem to be few limits on what this fat-tired beast can do and where it can take us. Few obstacles stand in its way, few boundaries slow its progress. Except for one—its own success. If trail closure means little to you now, read on and discover how a trail can be here today and gone tomorrow. With so many new off-road cyclists taking to the trails each year, it's no wonder trail access hinges precariously between universal acceptance and complete termination. But a little work on your part can go a long way to preserving trail access for future use. Nothing is more crucial to the survival of mountain biking itself than to read the examples set forth in the following pages and practice their message.

Without open trails, the maps in this book are virtually useless. Cyclists must learn to be responsible for the trails they use and to share these trails with others. This guidebook addresses such issues as why trail use has become so controversial, what can be done to improve the image of mountain biking, how to have fun and ride responsibly, on-the-spot trail repair techniques, trail maintenance hotlines for each trail, and the worldwide-standard Rules of the Trail.

Mountain Bike Beginnings

It seems the mountain bike, originally designed for lunatic adventurists bored with straight lines, clean clothes, and smooth tires, has become globally popular in as short a time as it would take to race down a mountain trail.

Like many things of a revolutionary nature, the mountain bike was born on the West Coast. But unlike Rollerblades, purple hair, and the peace sign, the concept of the off-road bike cannot be credited solely to the imaginative Californians—they were just the first to make waves.

The design of the first off-road-specific bike was based on the geometry of the old Schwinn Excelsior, a one-speed, camelback cruiser with balloon tires. Joe Breeze was the creator behind it, and in 1977 he built ten of these "Breezers" for himself and his Marin County, California, friends at $750 apiece—a bargain.

Breeze was a serious competitor in bicycle racing, placing thirteenth in the 1977 U.S. Road Racing National Championships. After races, he and friends would scour local bike shops hoping to find old bikes they could then restore.

It was the 1941 Schwinn Excelsior, for which Breeze paid just five dollars, that began to shape and change bicycling history forever. After taking the bike home, removing the fenders, oiling the chain, and pumping up the tires, Breeze hit the dirt. He loved it.

His inspiration, while forerunning, was not altogether unique. On the opposite end of the country, nearly 2,500 miles from Marin County, East Coast bike bums were also growing restless. More and more old, beat-up clunkers were being restored and modified. These behemoths often weighed as much as eighty pounds and were so reinforced they seemed virtually indestructible. But rides that take just forty minutes on today's twenty-five-pound featherweights took the steel-toed-boot-and-blue-jean-clad bikers of the late 1970s and early 1980s nearly four hours to complete.

Not until 1981 was it possible to purchase a production mountain bike, but local retailers found these ungainly bicycles difficult to sell and rarely kept them in stock. By 1983, however, mountain bikes were no longer such a fringe item, and large bike manufacturers quickly jumped into the action, producing their own versions of the off-road bike. By the 1990s the mountain bike had firmly established its place with bicyclists of nearly all ages and abilities, and it now commands nearly 90 percent of the U.S. bike market.

There are many reasons for the mountain bike's success in becoming the hottest two-wheeled vehicle in the nation. They are much friendlier to the cyclist than traditional road bikes because of their comfortable upright position and shock-absorbing fat tires. And because of the health-conscious, environmentalist movement of the late 1980s and 1990s, people are more activity minded and seek nature on a closer front than paved roads can allow. The mountain bike gives you these things and takes you far away from the daily grind—even if you're only minutes from the city.

Mountain Biking into Shape

If your objective is to get in shape and lose weight, then you're on the right track, because mountain biking is one of the best ways to get started.

One way many of us have lost weight in this sport is the crash-and-burn-it-off method. Picture this: You're speeding uncontrollably down a vertical drop that you realize you shouldn't be on—only after it is too late. Your front wheel lodges into a rut and launches you through endless weeds, trees, and pointy rocks before coming to an abrupt halt in a puddle of thick mud. Surveying the damage, you discover, with the layers of skin, body parts, and lost confidence littering the trail above, that those unwanted pounds have been shed—permanently. Instant weight loss.

There is, of course, a more conventional (and quite a bit less painful) approach to losing weight and gaining fitness on a mountain bike. It's called the workout, and bicycles provide an ideal way to get physical. Take a look at some of the benefits associated with cycling.

Cycling helps you shed pounds without gimmicky diet fads or weight-loss programs. You can explore the countryside and burn nearly 10 to 16 calories per minute or close to 600 to 1,000 calories per hour. Moreover, it's a great way to spend an afternoon.

No less significant than the external and cosmetic changes of your body from riding are the internal changes taking place. Over time, cycling regularly will strengthen your heart as your body grows vast networks of new capillaries to carry blood to all those working muscles. This will, in turn, give your skin a healthier glow. The capacity of your lungs may increase up to 20 percent, and your resting heart rate will drop significantly. The Stanford University School of Medicine reports to the American Heart Association that people can reduce their risk of heart attack by nearly 64 percent if they can burn up to 2,000 calories per week. This is only two to three hours of bike riding!

Recommended for insomnia, hypertension, indigestion, anxiety, and even for recuperation from major heart attacks, bicycling can be an excellent cure-all as well as a great preventive. Cycling just a few hours per week can improve your figure and sleeping habits, give you greater resistance to illness, increase your energy levels, and provide feelings of accomplishment and heightened self-esteem.

Be Safe—Know the Law

Occasionally, even the hard-core off-road cyclists will find they have no choice but to ride the pavement. When you are forced to hit the road, it's important for you to know and understand the rules.

Outlined below are a few of the common laws found in Oregon.

- In Oregon, you can pedal on any public road except urban freeways.
- Follow the same driving rules as motorists. Be sure to obey all road signs and traffic lights.
- Wear a helmet and bright clothing so you are more visible to motorists. Bright colors such as orange and lime green are also highly visible at night.
- Oregon law requires that riders and passengers under the age of sixteen wear a CPSC- (Consumer Product Safety Commission) approved helmet.

- Equip your bike with lights and wear reflective clothing if you plan on riding at night. When riding at night the bicycle or rider must have a white light visible at least 500 feet to the front and a red light or reflector visible at least 600 feet to the rear.
- Pass motorists on the left and not the right. Motorists are not expecting you to pass on the right and they may not see you.
- Ride single file on busy roads so motorists can pass you safely.
- Stop off the roadway.
- Use hand signals to alert motorists to what you plan on doing next.
- Ride with the traffic and not against it.
- Follow painted lane markings.
- Make eye contact with drivers. Assume they don't see you until you are sure they do.
- Ride in the middle of the lane at busy intersections and whenever you are moving at the same speed as traffic.
- Don't ride out to the curb between parked cars unless they are far apart. Motorists may not see you when you try to move back into traffic
- Turn left by looking back, signaling, getting into the left lane, and turning. In urban situations, continue straight to the crosswalk and walk your bike across the crosswalk when the pedestrian walk sign is illuminated.
- Never ride while under the influence of alcohol or drugs. DUI laws apply when you're riding a bicycle.
- Avoid riding in extreme foggy, rainy, or windy conditions.
- Watch out for parallel-slat sewer grates, slippery manhole covers, oily pavement, gravel, wet leaves, and ice.
- Cross railroad tracks as perpendicular as possible. Be especially careful when it's wet out. For better control as you move across bumps and other hazards, stand up on your pedals.
- Don't ride too close to parked cars—a person opening the car door may hit you.
- Avoid riding on sidewalks. Instead, walk your bike. Pedestrians have the right-of-way on walkways. By law, you must give pedestrians audible warning when you pass. Use a bike bell or announce clearly, "On your left/right."
- Slow down at street crossings and driveways.

The Mountain Bike Controversy

Are Off-Road Bicyclists Environmental Outlaws? Do We Have the Right to Use Public Trails?

Mountain bikers have long endured the animosity of folks in the backcountry who complain about the consequences of off-road bicycling. Many people believe that the fat tires and knobby tread do unacceptable environmental damage and that our uncontrollable riding habits are a danger to animals and other trail users. To the contrary, mountain bikes have no more environmental impact than hiking boots or horseshoes. This does not mean, however, that mountain bikes leave no imprint at all. Wherever man treads, there is an impact. By riding responsibly, though, it is possible to leave only a minimal impact—something we all must take care to achieve.

Unfortunately, it is often people of great influence who view the mountain bike as the environment's worst enemy. Consequently, we mountain bike riders and environmentally concerned citizens must be educators, impressing upon others that we also deserve the right to use these trails. Our responsibilities as bicyclists are no more and no less than those of any other trail user. We must all take the soft-cycling approach and show that mountain bicyclists are not environmental outlaws.

Etiquette of Mountain Biking

When discussing mountain biking etiquette, we are in essence discussing the soft-cycling approach. This term, as mentioned previously, describes the art of minimum-impact bicycling and should apply to both the physical and social dimensions of the sport. But make no mistake—it is possible to ride fast and furiously while maintaining the balance of soft-cycling. Here first are a few ways to minimize the physical impact of mountain bike riding.

- **Stay on the trail.** Don't ride around fallen trees or mud holes that block your path. Stop and cross over them. When you come to a vista overlooking a deep valley, don't ride off the trail for a better vantage point. Instead, leave the bike and walk to see the view. Riding off the trail may seem inconsequential when done only once, but soon someone else will follow, then others, and the cumulative results can be catastrophic. Each time you wander from the trail you begin creating a new path, adding one more scar to the earth's surface.

- **Do not disturb the soil.** Follow a line within the trail that will not disturb or damage the soil.

- **Do not ride over soft or wet trails.** After a rain shower or during the thawing season, trails will often resemble muddy, oozing swampland. The best thing to do is stay off the trails altogether. Realistically, however, we're all going to come across some muddy trails we cannot anticipate. Instead of blasting through each section of mud, which may seem both easier and more fun, lift the bike and walk past. Each time a cyclist rides through a soft or muddy section of trail, that part of the trail is permanently damaged. Regardless of the trail's conditions, though, remember always to go over the obstacles across the path, not around them. Stay on the trail.

- **Avoid trails that are considered impassable and impossible.** Don't take a leap of faith down a kamikaze descent on which you will be forced to lock your brakes and skid to the bottom, ripping the ground apart as you go.

Soft-cycling should apply to the social dimensions of the sport as well, since mountain bikers are not the only folks who use the trails. Hikers, equestrians, cross-country skiers, and other outdoors people use many of the same trails and can be easily spooked by a marauding mountain biker tearing through the trees. Be friendly in the forest and give ample warning of your approach.

- **Take out what you bring in.** Don't leave broken bike pieces and banana peels scattered along the trail.
- **Be aware of your surroundings.** Don't use popular hiking trails for race training.
- **Slow down!** Rocketing around blind corners is a sure way to ruin an unsuspecting hiker's day. Consider this: If you fly down a quick singletrack descent at 20 mph, then hit the brakes and slow down to only 6 mph to pass someone, you're still moving twice as fast as they are!

Like the trails we ride on, the social dimension of mountain biking is very fragile and must be cared for responsibly. We should not want to destroy another person's enjoyment of the outdoors. By riding in the backcountry with caution, control, and responsibility, our presence should be felt positively by other trail users. By adhering to these rules, trail riding—a privilege that can quickly be taken away—will continue to be ours to share.

Trail Maintenance

Unfortunately, despite all of the preventive measures taken to avoid trail damage, we're still going to run into many trails requiring attention. Simply put, a lot of hikers, equestrians, and cyclists use the same trails—some wear and tear is unavoidable. But like your bike, if you want to use these trails for a long time to come, you must also maintain them.

Trail maintenance and restoration can be accomplished in a variety of ways. One way is for mountain bike clubs to combine efforts with other trail users (i.e., hikers and equestrians) and work closely with land managers to cut new trails or repair existing ones. This not only reinforces to others the commitment cyclists have in caring for and maintaining the land, but also breaks the ice that often separates cyclists from their fellow trail mates. Another good way to help out is to show up, ready to work, on a Saturday morning with a few riding buddies at your favorite off-road domain. With a good attitude, thick gloves, and the local land manager's supervision, trail repair is fun and very rewarding. It's important, of course, that you arrange a trail-repair outing with the local land manager before you start pounding shovels into the dirt. They can lead you to the most needy sections of trail and instruct you on what repairs should be done and how best to accomplish the task. Perhaps the most effective means of trail maintenance, though, can be done by yourself and while you're riding. Read on.

On-the-Spot-Quick Fix

Most of us, when we're riding, have at one time or another come upon muddy trails or fallen trees blocking our path. We notice that over time the mud gets deeper and the trail gets wider as people go through or around the obstacles. We worry that the problem will become so severe and repairs too difficult that the trail's access may be threatened. We also know that our ambition to do anything about it is greatest at that moment, not after a hot shower and a plate of spaghetti. Here are a few on-the-spot quick fixes you can do that will hopefully correct a problem before it gets out of hand and get you back on your bike within minutes.

Muddy trails. What do you do when trails develop huge mud holes destined for the EPA's Superfund status? Corduroy (not the pants) is the term for roads made of logs laid down crosswise. Use small- and medium-size sticks and lay them side by side across the trail until they cover the length of the muddy section (break the sticks to fit the width of the trail). Press them into the mud with your feet, then lay more on top if needed. Keep adding sticks until the trail is firm. Not only will you stay clean as you cross, but the sticks may soak up some of the water and help the puddle dry. This quick fix may last as long as one month before needing to be redone. And as time goes on, with new layers added to the trail, the soil will grow stronger, thicker, and more resistant to erosion. This whole process may take fewer than five minutes, and you can be on your way, knowing the trail behind you is in good repair.

Leaving the trail. What do you do to keep cyclists from cutting corners and leaving the designated trail? The solution is much simpler than you may think. (No, don't hire an off-road police force.) Notice where people are leaving the trail and throw a pile of thick branches or brush along the path, or place logs across the opening to block the way through. There are probably dozens of subtle tricks like these that will manipulate people into staying on the designated trail. If executed well, no one will even notice that the thick branches scattered along the ground in the woods weren't always there. And most folks would probably rather take a moment to hop a log in the trail than get tangled in a web of branches.

Obstacle in the way. If there are large obstacles blocking the trail, try to remove them or push them aside. If you cannot do this by yourself, call the trail maintenance hotline to speak with the land manager of that particular trail and see what can be done.

We must be willing to sweat for our trails in order to sweat on them. Police yourself and point out to others the significance of trail maintenance. "Sweat Equity," the rewards of continued land use won with a fair share of sweat, pays off when the trail is "up for review" by the land manager and he or she remembers the efforts made by trail-conscious mountain bikers.

Rules of the Trail

The International Mountain Bicycling Association (IMBA) has developed these guidelines to trail riding. These "Rules of the Trail" are accepted worldwide and will go a long way in keeping trails open. Please respect and follow these rules for everyone's sake.

1. Ride only on open trails. Respect trail and road closures (if you're not sure, ask a park or state official first), do not trespass on private property, and obtain permits or authorization if required. Federal and state wilderness areas are off-limits to cycling. Parks and state forests may also have certain trails closed to cycling.

2. Zero impact. Be sensitive to the dirt beneath you. Even on open trails, you should not ride under conditions by which you will leave evidence of your passing, such as on certain soils or shortly after a rainfall. Be sure to observe the different types of soils and trails you're riding on, practicing minimum-impact cycling. Never ride off the trail, don't skid your tires, and be sure to bring out at least as much as you bring in.

3. Control your bicycle! Inattention for even one second can cause disaster for yourself or for others. Excessive speed frightens and can injure people, gives mountain biking a bad name, and can result in trail closures.

4. Always yield. Let others know you're coming well in advance (a friendly greeting is always good and often appreciated). Show your respect when passing others by slowing to walking speed or stopping altogether, especially in the presence of horses. Horses can be unpredictable, so be very careful. Anticipate that other trail users may be around corners or in blind spots.

5. Never spook animals. All animals are spooked by sudden movements, unannounced approaches, or loud noises. Give them extra room and time so they can adjust to you. Move slowly or dismount around animals. Running cattle and disturbing wild animals are serious offenses. Leave gates as you find them, or as marked.

6. Plan ahead. Know your equipment, your ability, and the area in which you are riding, and plan your trip accordingly. Be self-sufficient at all times, keep your bike in good repair, and carry necessary supplies for changes in weather or other conditions. You can help keep trails open by setting an example of responsible, courteous, and controlled mountain bike riding.

7. Always wear a helmet when you ride. For your own safety and protection, a helmet should be worn whenever you are riding your bike. You never know when a tree root or small rock will throw you the wrong way and send you tumbling.

Thousands of miles of dirt trails have been closed to mountain bicycling because of the irresponsible riding habits of just a few riders. Don't follow the example of these offending riders. Don't take away trail privileges from thousands of others who work hard each year to keep the backcountry avenues open to us all.

The Necessities of Cycling

When discussing the most important items to have on a bike ride, cyclists generally agree on the following four items:

Helmet. The reasons to wear a helmet should be obvious. Helmets are discussed in more detail in the "Be Safe—Wear Your Armor" section.

Water. Without it, cyclists may face dehydration, which may result in dizziness and fatigue. On a warm day, cyclists should drink at least one full bottle during every hour of riding. Remember, it's always good to drink before you feel thirsty—otherwise, it may be too late.

Cycling shorts. These are necessary if you plan to ride your bike more than 20 to 30 minutes. Padded cycling shorts may be the only thing preventing your derriere from serious saddle soreness by ride's end. There are two types of cycling shorts you can buy. Touring shorts are good for people who don't want to look like they're wearing anatomically correct cellophane. These look like regular athletic shorts with pockets, but they have built-in padding in the crotch area for protection from chafing and saddle sores. The more popular, traditional cycling shorts are made of skintight material, also with a padded crotch. Whichever style you find most comfortable, cycling shorts are a necessity for long rides.

Food. This essential item will keep you rolling. Cycling burns up a lot of calories and is among the few sports in which no one is safe from the "Bonk." Bonking feels like it sounds. Without food in your system, your blood sugar level collapses, and there is no longer any energy in your body. This instantly results in total fatigue and light-headedness. So when you're filling your water bottle, remember to bring along some food. Fruit, energy bars, or some other forms of high-energy food are highly recommended. Candy bars are not, however, because they will deliver a sudden burst of high energy, then let you down soon after, causing you to feel worse than before. Energy bars are available at most bike stores and are similar to candy bars, but they provide complex carbohydrate energy and high nutrition rather than fast-burning simple sugars.

Be Prepared or Die

Do you remember the Boy Scout motto? Be prepared. The following is a list of essential equipment that will keep you from walking out a long trail, being stranded in the woods, or even losing your life.

- Spare tube
- Tire irons
- Patch kit
- Pump
- Money: Spare change for emergency calls.
- Spoke wrench
- Spare spokes: To fit your wheel. Tape these to the chain stay.
- Chain tool
- Allen keys: Bring appropriate sizes to fit your bike.
- Compass/GPS
- Duct tape
- First-Aid kit: See First-Aid Kit sidebar.
- Rain gear: For quick changes in weather.
- Matches
- Guidebook: In case all else fails and you must start a fire to survive, this guidebook will serve as excellent fire starter!
- Food and water
- Jacket

To carry these items, you will need a backpack. There are currently many streamlined backpacks with hydration systems on the market that you can choose from. If you're carrying lots of equipment, you may want to consider a set of panniers. These are much larger and mount on either side of each wheel on a rack.

Be Safe—Wear Your Armor

While on the subject of jerseys, it's crucial to discuss the clothing you must wear to be safe, practical, and—if you prefer—stylish. The following is a list of items that will save you from disaster, outfit you comfortably, and most important, keep you looking cool.

Helmet. A helmet is an absolute necessity because it protects your head from complete annihilation. It is the only thing that will not disintegrate into a million pieces after a wicked crash on a descent you shouldn't have been on in the first place. A helmet with a solid exterior shell will also protect your head from sharp or protruding objects. Of course, with a hard-shelled helmet, you can paste several stickers of your favorite bicycle manufacturers all over the outer shell, giving companies even more free advertising for your dollar.

Shorts. Padded cycle shorts provide cushioning between your body and the bicycle seat. Cycle shorts also wick moisture away from your body and prevent chafing. Form-fitting shorts are made from synthetic material and have smooth seams to avoid chafing. If you don't feel comfortable wearing form-fitting shorts, baggy-style padded shorts with pockets are available.

Gloves. You may find well-padded cycling gloves invaluable when traveling over rocky trails and gravelly roads for hours on end. When you fall off your bike and land on your palms, gloves are your best friend. Long-fingered gloves may also be useful, as branches, trees, assorted hard objects, and, occasionally, small animals will reach out and whack your knuckles. Insulated gloves are essential for winter riding.

Glasses. Not only do sunglasses give you an imposing presence and make you look cool (both are extremely important), they also protect your eyes from harmful ultraviolet rays, invisible branches, creepy bugs, dirt, and may prevent you from being caught sneaking glances at riders of the opposite sex also wearing skintight, revealing Lycra.

Shoes. Mountain bike shoes are constructed with stiff soles in order to transfer more of the power from a pedal stroke to the drive train and to provide a solid platform to stand on, thereby decreasing fatigue in your feet. You can use virtually any good, light, outdoor hiking footwear, but specific mountain bike shoes (especially those with inset cleats) are best. They are lighter, breathe better, and are constructed to work with your pedal strokes instead of the natural walking cadence.

Other Clothing. To prepare for northwest Oregon's weather, it is best to dress in layers that can be added or removed as weather conditions change. In cold weather wear next to your skin a wicking layer made of a modern synthetic fiber. Avoid wearing cotton of any type. It dries slowly and does not wick moisture away from your skin, so it chills you directly as it evaporates. The next layer should be a wool or synthetic insulating layer that helps keep you warm but also is breathable. A fleece jacket or vest works well as an insulating layer. The outer layer should be a jacket and pants that are waterproof, windproof, and breathable. Your ears will also welcome a fleece headband when it's cold out.

First-Aid Kit

- Band-Aids
- mole skin
- various sterile gauze and dressings
- white surgical tape
- an Ace bandage
- an antihistamine
- aspirin
- Betadine solution
- First-Aid book
- Tums
- tweezers
- scissors
- antibacterial wipes
- triple-antibiotic ointment
- plastic gloves
- sterile cotton tip applicators
- syrup of ipecac (to induce vomiting)
- thermometer
- wire splint

Oh, Those Cold, Wet Northwest Oregon Days

If the weather chooses not to cooperate on the day you've set aside for a bike ride, it's helpful to be prepared.

Tights or leg warmers. These are best in temperatures below 55 degrees F. Knees are sensitive and can develop all kinds of problems if they get cold. Common problems include tendinitis, bursitis, and arthritis.

Plenty of layers on your upper body. When the air has a nip in it, layers of clothing will keep the chill away from your chest and help prevent the development of bronchitis. If the air is cool, a Polypropylene or Capilene long-sleeved shirt is best to wear against the skin beneath other layers of clothing. Polypropylene or Capilene, like wool, wicks away moisture from your skin to keep your body dry. Try to avoid wearing cotton or baggy clothing when the temperature falls. Cotton, as mentioned before, holds moisture like a sponge, and baggy clothing catches cold air and swirls it around your body. Good cold-weather clothing should fit snugly against your body, but not be restrictive.

Wool socks. Don't pack too many layers under those shoes, though. You may stand the chance of restricting circulation, and your feet will get real cold, real fast.

Thinsulate or Gortex gloves. We may all agree that there is nothing worse than frozen feet—unless your hands are frozen. A good pair of Thinsulate or Gortex gloves should keep your hands toasty and warm.

Hat or helmet on cold days. Sometimes, when the weather gets really cold and you still want to hit the trails, it's tough to stay warm. We all know that 130 percent of the body's heat escapes through the head (overactive brains, I imagine), so it's important to keep the cranium warm. Ventilated helmets are designed to keep heads cool in the summer heat, but they do little to help keep heads warm during rides in subzero temperatures. Cyclists should consider wearing a hat on extremely cold days. Capilene Skullcaps are great head and ear warmers that snugly fit over your head beneath the helmet. Head protection is not lost. Another option is a helmet cover that covers those ventilating gaps and helps keep the body heat in. These do not, however, keep your ears warm. Some cyclists will opt for a simple knit cycling cap sans the helmet, but these have never been shown to be very good cranium protectors.

All of this clothing can be found at your local bike store, where the staff should be happy to help fit you into the seasons of the year.

To Have or Not to Have—Other Very Useful Items

There is no shortage of items for you and your bike to make riding better, safer, and easier. We have rummaged through the unending lists and separated the gadgets from the good stuff, coming up with what we believe are items certain to make mountain bike riding easier and more enjoyable.

Tires. Buying a good pair of knobby tires is the quickest way to enhance the off-road handling capabilities of a bike. There are many types of mountain bike tires on the market. Some are made exclusively for very rugged off-road terrain. These big-knobbed, soft rubber tires virtually stick to the ground with magnetlike traction, but they tend to deteriorate quickly on pavement. There are other tires made exclusively for the road. These are called "slicks" and have no tread at all. For the average cyclist, though, a good tire somewhere in the middle of these two extremes should do the trick. Realize, however, that you get what you pay for. Do not skimp and buy cheap tires. As your primary point of contact with the trail, tires may be the most important piece of equipment on a bike. With inexpensive rubber, the tire's beads may unravel or chunks of tread actually rip off the tire. If you're lucky, all you'll suffer is a long walk back to the car. If you're unlucky, your tire could blow out in the middle of a rowdy downhill, causing a wicked crash.

Clipless pedals. Clipless pedals, like ski bindings, attach your shoe directly to the pedal. They allow you to exert pressure on the pedals during the down- and up-strokes. They also help you to maneuver the bike while in the air or climbing various obstacles. Toe clips may be less expensive, but they are also heavier and harder to use. Clipless pedals and toe clips take a little getting used to, but they're definitely worth the trouble.

Bar ends. These clamp-on additions to your original straight bar will provide more leverage, an excellent grip for climbing, and a more natural position for your hands. Be aware, however, of the bar end's propensity for hooking trees on fast descents, sending you, the cyclist, airborne. Opinions are divided on the general usefulness of bar ends these days and, over the last few years, bar ends have fallen out of favor with manufacturers and riders alike.

Back pack. These bags are ideal for carrying keys, extra food and water, guidebooks, foul-weather clothing, tools, spare tubes, and a cellular phone, in case you need to call for help.

Suspension forks. For off-roaders who want nothing to impede their speed on the trails, investing in a pair of suspension forks is a good idea. Like tires, there are plenty of brands to choose from, and they all do the same thing—absorb the brutal beatings of a rough trail. The cost of these forks, however, is sometimes more brutal than the trail itself.

Bike computers. These are fun gadgets to own and are much less expensive than in years past. They have such features as trip distance, speedometer, odometer, time of day, altitude, alarm, average speed, maximum speed, heart rate, global satellite positioning, etc. Bike computers will come in handy when following these maps or to know just how far you've ridden in the wrong direction.

Hydration Pack. This is quickly becoming an essential item for cyclists pedaling for more than a few hours, especially in hot, dry conditions. The most popular brand is, of course, the Camelback, and these water packs can carry in their bladder bags as much as 100 ounces of water. These packs strap on your back with a handy hose running over your shoulder so you can be drinking water while still holding onto the bars with both hands on a rocky descent. These packs are a great way to carry a lot of extra liquid on hot rides in the middle of nowhere, as well as keys, a camera, extra food, guidebooks, tools, spare tubes, and a cellular phone, in case you need to call for help.

Types of Off-Road Terrain

Before roughing it off-road, we may first have to ride the pavement to get to our destination. Please don't be dismayed. Some of the country's best rides are on the road. Once we get past these smooth-surfaced pathways, though, adventures in dirt await us.

Rails-to-Trails. Abandoned rail lines are converted into usable public resources for exercising, commuting, or just enjoying nature. Old rails and ties are torn up and a trail, paved or unpaved, is laid along the existing corridor. This completes the cycle from ancient Indian trading routes to railroad corridors and back again to hiking and cycling trails.

Unpaved roads are typically found in rural areas and are most often public roads. Be careful when exploring, though, not to ride on someone's unpaved private drive.

Forest roads. These dirt and gravel roads are used primarily as access to forestland and are generally kept in good condition. They are almost always open to public use.

Singletrack can be the most fun on a mountain bike. These trails, with only one track to follow, are often narrow, challenging pathways. Remember to make sure these trails are open before zipping into the woods. (At the time of this printing, all trails and roads in this guidebook were open to mountain bikes.)

Open land. Unless there is a marked trail through a field or open space, you should not plan to ride here. Once one person cuts his or her wheels through a field or meadow, many more are sure to follow, causing irreparable damage to the landscape.

Techniques to Sharpen Your Skills

Many of us see ourselves as pure athletes—blessed with power, strength, and endless endurance. However, it may be those with finesse, balance, agility, and grace who get around most quickly on a mountain bike. Although power, strength, and endurance do have their places in mountain biking, these elements don't necessarily form the complete framework for a champion mountain biker.

The bike should become an extension of your body. Slight shifts in your hips or knees can have remarkable results. Experienced bike handlers seem to flash down technical descents, dashing over obstacles in a smooth and graceful effort as if pirouetting in Swan Lake. Here are some tips and techniques to help you connect with your bike and float gracefully over the dirt.

Braking. Using your brakes requires using your head, especially when descending. This doesn't mean using your head as a stopping block, but rather to think intelligently. Use your best judgment in terms of how much or how little to squeeze those brake levers.

The more weight a tire is carrying, the more braking power it has. When you're going downhill, your front wheel carries more weight than the rear. Braking gently with the front brake will help keep you in control without going into a skid. Be careful, though, not to overdo it with the front brakes and accidentally toss yourself over the handlebars. And don't neglect your rear brake! When descending, shift your weight back over the rear wheel, thus increasing your rear braking power as well. This will balance the power of both brakes and give you maximum control.

Good riders learn just how much of their weight to shift over each wheel and how to apply just enough braking power to each brake, so not to "endo" over the handlebars or skid down a trail.

Going Uphill—Climbing Those Treacherous Hills

Shift into a low gear. Before shifting, be sure to ease up on your pedaling so there is not too much pressure on the chain. With that in mind, it's important to shift before you find yourself on a steep slope, where it may too late. Find the best gear for you that matches the terrain and steepness of each climb.

Stay seated. Standing out of the saddle is often helpful when climbing steep hills on a bike, but you may find that on dirt, standing may cause your rear tire to lose its grip and spin out. Climbing is not possible without traction. As you improve, you will likely learn the subtle tricks that make out-of-saddle climbing possible. Until then, have a seat.

Lean forward. On very steep hills, the front end may feel unweighted and suddenly pop up. Slide forward on the saddle and lean over the handlebars. Think about putting your chin down near your stem. This will add more weight to the front wheel and should keep you grounded. It's all about using the weight of your head to your advantage. Most people don't realize how heavy their noggin is.

Relax. As with downhilling, relaxation is a big key to your success when climbing steep, rocky climbs. Smooth pedaling translates into good traction. Tense bodies don't balance well at low speeds. Instead of fixating grimly on the front wheel, look up at the terrain above, and pick a good line.

Keep pedaling. On rocky climbs, be sure to keep the pressure on, and don't let up on those pedals! You'll be surprised at what your bike will just roll over as long as you keep the engine revved up.

Going Downhill—The Real Reason We Get Up in the Morning

Relax. Stay loose on the bike, and don't lock your elbows or clench your grip. Your elbows need to bend with the bumps and absorb the shock, while your hands should have a firm but controlled grip on the bars to keep things steady. Breathing slowly, deeply, and deliberately will help you relax while flying down bumpy singletrack. Maintaining a death-grip on the brakes will be unhelpful. Fear and tension will make you wreck every time.

Use your eyes. Keep your head up and scan the trail as far forward as possible. Choose a line well in advance. *You* decide what line to take—don't let the trail decide for you. Keep the surprises to a minimum. If you have to react quickly to an obstacle, then you've already made a mistake.

Rise above the saddle. When racing down bumpy, technical descents, you should not be sitting on the saddle, but hovering just over it, allowing your bent legs and arms, instead of your rear, to absorb the rocky trail. Think jockey.

Remember your pedals. Be mindful of where your pedals are in relation to upcoming obstacles. Clipping a rock will lead directly to unpleasantness. Most of the time, you'll want to keep your pedals parallel to the ground.

Stay focused. Many descents require your utmost concentration and focus just to reach the bottom. You must notice every groove, every root, every rock, every hole, every bump. You, the bike, and the trail should all become one as you seek singletrack nirvana on your way down the mountain. But if your thoughts wander, however, then so may your bike, and you may instead become one with the trees!

Watch Out!

Back-Road Obstacles

Logs. When you want to hop a log, throw your body back, yank up on the handlebars, and pedal forward in one swift motion. This clears the front end of the bike. Then quickly scoot forward and pedal the rear wheel up and over. Keep the forward momentum until you've cleared the log, and by all means, don't hit the brakes, or you may do some interesting acrobatic maneuvers!

Rocks and roots. Worse than highway potholes! Stay relaxed and let your elbows and knees absorb the shock. Staying seated will keep the rear wheel weighted to prevent slipping, and a light front end will help you to respond quickly to each new obstacle.

Water. Before crossing a stream or puddle, be sure to first check the depth and bottom surface. There may be an unseen hole or large rock hidden under the water that could wash you up if you're not careful. You should also consider that riding through a mountain stream can cause great damage to the stream's ecosystem. If you still want to try, hit the water at a good speed, pedal steadily, and allow the bike to steer you through. Once you're across, tap the brakes to squeegee the water off the rims and the guilt off your conscience.

Leaves. Be careful of wet leaves. They may look pretty, but a trail or bridge covered with leaves may cause your wheels to slip out from under you. Leaves are not nearly as unpredictable and dangerous as ice, but they do warrant your attention on a rainy day.

Mud. If you must ride through mud, hit it head on and keep pedaling. You want to part the ooze with your front wheel and get across before it swallows you up. Above all, don't leave the trail to go around the mud. This just widens the path even more and leads to increased trail erosion.

Urban Obstacles

Curbs are fun to jump, but as with logs, be careful.

Curbside drains. Be careful not to get a wheel caught in the grate.

Dogs make great pets, but they seem to have it in for mountain bikers. If you think you can't outrun a dog that's chasing you, stop and walk your bike out of its territory. A loud yell to "Get!" or "Go home!" often works, as does a sharp squirt from your water bottle right between the eyes.

Cars are tremendously convenient when we're in them, but dodging irate motorists in big automobiles becomes a real hazard when riding a bike. As a cyclist, you must realize most drivers aren't expecting you to be there and often wish you weren't. Stay alert and ride carefully, clearly signaling all of your intentions.

Potholes, like grates and back-road canyons, should be avoided. Just because you're on an all-terrain bicycle doesn't mean you're indestructible. Potholes regularly damage rims, pop tires, and sometimes lift unsuspecting cyclists into a spectacular swan dive over the handlebars.

Last-Minute Checkover

Before a ride, it's a good idea to give your bike a once-over to make sure everything is in working order. Begin by checking the air pressure in your tires before each ride to make sure they are properly inflated. Mountain bikes require about 45 to 55 pounds per square inch of air pressure. If your tires are underinflated, there is greater likelihood that the tubes may get pinched on a rock, causing the tire to flat.

Looking over your bike to make sure everything is secure and in its place is the next step. Go through the following checklist before each ride.

- **Pinch the tires to feel for proper inflation.** They should give just a little on the sides but feel very hard on the treads. If you have a pressure gauge, use that.
- **Check your brakes.** Squeeze the rear brake and roll your bike forward. The rear tire should skid. Next, squeeze the front brake and roll your bike forward. The rear wheel should lift into the air. If this doesn't happen, then your brakes are

too loose. Make sure the brake levers don't touch the handlebars when squeezed with full force.

- **Check all quick releases on your bike.** Make sure they are all securely tightened.
- **Lube up.** If your chain squeaks, apply some lubricant.
- **Check your nuts and bolts.** Check the handlebars, saddle, cranks, and pedals to make sure that each is tight and securely fastened to your bike.
- **Check your wheels.** Spin each wheel to see that they spin through the frame and between brake pads freely.
- **Have you got everything?** Make sure you have your spare tube, tire irons, patch kit, frame pump, tools, food, water, foul-weather gear, and guidebook.

Need more info on mountain biking? Consider reading *Basic Essentials Mountain Biking.* You'll discover such things as choosing and maintaining a mountain bike; useful bike-handling techniques; preparing for long rides; overcoming obstacles such as rocks, logs, and water; and even preparing for competition.

Repair and Maintenance

Fixing a Flat

TOOLS YOU WILL NEED

- Two tire irons
- Pump (either a floor pump or a frame pump)
- No screwdrivers!!! (This can puncture the tube.)

REMOVING THE WHEEL

The front wheel is easy. Simply disconnect the brake shoes, open the quick release mechanism or undo the bolts with the proper sized wrench, then remove the wheel from the bike.

The rear wheel is a little more tricky. Before you loosen the wheel from the frame, shift the chain into the smallest gear on the freewheel (the cluster of gears in the back). Once you've done this, removing and installing the wheel, like the front, is much easier.

REMOVING THE TIRE

Step one: Insert a tire iron under the bead of the tire and pry the tire over the lip of the rim. Be careful not to pinch the tube when you do this.

Step two: Hold the first tire iron in place. With the second tire iron, repeat step one, 3 or 4 inches down the rim. Alternate tire irons, pulling the bead of the tire over the rim, section by section, until one side of the tire bead is completely off the rim.

Step three: Remove the rest of the tire and tube from the rim. This can be done by hand. It's easiest to remove the valve stem last. Once the tire is off the rim, pull the tube out of the tire.

CLEAN AND SAFETY CHECK

Step four: Using a rag, wipe the inside of the tire to clean out any dirt, sand, glass, thorns, etc. These may cause the tube to puncture. The inside of a tire should feel smooth. Any pricks or bumps could mean that you have found the culprit responsible for your flat tire.

Step five: Wipe the rim clean, then check the rim strip, making sure it covers the spoke nipples properly on the inside of the rim. If a spoke is poking through the rim strip, it could cause a puncture.

Step six: At this point, you can do one of two things: replace the punctured tube with a new one, or patch the hole. It's easiest to just replace the tube with a new tube when you're out on the trails. Roll up the old tube and take it home to repair later that night in front of the TV. Directions on patching a tube are usually included with the patch kit itself.

INSTALLING THE TIRE AND TUBE

(This can be done entirely by hand.)

Step seven: Inflate the new or repaired tube with enough air to give it shape, then tuck it back into the tire.

Step eight: To put the tire and tube back on the rim, begin by putting the valve in the valve hole. The valve must be straight. Then use your hands to push the beaded edge of the tire onto the rim all the way around so that one side of your tire is on the rim.

Step nine: Let most of the air out of the tube to allow room for the rest of the tire.

Step ten: Beginning opposite the valve, use your thumbs to push the other side of the tire onto the rim. Be careful not to pinch the tube in between the tire and the rim. The last few inches may be difficult, and you may need the tire iron to pry the tire onto the rim. If so, just be careful not to puncture the tube.

BEFORE INFLATING COMPLETELY

Step eleven: Check to make sure the tire is seated properly and that the tube is not caught between the tire and the rim. Do this by adding about five to ten pounds of air, and watch closely that the tube does not bulge out of the tire.

Step twelve: Once you're sure the tire and tube are properly seated, put the wheel back on the bike, then fill the tire with air. It's easier squeezing the wheel through the brake shoes if the tire is still flat.

Step thirteen: Now fill the tire with the proper amount of air, and check constantly to make sure the tube doesn't bulge from the rim. If the tube does appear to bulge out, release all the air as quickly as possible, or you could be in for a big bang. Place the wheel back in the dropost and tighten the quick release lever Reconnect the brake shoes.

When installing the rear wheel, place the chain back onto the smallest cog (farthest gear on the right), and pull the derailleur out of the way. Your wheel should slide right on.

Lubrication Prevents Deterioration

Lubrication is crucial to maintaining your bike. Dry spots will be eliminated. Creaks, squeaks, grinding, and binding will be gone. The chain will run quietly, and the gears will shift smoothly. The brakes will grip quicker, and your bike may last longer with fewer repairs. Need I say more? Well, yes. Without knowing where to put the lubrication, what good is it?

THINGS YOU WILL NEED
- One can of bicycle lubricant, found at any bike store
- A clean rag (to wipe excess lubricant away)

WHAT GETS LUBRICATED
- Front derailleur
- Rear derailleur
- Shift levers
- Front brake
- Rear brake
- Both brake levers
- Chain

WHERE TO LUBRICATE

To make it easy, simply spray a little lubricant on all the pivot points of your bike. If you're using a squeeze bottle, use just a drop or two. Put a few drops on each point wherever metal moves against metal, for instance, at the center of the brake calipers. Then let the lube sink in.

Once you have applied the lubricant to the derailleurs, shift the gears a few times, working the derailleurs back and forth. This allows the lubricant to work itself into the tiny cracks and spaces it must occupy to do its job. Work the brakes a few times as well.

LUBING THE CHAIN

Lubricating the chain should be done after the chain has been wiped clean of most road grime. Do this by spinning the pedals counterclockwise while gripping the chain with a clean rag. As you add the lubricant, be sure to get some in between each link. With an aerosol spray, just spray the chain while pedaling backwards (counterclockwise) until the chain is fully lubricated. Let the lubricant soak in for a few seconds before wiping the excess away. Chains will collect dirt much faster if they're loaded with too much lubrication.

Ride Index

Trails by Feature

Best Singletrack

Ride 2: Tarbell Trail

Ride 3: Ape Canyon–Plains of Abraham–Windy Point

Ride 8: Riverside Trail

Ride 12: Hagg Lake

Honorable Mention Ride B: Lewis River

Ride 17: Surveyor's Ridge

Ride 18: Fifteen Mile Creek

Ride 19: East Fork Hood River

Ride 21: Timothy Lake

Ride 26: McKenzie River

Honorable Mention Ride X: Moon Point–Youngs Rock Loop

Honorable Mention Ride Y: Waldo Lake Loop

Ride 37: Deschutes River Trail

Ride 39: Lava Lake Loop

Ride 40: Cultus Lake Loop

Ride 44: Newberry Crater Rim Loop

Honorable Mention Ride AA: Mzarek

Best Climbs

Ride 1: Three Corner Rock

Ride 2: Tarbell Trail

Ride 3: Ape Canyon–Plains of Abraham–Windy Point

Honorable Mention Ride G: Dan's Trail–Dimple Hill

Honorable Mention Ride H: Mary's Peak

Ride 17: Surveyor's Ridge

Ride 18: Fifteen Mile Creek

Ride 22: Gunsight Ridge

Honorable Mention Ride O: Crosstown–Pioneer Bridle–Still Creek Loop

Honorable Mention Ride T: Hardesty Trail

Honorable Mention Ride V: Larison Rock

Honorable Mention Ride X: Moon Point–Youngs Rock Loop

Ride 29: Gray Butte Loop

Ride 30: Smith Rock State Park

Ride 41: Charlton Lake Trail

Ride 43: Peter Skene Ogden Trail

Ride 44: Newberry Crater Rim Loop

Honorable Mention Ride CC: North Fork–South Fork–Flagline Loop

Honorable Mention Ride DD: Edison–Lava–Kwolh Butte

Honorable Mention Ride II: Coyote Creek

Honorable Mention Ride JJ: Round Mountain

Ride 47: Neahkahnie Mountain

Honorable Mention Ride MM: Cummins Creek Loop

Best Technical Challenges and Descents

Ride 1: Three Corner Rock

Ride 2: Tarbell Trail

Ride 3: Ape Canyon–Plains of Abraham–Windy Point

Ride 11: Tillamook State Forest

Honorable Mention Ride A: Larch Mountain

Ride 18: Fifteen Mile Creek

Honorable Mention Ride J: Post Canyon Loop

Honorable Mention Ride N: Ski Bowl

Honorable Mention Ride P: Umbrella
Falls–Sahalie Falls Loop

Ride 25: Larison Creek

Honorable Mention Ride T: Hardesty
Trail

Honorable Mention Ride V: Larison
Rock

Honorable Mention Ride X: Moon
Point–Youngs Rock Loop

Ride 39: Lava Lake Loop

Ride 41: Charlton Lake Trail

Honorable Mention Ride DD:
Edison–Lava–Kwolh Butte

Best Adventure Rides

Ride 2: Tarbell Trail

Ride 3: Ape Canyon–Plains of
Abraham–Windy Point

Honorable Mention Ride B: Lewis
River

Ride 17: Surveyor's Ridge

Ride 18: Fifteen Mile Creek

Ride 26: McKenzie River

Honorable Mention Ride X: Moon
Point–Youngs Rock Loop

Honorable Mention Ride Y: Waldo
Lake Loop

Ride 39: Lava Lake Loop

Ride 44: Newberry Crater Rim Loop

Honorable Mention Ride DD: Edison–Lava–Kwolh Butte

Best Beach Rides

Ride 45: Fort Stevens State Park

Ride 46: Cannon Beach

Best Rides with Mountain Views

Ride 1: Three Corner Rock

Ride 2: Tarbell Trail

Ride 3: Ape Canyon–Plains of Abraham–Windy Point

Honorable Mention Ride G: Dan's
Trail–Dimple Hill

Ride 17: Surveyor's Ridge

Ride 22: Gunsight Ridge

Honorable Mention Ride X: Moon
Point–Youngs Rock Loop

Ride 29: Gray Butte Loop

Ride 30: Smith Rock State Park

Ride 38: Swampy Lakes–Swede Ridge
Loop

Ride 39: Lava Lake Loop

Ride 44: Newberry Crater Rim Loop

Honorable Mention Ride DD: Edison–Lava–Kwolh Butte

Honorable Mention Ride JJ: Round
Mountain

Ride 47: Neahkahnie Mountain

Best Rides for Lake Lovers

Ride 12: Hagg Lake

Ride 21: Timothy Lake

Honorable Mention Ride Y: Waldo
Lake Loop

Ride 28: Haystack Reservoir

Ride 32: Suttle Tie–Suttle Lake Loop

Ride 39: Lava Lake Loop

Ride 40: Cultus Lake Loop

Ride 41: Charlton Lake Trail

Honorable Mention Ride FF: Twin
Lakes

Ride 48: Siltcoos Lake

Best Rides for Creek and River Lovers

Ride 8: Riverside Trail

Honorable Mention Ride B: Lewis
River

Honorable Mention Ride C: Siouxan
Creek–Horseshoe Creek Falls–
Chinook Falls

Ride 18: Fifteen Mile Creek

Ride 19: East Fork Hood River

Best Rides for Dogs

Trails by Difficulty

EASY
Southwest Washington, Portland, and Salem

Columbia River Gorge, Hood River, and Mount Hood

Eugene and Oakridge

Bend and Central Oregon

Ride 28: Haystack Reservoir

Ride 35: Deschutes River Trail–First
Street Rapids Park

Ride 42: Fall River Trail

Honorable Mention Ride FF: Twin
Lakes

Honorable Mention Ride GG: La Pine
State Park

Oregon Coast

Ride 45: Fort Stevens State Park

Ride 46: Cannon Beach

Honorable Mention Ride KK:
Nehalem Bay State Park

Honorable Mention Ride LL: South
Beach State Park

MODERATE
Southwest Washington, Portland, and Salem

Ride 1: Three Corner Rock

Ride 2: Tarbell Trail

Ride 5: Leif Erikson Drive–Firelane 1

Ride 7: Powell Butte Nature Park

Ride 8: Riverside Trail

Ride 9: Molalla River Trail System

Ride 11: Tillamook State Forest

Honorable Mention Ride B: Lewis
River

Honorable Mention Ride C: Siouxan
Creek–Horseshoe Creek Falls–Chinook Falls

Ride 12: Hagg Lake

Ride 13: Silver Falls State Park

Honorable Mention Ride D: Gales
Creek

Honorable Mention Ride G: Dan's
Trail–Dimple Hill

Columbia River Gorge, Hood River, and Mount Hood

Ride 15: Gorge Trail 400

Honorable Mention Ride K: Knebal
Springs Loop

Ride 17: Surveyor's Ridge

Ride 18: Fifteen Mile Creek

Ride 19: East Fork Hood River

Honorable Mention Ride K: Knebal
Springs Loop

Honorable Mention Ride L: Eightmile
Creek

Honorable Mention Ride Q: Clear
Creek–Camas Trail

Eugene and Oakridge

Ride 26: McKenzie River

Honorable Mention Ride S: Goodman
Trail

Honorable Mention Ride U: Flat
Creek–Dead Mountain Trail

Honorable Mention Ride W: Middle
Fork Willamette River

Honorable Mention Ride Z: Brice
Creek

Bend and Central Oregon

Ride 31: Peterson Ridge–Eagle Rock
Loops

Ride 32: Suttle Tie–Suttle Lake Loop

Ride 33: Upper Black Butte Loop

Ride 34: Shevlin Park

Ride 36: Phil's Trail–Kent's Trail Loop

Ride 37: Deschutes River Trail

Ride 38: Swampy Lakes–Swede Ridge
Loop

Ride 40: Cultus Lake Loop

Honorable Mention Ride AA: Mzarek

Honorable Mention Ride BB: Tumalo
Creek–Tumalo Falls

Clubs and Trail Groups

Central Oregon Trails Alliance (COTA)
1293 NW Wall, #72
Bend, OR 97701
(541) 385–1985
www.cotamtb.org

Mid-Valley Bicycle Club
P.O. Box 1373
Corvallis, OR 97339–1373
www.mvbc.com/index.html

Portland United Mountain Pedalers
(PUMP)
818 SW Third, #228
Portland, OR 97204
(503) 690–5259
www.pumpclub.org

Salem Merry Cranksters
Salem, OR 97301
(503) 365–8914
www.merrycranksters.org

Southern Oregon Mountain Bike
Association (SOMBA)
P.O. Box 903
Ashland, OR 97420
(541) 552–0427
www.somba.org

About the Author

Lizann Dunegan is a freelance writer and photographer who specializes in writing about outdoor activities and travel. She has been riding trails in the Northwest for more than ten years and is often accompanied by her two border collies, Levi and Sage. Lizann also loves trail running, hiking, cross-country skiing, sea kayaking, and playing the violin and cello.